THE RIGHTSIZING REMEDY

HOW MANAGERS CAN RESPOND TO THE DOWNSIZING DILEMMA

THE RIGHTSIZING REMEDY

HOW MANAGERS CAN RESPOND TO THE DOWNSIZING DILEMMA

Charles F. Hendricks

Copublished by
Society for Human Resource Management
Alexandria, Virginia 22314
and
BUSINESS ONE IRWIN
Homewood, Illinois 60430

Sponsoring editor: Cynthia A. Zigmund
Project editor: Ethel Shiell
Production manager: Irene H. Sotiroff
Designer: Larry J. Cope
Jacket designer: Annette Vogt
Compositor: Graphic Sciences Corporation
Typeface: 11/13 Times Roman
Printer: Arcata Graphics/Kingsport

Library of Congress Cataloging-in-Publication Data

Hendricks, Charles F.
    The rightsizing remedy: how managers can respond to the downsizing dilemma / Charles F. Hendricks.
        p.   cm.
    ISBN 1-55623-654-9
    1. Industries, Size of—United States.   2. Corporate reorganizations—United States.   3. Organizational change—United States.   4. Career development—United States.   I. Title.
HD69.S5H46   1992
658.1'6—dc20   91–37138

Printed in the United States of America

1 2 3 4 5 6 7 8 9 0 AG-K 98 7 6 5 4 3 2

For two wonderful human beings:

Aloysius, my late father, who loved his time on this earth thanks to Dorothy, a loving wife and mother.

FOREWORD

Downsizing has become a fact of life for Corporate America that transcends these times of economic slowdown. Because of increased global competition and mergers and acquisitions, companies that for years boasted a "no-layoff" policy, have been forced into the cutback mode.

In the late 1980s and early 1990s, middle- and senior-management positions, once considered inviolate territory, were especially hard hit. In 1990 alone, nearly a million U.S. managers with yearly salaries of more than $40,000 lost their jobs.

Downsizing of American corporations, while considered essential for survival, remains difficult for companies wishing to balance the interests of their employees with the needs of the business. During the 1980s, clumsy and insensitive downsizing strategies virtually destroyed employee morale at many top U.S. companies, creating a climate of worker fear and insecurity that has seriously eroded management–employee relations.

One of the worst casualties arising out of corporate restructuring is employee loyalty. Recent studies have shown that employee loyalty has drastically plummeted over the last decade— because workers no longer feel that they can trust their companies to be concerned about their well-being. This is in sharp contrast to the position of Japanese workers, many of whom remain with the same company for the duration of their working lives because they are confident that their employers will consider their interests.

The leveraged buyouts and hostile takeovers of the 1980s, which forced many workers into the unemployment lines, have contributed to serious management–employee tensions and caused many workers to adopt a "Take what you can while you can" attitude. "Job hopping" and radical career changes have become socially acceptable and even expected in today's rapidly changing and uncertain job market. Entrepreneurship and self-employment continue to rise because many feel that—even with the risks attached—it is safer to work for themselves than for someone else.

All of this is happening at a time when America desperately needs a motivated, creative, and innovative work force. *Time* magazine recently reported that, "In an economy increasingly based on information and technology, ideas and creativity often embody most of a company's wealth."

Corporate restructuring does not have to be a nightmare. Downsizing has forced many bloated and inefficiently run corporations to eliminate wasteful spending and management practices, thereby gaining greater competitiveness in a global economy.

As Charles Hendricks points out in this book, the "Quick Fix" approach to restructuring needs to be replaced with a more holistic, intuitive, and humanistic approach. He argues that continuous restructuring is the wave of the future and that restructured companies will require fiercely loyal employees who will support new ideas and take risks because their jobs are not always on the line.

The concept of "rightsizing," according to Hendricks, encompasses much more than extrapolating "business as usual" approaches into an uncharted future. Business conditions are fundamentally changing the employment relationship between American workers and the large companies. This means that corporations must rethink their entire operational strategy, including hiring and promotional policies, pay scales, and management practices. "Managers—throw out your script. Your 'role' is changing. Get out of the way of your people. Lead for once by following their advice, facilitating their movement, and franchising their futures."

Hendricks believes the human resource management profession is critical to achieving a positive corporate future because practitioners have had to deal with the downsizing victims and the survivors as human beings, not as just financial numbers on a profit and loss statement. "What HR practitioners need to do now is to take the lead in forging new employment relationships for their companies' employees."

At the Society for Human Resource Management, we have long known that the human resource management profession can play a major role in helping companies take a more intelligent approach to restructuring by encouraging management to see their employees as corporate assets rather than as corporate liabilities, and by promoting long-term as opposed to short-term solutions.

Mr. Hendricks' book will be a valuable resource for companies looking to ease their dilemma in downsizing. It raises many thought-provoking and stimulating questions as to how we can manage human resources into the 21st century and beyond.

Michael R. Losey, SPHR
President and CEO
Society for Human Resource Management
Alexandria, Virginia

PREFACE

My compulsion to write *The Rightsizing Remedy* began in early 1988 after reading a February article in *The Washington Post* about the growing contingency work force. Although corporate restructuring had been going on for some time, this was the first indication, at least to me, that an ever increasing number of highly educated people were being permanently pushed out of the mainstream of corporate life. And, as I would later learn, there was nothing they could do about it because they were at-will employees. The more I read and observed this phenomena, the more obvious it became that a fundamental change was occurring in American employment relations. And while news commentators, business experts, and others were talking about this new employment relationship, all of the remedies seemed like business-as-usual.

When I started working on this book, my focus was on questioning the employment-at-will legal doctrine, which struck me as unduly harsh, one-sided, and out-of-line with the welfare-like employment systems in place in many corporations. However, I soon came to realize that these "welfare webs," which lock employees into corporations, may also be out-of-line with the realities of an ever competitive marketplace which has been forcing managements to downsize and restructure. However, employment-at-will and "welfare webs" were not the only culprits. The approach to *downsizing* and *restructuring* followed by many companies has been shown to be unimaginative, reactive, and mechanical quick fixes, driven by linear reasoning and, most disturbingly, by numbers! And where many had initially believed that downsizing was to be a one-time event, it was now becoming an annual rite of head counting and cutting.

Downsizing, the proclaimed cure for what ails American business, has become a dilemma to managers. It has not delivered tangible long-term results; instead, it has weakened intangible long-term values. The rightsizing remedy is a wake-up call to managers—particularly human resource practitioners—and employees, alike, on how to respond to the downsizing dilemma by taking a more holistic, intuitive, and most of all, humanistic approach to human resource management.

As the chapter references demonstrate, this book is based on a wide range of sources, from newspaper reports, business and general interest periodicals, interviews, and books on management and related topics. I feel particularly indebted to Peter Drucker, Thomas Peters, Robert Waterman, Alvin Toffler, David Halberstam, Robert Tomasko, Paul Hirsch, Charles Handy, Thomas Horton and Peter Reid, John Naisbitt, Robert Reich, Dan Lacey, and Robert Samuelson, and to numerous other authors, columnists, and reporters whose writings have helped me to develop and express the conceptual underpinnings of *The Rightsizing Remedy*.

I would like to acknowledge the support and assistance of many people who urged me on in writing and seeing that this book is published—Janet Jordan, Jim Rowbotham, Jan Clarkson, Rebecca Ford Myers, Karen White-Johnson, Gayla Kraetsch Hartsough, and my brother, John Hendricks, who offered me early encouragement; Mai Fleury, who pushed me through my first drafts; Robert Tomasko, Monsignor Thomas Duffy, Reverend James Connor, and my father-in-law, Donald Gray, who critically reviewed my initial efforts; and Marty Lobel, whose legal and publishing advice, and friendship, has been invaluable. I would also like to acknowledge the contribution of many of my professional acquaintances, colleagues, and clients, including Jim Buttimer, Tom Cody, Doug Huron and Jim Heller, Tom Lewis, Jack Tuttle, and many other individuals whom I have worked with over the years. I would particularly like to thank John Adams, Ceel Pasternak, and Michelle Neely Martinez of the Society for Human Resource Management who got behind the book to make its publication a reality; and my editor, Cynthia Zigmund, marketing specialist, Melanie Chionis, and the staff of Business One Irwin for their patience, guidance, and support.

Most of all, I want to thank my wife, Tricia, and our son, Charles, for their loving companionship and support, and for putting up with me throughout all of this.

Charles F. Hendricks

TABLE OF CONTENTS

PROLOGUE—A LEGACY
FOR FUTURE EMPLOYEES

The Age of Reason. The Industrial Age. The Post-Industrial Age. And now the Age of Uncertainty. With a resounding boom, General Motors Corp. has declared the end of an era and the beginning of a new one. Its plan to cut 74,000 jobs . . . marks a dramatic end to employment as we've known it.[1]

THE DOWNSIZING DILEMMA

"I'm sorry, but we don't have a job for you here anymore."[2] It was reported, back in 1982, that it's the toughest thing a manager ever had to say to an employee. Today, many managers are saying it a lot more and many are even finding it even tougher to hear it said. In 1990, an outplacement counselor is reported to be telling graduate business students that "each one of you is going to be fired at least once during your careers. That simply reflects the brutality and competitiveness of the world economy."[3]

It was said as far back as 1951 that the United States of America had become "a nation of employees" with "the substance of life" now in "another man's hands"! More than a generation later, the substance of life is still in another man's hands for 9 out of 10 American workers. Almost all of us, even if we are "managers," are still employees. And, at least two out of every three of us can be terminated at the "will" of our employers.[4] The livelihood of "at-will" employees depends on their remaining in good standing with their employers. Increasingly, however, many employees have fallen from grace.

Downsizing has become a national fact of life! Over the past decade, millions of managers and professional employees have lost their jobs because of corporate restructuring. Corporate planners, economists, personnel specialists, market researchers, purchasing agents, financial analysts, "middle" managers, and "deep thinkers" have become "endangered species." It is reported that these actions are destroying the lives of loyal long-term employees who know the business best and have been most committed to its continued success.[5] According to the Department of Commerce, between 1983 and 1990 nearly 5 million workers who had held their jobs for at least three years have been dismissed; about a third of them took pay cuts of at least 20 percent in their next position.[6] As a result, fear has spread to those who survive these waves of cutbacks.

With growing competition from abroad, this is believed to be only the tip of the iceberg. An article entitled "White-Collar Layoffs Open 1990, and May Close It, Too" reported that the "fresh flood of managerial cutbacks" is expected to be "much broader in scope and range than previous streamlining waves ... striking deeply at top-level and middle-level managers, and at a cross section of corporate America."[7] And the layoffs go on, as *Business Week* reported, in late 1991:

> Corporate America's workplace is undergoing tumultuous change. Every week brings news of yet another corporation cutting 10 percent of its work force. Most of the layoffs are taking place in the service sector, and most are of white-collar employees.[8]

Notably, International Business Machines Corp., a company which had always cherished its employees and was noted for its "no-layoff" policy, announced in late 1991 that it will be forced to lay off another 20,000 employees. *The Washington Post* reported that "such an announcement would hardly be news in this time of widespread corporate cutbacks if it weren't happening at IBM, a company that for generations has been an icon for all that is fair and honorable about corporate paternalism."[9] Some management experts estimate that one in four management jobs have disappeared in the last decade.[10] But the downsizing of American management goes on.

A QUESTION OF VALUES

As downsizing continues, corporate loyalty is disappearing from employment relationships. They are now viewed as "arm's-length, hard-nose" agreements. The absence of loyalty has become quite a topical issue over the past several years. Critics are questioning the loyalty of former White House insiders who have cashed in on their years with each recent administration. Ironically, Donald Regan—the man who gave new life to star gazing—when questioned about his loyalty back in the late 80s, said that you cannot expect subordinates to be "loyal up" the organization if they don't get "loyalty down."[11] No doubt Regan must have been reading a few astrological stars of his own because he was clairvoyant about the values of the commander of "Desert Storm", Norman Schwarzkopf, who showed in the Persian Gulf that "loyalty also runs from top down to the troops." David Gergen, another former White House insider, believes that the military has adopted values that companies sorely need. Gergen asks, "Apart from IBM and a few other blue-chip firms, how many private companies can claim as much dedication to employee loyalty?" His conclusion, "Not many."[12]

Loyalty-up, loyalty-down—an old Marine Corps motto—no longer applies to American business. For the past several years, business articles and publications have been reporting on the "end of corporate loyalty."[13] It is believed that "managers had the closest thing to a social contract that America had to offer."[14] Regrettably, the contract is now null and void.

Restructuring has done away with traditional notions of "years of service" and "demonstrated loyalty." Alvin Toffler comments about the "devastating decline of personal and collective power" afflicting many professionals: "programmers and space engineers have learned that they, exactly like punch-press operators and assembly-line hands, can be pink-slipped without ceremony, while their bosses vote themselves 'golden parachutes'."[15] Because of this "lack of ceremony," laid-off victims as well as the survivors are avoiding loyalty-up commitments, as loyalty-down career employment bargains are being broken.

Unfortunately for these victims and survivors—and their corporate employers—a new employment relationship is being forged out of anxiety, miscommunication, and a general lack of employer trust, as job security and paternalism are being replaced by "take charge of your career" and "get what you can while you can." All managers, particularly those in the human resource profession, are finding themselves on the front lines of an employment relations "battleground." On the one hand, managers must be careful what they promise to employees because employers are increasingly being dragged into court for having broken some "implicit contract," and they are literally paying out millions of dollars in attempting to resolve employee claims. On the other hand, managers are finding it difficult not to promise "something" to the survivors who are asking, "what is in it for me to stay here?" Ironically, the well-meaning attempts at quality and productivity improvement are being eroded by this new "arm's-length" employment relationship, thus further exasperating the very challenge that corporate restructuring is attempting to address—to assure America's global competitiveness into the next century.

MUDDLING TOWARD THE MILLENNIUM

According to David Halberstam, "It is our not-very-secret secret that the American Century is over."[16] What kind of world will it be for our children—the employees of the 21st century? It is hard to be optimistic. During the 80s, the national debt tripled, from $909 billion to almost $2.9 trillion. The interest on the debt alone is over $165 billion a year. And the U.S. trade deficit runs over $150 billion a year[17], with growing competition from abroad!

During the late 1980s, the year 2000 was described as the beginning of "the Pacific Century"[18] with a variety of Asian countries outcompeting the United States in an ever competitive global marketplace. *Fortune* reports that "Japan's share of high-tech markets worldwide is surging while the U.S. share is declining. . . . Japan's rise as an economic superpower has reawakened Japanese nationalism in the form of anti-Americanism. . . . In comic books and on television, American executives have become the butt of jokes."[19] For example, a Japanese best-selling comic book pictures "inept American executives being shown what to do by a Japanese executive."[20] More recent events—the creation of a European common market and now the reunification of Eastern and Western Europe—argue for the continuation of the "Atlantic Century" but not from America's shores. The prospective decline of American business in the next century is consistent with a broader view that

American economic influence is momentary and fleeting.[21] Paul Kennedy, the most widely known of the "School of Decline" or "Solvency" intellectual movement, has argued that America is failing to address the demands of its maturing economy.[22]

LOOKING BEYOND THE NUMBERS

Is the future this bleak? Not necessarily; just this "linear" prediction of the future! "Linear thinking" in fact has created a dilemma for "downsizers." To survive in the 21st century, there is a belief that corporate restructuring is needed to make U.S. corporations more flexible to compete in an era of global competition. However, "flexibility" has often been equated with "leanness and meanness." And the linear interpretation of "leanness" has been to shed people. It is reported that "80 percent of companies with 5,000 or more employees have reduced their work forces in the past four years . . . [and] show no sign of slowing. Corporate restructuring or downsizing is now seen as an "annual edgy rite" of "cutting" people.[23] A bottom-line "numbers game"!

As a result of these annual quick fixes of the numbers, the linear interpretation of "meanness" has been this new employment "bargain." It is founded on a lack of trust that nobody—not employees, human resource professionals, or managers, in general— seems to want. Thomas Horton, the chairman of the American Management Association, and Peter Reid, in their 1991 book, *Beyond the Trust Gap,* argue this very point—that the trust gap between employer and employee was created by "quick fixes and by-the-numbers management."[24]

Even some who have reacted by replacing "downsizing" with the more positive term—"rightsizing"[25]—continue to focus on the same linear outcome—the right "quantity" of workers in the workplace. According to the president of a California-based think tank, "Companies are more comfortable . . . with simple quantification because it reduces the complexity of a problem. . . . Most managers believe that if they get the right spreadsheet, the right formula, all that complexity will disappear."[26] What these quantifiers seem to miss is the human element. Restructured companies need fiercely loyal employees who will support new ideas and take risks—because their jobs are not always on the line.

In effect, we have two strategies for the future. One strategy calls for "flexibility" through constant restructuring; the other requires "stability" to produce superior quality products. To make this work, managers and human resource practitioners need to make each strategy mutually reinforcing, not mutually exclusive. The challenge is to fit the lives of working people into this simultaneous equation with some "clearer" measure of loyalty-up/loyalty-down. This is the "rightsizing remedy."

THE RIGHTSIZING REMEDY—BUILDING A NEW EMPLOYMENT RELATIONSHIP

The rightsizing remedy is built on the following premise: The employment relationship between American workers and their employers is changing *fundamentally.* However, most employer and employee reactions have been defensive, "knee-jerk" quick fixes, failing to look beneath and beyond the surface of the present turmoil. Increased American protectionism, legal disclaimers in employee handbooks, and "free-agent management"[27] are short-term fixes that do not get at the fundamental problem of restoring American economic influence. Because of evolutionary shifts which have occurred in American employment, broader and more fundamental remedies will be needed.

To fully understand and deal with the problem, this book attempts to answer six questions:

- What has gone wrong?
- Why are today's solutions not working?
- How are today's realities shaping tomorrow's opportunities?
- What choices will employees have?
- How can human resource systems be changed?
- How should managers follow the rightsizing remedy?

These six questions are answered in the six chapters of this book—and are summarized here.

What Has Gone Wrong?

To understand the roots of this crisis, consider that legal concepts, personnel systems, and business conditions are no longer in harmony. Each comes out of a different stage of American employment relations. Chapter 1, "Remembering the Past—Pioneers, Paternalists, and Parachutes," traces the evolution of employment law, personnel systems, and current business conditions in Frontier, Welfare, and Restructured America.

Stage 1: Frontier America. This period extends almost 100 years from the early part of 19th-century America to the Great Depression of the 1930s. In the early 19th century, at least four out of five people were self-employed. As a result, there was very little reason to regulate employment relations. This laissez-faire view of employment relations continued into the early 20th century, even though the ratio of self-employed to employed workers had reversed.

Stage 2: Welfare America. This period starts with the introduction of the 1930s' New Deal legislation to regulate an increasingly employer-dominated workplace. With the growth of larger corporations and increasing American worldwide economic dominance, it gave structure and life to "organization man" or "company man" analogies made popular from the 1950s to the middle 1970s. During this time, increasing legal inroads were made to make the workplace a better and fairer place to work. Despite these "welfare" advances, employers and employees could still terminate the employment relationship at any time and for any reason.

Stage 3: Restructured America. This is the downsizing period that American corporations are now in as a means of addressing turbulent business conditions. It is best characterized by the layoffs and turmoil affecting employees and many businesses. It is best represented by a new consciousness on the part of all concerned that we have come to the end of the postwar era of boundless American optimism. Because of its overwhelming effects on workers at all levels, it will be followed by fundamental changes in employer/employee relations.

Why Are Today's Solutions Not Working?

We all know that screaming "fire" in a crowded theater will only lead to chaos. However, the current employment crisis of "firings" is leading to more than chaos as the screams cause everyone to run in several different directions all at once. Chapter 2, "Forsaking the Present—Old Solutions for Insoluble Problems," reacts to the chaotic array of defensive actions we are now seeing.

- **A misguided search for villains:** Critics are embarked on a witch hunt, blaming other countries, Wall Street investors, the fired employees, and their companies.
- **Pioneering the last American frontier:** Employees are dragging their former employers to court and developing modern-day precedents to its 200-year-old employment laws.
- **A case of corporate schizophrenia:** Employers are circling their wagons in defense of their behavior, which varies from legally disclaiming responsibility to predicting that restructuring is over.
- **Crash course in becoming airborne:** Individuals are fighting for parachutes and life preservers and then focusing singularly on their own careers.

The net result is further employee alienation and distrust of American employers—already believed to be at an all-time low. This chaotic behavior is doing little to restore America's competitive position in the global marketplace.

**How Are Today's Realities Shaping
Tomorrow's Opportunities?**

The Rightsizing Remedy is not about solving insoluble problems, but identifying new opportunities that will make these problems fade away. It means that we fight our tendency to think in deductive "straight lines," but instead look at a situation "holistically" and with "a blank sheet of paper." Fortunately, General "Hail Mary" Schwarzkopf and his staff did not think in straight lines in carrying out their ground offensive; they sensed an opportunity from a holistic view of the situation and made solving the problem of a frontal assault on Kuwait fade away.

We need to ask ourselves what are some of today's realities and what are their implications for tomorrow's workplace? What is happening now? How is it different from what managers and employees are used to? And what will it mean for employment relationships? Chapter 3, "Visioning the Future—New Workplace Trends and Opportunities," discusses 10 developments, for which these expressions have been coined:

- **The sprouting spiritualism:** A growing spiritual revival which could have a profound effect on the "ethical climate" of American institutions and, in turn, employment relations.
- **The global glue:** The increasing global economy, which is blending first, second, and third country "nationals" and blurring national boundaries in employment law.
- **The fickle future:** The acceleration of events pulsating at people and institutions and causing renewal to become routine.
- **The quality quest:** The search for the candle of American enterprise—the quality of American-made goods and services.
- **The downsized demographics:** America's "hourglass" population, which could result in there being three generations in the early 21st-century work force at the same time.
- **The high-tech households:** The "age of the smart machine,"[28] which is transforming an employee from technology's servant to its master.
- **The professionalization push:** The growth of "institutional professionalism" as professional societies become more equal in power to major corporations.
- **The grass roots grip:** The growing importance of state and local governments in representing the economic interests of their citizens against transnational corporations.
- **The information implosion:** The information phase of work force "democratization" as knowledge workers demand to know what is going on inside their corporations.

- **The constitutionalized company:** The final American "work-place" revolution as "autonomous" employees fight employ-ers for their own "bill of rights."

These workplace changes are not only eroding the employment-at-will doctrine but are contributing to the development of a new "independent" employee.

What Choices Will Employees Have?

Five hundred years ago, Christopher Columbus had a vision which—rightly and/or wrongly—changed the course of history; however, his vision would not have mattered if Queen Isabella had not empowered him to do something about it or if he had chosen a different sailing route. Chapter 4, "Empowering the Autonomous Employee—A Time of Choices," focuses on the myriad of choices that independent employees will face from their—not their employer's—perspective.

- **Long-term versus short-term employment:** How long should employment relationships last? What does life-time employment mean today? How do you determine whether a short-term or a long-term employment relationship is better for you? What do you want from your employer? What are you willing to give up in return? How you can determine when it's time to leave?
- **Implied versus expressed bargains:** When should contractual terms and conditions be applied to an employment relationship? What is an implied agreement? When is it sufficient and when is it not? What good will it do to have an explicit agreement and what are the potential drawbacks? What to look for and what not to look for in employee handbooks? Why is truth-in-advertising important to corporate communications? What value are employee agreements as a potential "poison pill" against hostile takeovers? Why should disputes be quickly handled in a new "people's court"?
- **Big versus small employers:** What difference does employer size mean to you? What are the economies of scale? When is big "too big" and small "too small"? What should you expect

from a large company and what are you willing to put up with? What should you look out for in working for a small company? Why are market niche and growth important? What are "motherships" and "satellites"? Why are "networked organizations" important to your career?

- **Company versus profession:** What choice do you have and why is it important? What does your company do for your profession and what does your profession do for your company? What is the occupational core of your company? What are the shaky limbs and branches? Who is your "consigleone" inside the organization? And who is your player-rep?

- **Full-time versus part-time employment:** What does full-time mean? Is it "quality" or "quantity" time? What is the difference between moonlighting and free-lancing? Should part-time employment refer to the employer as well as the employee? Who owns the "intellectual capital" of the knowledge worker? What is leisure time? Why is time so important?

Although a book for managers, *The Rightsizing Remedy* is also a wake-up call to employees; the intent of Chapter 4 is to awaken employees to a world of new possibilities and to realize their potential instead of merely surviving as at-will employees in arm's-length relationships.

How Can Human Resource Systems Be Changed?

Despite his vision and strategy, Columbus would have never reached America if his ship's systems were not working. What if the ship sprang a leak? The best vision and strategies are doomed to failure if the systems in place are not supportive. For example, Robert Tomasko, an authority on restructuring, has criticized conventional job evaluation systems for the "bulge" they have caused in many corporations. For example, salary advancement only comes with more "management responsibility points," which leads to excessive management layers and narrow spans of control.[29] Unfortunately, many human resource systems in Restructured America's companies are products of Welfare America's "paternalism," long tenure, and job security. Chapter 5, "Human Beings at Work—A Voyage Back to the Future," examines what changes may be needed as people move through the employment system of a different 21st-century corporation.

- **Coming on board** discusses how to rightsize an organization (so that later downsizing can be avoided) and how to recruit qualified (not quantified) people in a straightforward and flexible manner. It also introduces the notion of "continuing commissions" and "endable enlistments" as part of the employment bargain. The net result is a lean and mean organization with any meanness directed to competitors, not customers and employees.

- **Going to work** discusses ways to assign people to work. It discusses how to replace bureaucratic position descriptions with a more team-oriented "job" proposal. It also will examine the difference between pay "ranks" and pay "rates" and how the wrong emphasis in the past often led to "position paralysis."

- **Getting rewarded** discusses why managing and measuring performance are not the same and why the difference leads to conflict. It will also demonstrate the need for win–win appraisal strategies, loss sharing, and bottom-up bonuses to rebuild loyalty and commitment.

- **Moving through** outlines a mission-driven approach to building broadly defined career paths by combining occupational "core" and "corps" concepts, and how slow-track career advancement can start a "quality revolution" in regaining worldwide competitive advantage. It also discusses "sidemotion" career management strategy and envisions a front-end "intracker" role for what used to be rear-end outplacers.

- **Preparing to leave** discusses termination strategies that restore human dignity along with some degree of financial security to "terminating" employees. It discusses "fast-track" defined-benefit retirement programs to maintain flexibility for future restructuring so that "emeritus employees" can move on to second and third careers every 10 years.

This future scenario is not what reasonable people would predict today; it is not a linear extrapolation of the present. However, Charles Handy, author of *The Age of Unreason,* believes that "the future we predict today is not inevitable. We can influence it, if we know what we want it to be."[30] Therefore, managers can invent this future for their company if they know what they want the future to be!

How Should Managers Follow the Rightsizing Remedy?

Linear patterns of management thought and action inevitably lead to "extrapolated" outcomes. The challenge is to be bold and unreasonable. There are so many roads to the future that there really are no roads or roadmaps. Because of this, Chapter 6, "Following the Rightsizing Remedy—An Integrated Human Resource Management Approach," although presenting a five-step program for managers, is not a road map but a multidimensional guide:

Step 1. Internalize Your Environment: Discusses why managers should start with a blank piece of paper to "reframe" their company's present situation, think holistically, invent their own future(s), and quantify the unquantifiable.

Step 2. Externalize Your Culture: Outlines why it is important to abandon out-dated patterns of behavior, practice management-by-neglect, become the perfect audience, and "customerize" a code of ethics.

Step 3. Upsize Your People: Discusses "A," "B," and "C" employees, why "F" is important, how to perfect the three R's, and what is as American as apple pie and baseball.

Step 4. Downsize Your Systems: Takes a contrarian view of systems such as performance appraisal, position evaluation, and employee benefits.

Step 5. Flexsize Your Structure: Reviews nonpapered approaches to organization structure, the invisible and the adaptive organization, relational networks for wealth creation, and the importance of nurturing autonomous employees.

AN ALERT TO HUMAN RESOURCE MANAGERS
AND A WARNING TO READERS

The human resource management (HRM) profession is critical to achieving this kind of a future. HRM practitioners have had to deal with downsizing victims and survivors as "flesh and blood" human beings, not as just financial numbers on a profit and loss statement. What HRM practitioners need to do now is to take the lead in forging new employment relationships for their companies' employees. Although this book is meant to help, it is not a technical management book that focuses on "doing things right" or even "doing the right thing." It is about "doing the right things differently" within the context of a new era of employment relations.

In providing this broad context, this book attempts to demystify a complicated subject which, like nuclear disarmament, affects all of us. Next to death or divorce, job loss—even the fear of job loss—is a serious and highly stressful event not only for the people who are the downsizing victims but also for all who remain with the surviving corporation. These situations are even more stressful when the average person caught in the crisis (manager as well as employee) does not understand why it happens and what he or she can do about it. Even though the content of the message is serious, the tone and delivery is not technical, but attempts to be entertaining and informative.

Remember another Donald Regan remark: that women are not interested in technical "throw-weight" issues of nuclear disarmament. If you are looking for a technical throw-weight discussion, this book will probably not serve you. However, Regan found out that women and men do not have to understand throw-weights to be concerned about nuclear survival. This book is for men and women concerned about not only surviving but thriving on the future of American employment.

CHAPTER 1

REMEMBERING THE PAST— PIONEERS, PATERNALISTS, AND PARACHUTES

We have broken a sacred covenant between employers and their managers, an agreement that tacitly but strongly existed for three decades, a 30-year period in America's standard of living that made us the envy of the world.

Thomas R. Horton and Peter C. Reid[1]

To understand the roots of the crisis we need to go back nearly 200 years. We also need to think of this "sacred covenant" no differently than the joining together of two parties, for example, a husband and wife by a third party, a minister. The minister presides and, in effect, lays out the rules for joining the couple together. The marriage is a blending of the needs, values, and expectations of the two newlyweds, and their duties and responsibilities to each other "till [fill in the blank] does us part." *The problem is that the three parties have a different idea of "to fill in the blank."* The minister's belief is derived from a legal concept of the early 19th century, one spouse's belief is based on personnel systems in place since 1930, and the other spouse's belief is based on business conditions affecting the relationship since 1980. Legal concepts, personnel systems, and business conditions are no longer in harmony. Each comes out of a different stage of American employment relations. The following sections chronologize each employment stage and how it has contributed to America's present crisis.

FRONTIER AMERICA

AMERICA—A NEW BEGINNING IN EMPLOYMENT LAW

America—the land of opportunity! This dream drove waves of people from foreign lands to come here to a better life. For the people who came here, this nation represented a new start, a second chance, a break from the past. In this new land, they were no longer bound by authority, customs, and traditions of other lands. Our national heritage is rich with stories of how our forefathers immigrated to America and pioneered westward.

Immigrants came to America because there were no masters; all men were created equal and possessed free will. The boundless frontier enabled people to be free of traditional authorities—not only to break from the feudal master but also the oppressive laws and courts which interfered with man's natural rights. One important break was with English common law and its traditional notions of the natural rights and responsibilities of feudal masters and servants.[2] Unlike their masters, servants were not men of free will. Hence, the relationship between master and servant was based on the rights and duties attached to each's status. There was no room for negotiation. While the master–servant relationship was hardly balanced, it was not entirely one-sided. Accepting the harshness of work and working conditions, servants depended on these feudal lords for food, clothing, and shelter. This responsibility of masters to their servants was codified in the 1562 English Statute of Laborers. In effect, English common law offered some job security because servants could not be terminated without reasonable cause.

THE NOBLE INDIVIDUAL—SELF-RELIANT AND MOBILE

To fully understand this radical transformation of the traditional master–servant concept which occurred in the 19th century, just go back to the heroes of early America. According to Charles Reich, "the heroes of this new land were people of ordinary virtues— plainness, character, honesty, and hard work."[3] The individual was a man of innocence in a great uncharted wilderness—alone and self-reliant. Success was ultimately determined by character, hard work, and self-denial—a timeless morality play.

The triumphant individual remains an important part of American folklore. Many famous screen actors—Gary Cooper, Jimmy Stewart, John Wayne, and Ronald Reagan—have become embodiments of the noble individual by their collective screen roles. In 19th-century westerns, such as *High Noon,* good man was pitted against bad man, or in the 20th century, good man was pitted against bad system, as in *Mr. Smith Goes to Washington.*

In Frontier America, the self-reliant individual was self-employed. He was a pioneer, a settler, a rancher, a cattleman, or a farmer. Or, he settled in a small town as a self-proprietor of a small store. When he worked for others, the job and the pay were straightforward. ("Help me deliver these cattle to market and I will feed you and pay you 'x' dollars.") This was negotiated between two relatively equal parties—there were no fringe benefits, retirement plan, or job evaluation points to determine salary range. Life was harsh, but simple and direct.

Opportunity was there because the country was big and open, and people were mobile. Just as their immigrant parents voted against oppression with their feet, Americans moved westward to find opportunity. Roots in a community came with self-employment by claiming land or establishing a business. In these small towns and villages, it was likely that those who were not self-employed were drifters in search of their fortune. In *Paint Your Wagon,* Lee Marvin sings "I was born under a wandering sky," as he and his no-account group set out for No-Name City in search of gold. The 19th-century individual is remembered for his mobility. The American legal system of "at-will" employment relations stems from this view of self-reliance and mobility.

THE EMERGENCE OF THE DOCTRINE OF EMPLOYMENT AT-WILL

So a new nation which had declared its independence from England, after two bitterly fought wars, also broke with tradition. Free men, distrustful of government rule and any kind of authority, took responsibility for their own survival and well-being by grabbing a stake in America. Many were determined to go it alone, no longer to be the servant of any master, but their own ambition.

Without conventional guarantees of law and order, people were suspicious of one another. Many saw another's fortune as their own loss—the world being a rat race with no rewards for the losers.[4] Competition emerged on the most basic level. People became "street smart" before there were streets.

Communities were formed because it was to everyone's advantage to band together against a more formidable enemy or to exchange goods and services. These transactions were straightforward and simple—services (work) for goods (food and shelter), goods (livestock) for other goods (food, farm supplies, clothing) or money, and service for money. A man's handshake was his contract—signifying the intent of the two parties. When such transactions ended in a dispute they were settled—without lawyers—one way or another.

Agreements were reached out of need, not trust, and because each party thought they had equal bargaining power—whether it was a gun or physical strength. Such agreements were also true between employer and employee, whether rancher and cowboy or proprietor and stock boy. And the employment relationship could be broken at will by either party, despite the power and influence of the employer. After all, the employee could vote with his (or his horse's) feet by walking, running, or riding away. What court was available to oversee and enforce the agreement which affected such a small part of the population? What long-term career damage and monetary loss was at stake?

And so, a contract theory of employment relations emerged, giving full recognition to the notion that people of free will, with relatively equal power, could negotiate their employment relationship. This freedom to contract would eventually be recognized by the U.S. Supreme Court as a constitutional right of the individual.[5]

THE DAWN OF THE INDUSTRIAL ERA

In Frontier America, all men were born equal but there was no constitutional rule that it had to remain that way. The Calvinistic view of the harshness and competitiveness of life would take form in the

American Industrial Revolution. The Industrial Revolution started a real "rat race," with some truly coming out ahead. Just as the end of the Civil War began a century-long process of eliminating America's black underclass, the birth of the Industrial Revolution started the rise of an American "super-rich" upper class.

Frontier America was opportunistic, but also a harsh and unregulated land. Its virtue was its unlimited promise and its belief in the natural goodness of man and his ability to triumph based on hard work. Its downfall was that a few men, left unregulated, triumphed too much at the expense of too many others. Because of the Industrial Revolution, wealth became extremely concentrated in the hands of a relative few who became increasingly out-of-touch. Corruption and a variety of abuses became rampant and a new consciousness for reform slowly took hold at the turn of the century.

After having regained their independence from foreign oppressors, men would lose it to the robber baron, the factory manager, or the industrialist. The individual would no longer be self-reliant as self-employment diminished. The small-town village, community, or farm would begin to fade into our American folklore, as men, women, and children were forced to migrate to the larger cities in search of jobs in factories.

However, folklore provides comfort in dealing with the uncertainty of the future, so myths live on. One myth which survived into the industrial era was the doctrine of employment-at-will and the notion that employee and employer were still equal bargaining partners. In reality, the individual was no longer competing against the success of other individuals but against "the system" or "the house." The myth is that the individual is divinely incarnate, a natural underdog who can still win despite the odds.[6]

On a more rational level, the employment-at-will doctrine served to facilitate the American industrial revolution. It also permanently shifted the balance of power to employers who emerged to control work forces of the hundreds and thousands. The economics and technology of mass production diminished the importance of the individual worker. Specialization and division of "labor" (as individual employees would now be called) resulted in the factory worker becoming a "cog in the wheel" or an "interchangeable element of production." Industrialists were ready to accept the risks of investing in new plant and equipment as a fixed cost. After all, the workers absorbed all the risk for their labor. Workers were a variable cost because they could be terminated at-will in a fast changing economy.[7] Workers also benefitted however, because their standard of living was raised by the abundance of material goods produced through mass technology. And they still were mobile.

REFORM TO WELFARE: THE BEGINNING OF THE END

At first, reform measures were highly targeted at specific industries and specific practices (e.g., unhealthy practices in the food industry, monopolies and monopolistic practices, unfair competition, dishonest advertising, and unfair and unsafe employment practices). The frontier was now settled and the settlement needed to be policed.

Although the sun was already setting on Frontier America, the Great Depression ushered in the darkness. Hope and opportunity had turned to despair. Migration replaced mobility. Self-reliance was lost in the bread and soup lines. Individuals became mobs. The American dream was bankrupt because of the excesses of selfish men.

A new collective force sprang out of the depths of the depression—people binding together to rebuild the country by putting in checks and balances so that this could never happen again. The New Deal, bringing together all facets of the American reform movement,[8] formed the basis of a new era.

This new era would touch on all phases of American life and, in particular, would bring about fundamental changes in employment relations. Employment security would be fostered through a "safety net" of unemployment compensation, welfare, and social security legislation to provide a sustenance floor so that no one was left out in the cold. Business power would be countervailed through unions and big government. In turn, other changes would come about. Major corporations, in a spirit of enlightened self-interest, would become more benevolent employers and would improve the welfare of their employees. However, the at-will employment doctrine would remain substantially intact.

Thus, Stage II Employment—Welfare America began.

WELFARE AMERICA

THE AGE OF INSTITUTIONS

Frontier America was the age of the individual; the new era would be the age of the organization—big government, other large public institutions (schools and universities, hospitals, and other non-profits) and goliath corporations. In the early 19th century, no one could have envisioned that large corporations—rather than partnerships and self-proprietorships—would become the dominant employers in American society. Nor could anyone imagine that government would, in time, take on such a pervasive role as a regulator and protector of American society.

To be sure, major corporations were not born in the 1930s and 40s, but they did come of age in this period. Although there were a few hundred American corporations in the early 19th century, almost all were devoted to quasi-public activities, such as running turnpikes or building canals.[9] The business corporation took form with the growth of the industrial revolution. The concept of corporate "limited liability" encouraged investors to finance plant and equipment needed for mass production—since it limited individual risk. By 1920, some of these corporations had grown to a billion dollars in revenues. These early corporations personified their founders; their identities were synonymous. Their authoritarian leaders were still pioneers on a harsh frontier in a classic competitive struggle. Employee welfare was not their concern. This would all change, because unlike its founder, the Corporation was immortal.

The age of Welfare America was now well under way by a culmination of events external to the Corporation—the Federal Child Labor Law of 1916; the Railway Labor Act of 1926; the Norris–La Guardia Act of 1932; the National Labor Relations Act of 1935; the Walsh-Healy Public Contracts Act of 1936, and the Fair Labor Standards Act of 1938.[10] Beyond these reforms, real change was internal. A more detached manager would replace a very impassioned and dictatorial founder. Because of externally imposed reform, corporations could become more friendly places at which to work—inventing *personnel management.*

THE INSTITUTIONAL INDIVIDUAL—COMMITTED AND DEPENDENT

A profound change was occurring in the values and aspirations of the American worker. No longer first-generation Americans, mid-20th-century man's experience was collective, not singular. He had grown up in the Great Depression and fought in World War II—two events which bonded people against forces of darkness, one internal, one external. Through this experience, he learned to rely on others, most notably major American institutions. Although still fueled by the enterprising spirit of his ancestors, *his* pioneering journey would be a climb through the pyramid of the corporate organization.

Unlike his forefathers however, he would become the anti-hero of American folklore. In the middle 1950s, he was the "organization man" who had left home, spiritually as well as physically, to take the vows of organization life.[11] In the late 60s he was "institutional man," the epitome of "Consciousness II," who relies on institutions to certify the meaning and value of his life, by rewarding accomplishment and conferring titles, office, respect, and honor" and providing "personal security in terms of tenure, salary, and retirement benefits."[12] By 1976 he would become the "company man" who "equates personal interest with the corporation's long-term development and success and whose belief in the company may transcend self-interest."[13] In sum, the hero of Welfare America certainly was not John Wayne.

Like his ancestors in Frontier America, the institutional individual struck a deal with another individual, forming the basis of an employment relationship. However, the new employer was an immortal Goliath, either a Corporation or the Government. The relationship was clearly out-of-balance; no longer adult–adult but parent–child. This is the essence of Welfare America.

A GROWING WELFARE WEB

As part of this parent-child relationship, employees began to expect more than just a "fair day's pay for a fair day's work." Jobs were positions and positions were rungs in a career ladder. "Cultural relativism"[14] had come to the workplace—a job had little meaning out of context of its place within the corporate hierarchy or timing within one's career. Sure, employees were paid for their work but these wages and salaries were determined based on rational job evaluation techniques to determine relative fit. Career progress was tracked through salary advancement and promotion. Success meant grabbing a stake in this new landscape. However, hard work and perseverance were not enough. Institutions were made of people, their values and expectations. Through work experience, these values and expectations were "shared." Over time, a "culture" would emerge through these shared experiences. Not unlike the small towns and villages of Frontier America, corporate life would develop its own folklore of heros and villains and "shared values," including loyalty, trust, teamwork, and commitment. Institutional individuals did not just work for a company, they belonged to it.

In return, the Corporation took care of the welfare of these employees by removing much of their financial risk. In addition to cash salaries, other benefits were provided to ensure against untimely death or disability or any major medical and hospital needs. Furthermore, employers guaranteed a post-retirement level of income through "defined benefit" retirement plans. In return for spending a 20-to 30-year career with a company, institutional employees could anticipate receiving 60 to 70 percent of their salary for the rest of their life. The federal government promoted corporate welfare by subsidizing employer-provided health benefits by excluding their employee value from ordinary income tax.

So the employment relationship was complete. In return for their hard work, commitment, and trust, employees were provided with social standing, a future career, and a financial risk-free environment. The only aspect of the employment relationship still at risk was how long it would last.

A NATION OF AT-WILL EMPLOYEES

By 1980, over 90 percent of the nation's work force were counted as employees; a complete reversal from the early 1900s when over 80 percent were self-employed. Self-employment was on the ropes in Welfare America. The odds against success were overwhelming. For every new business which opened each year, eight or nine were destined to failure.[15] Despite establishing an institution to promote small business, Welfare America did little to help the pioneer self-starter. The country was now settled with tax breaks and special allowances for large corporations with powerful lobbyists. Relative to its small size, a new business would have to absorb a disproportionate share of Welfare America's costs—social security, unemployment insurance, workers' compensation, internal revenue regulations, and other government intervention. It is no wonder the institutional employee felt locked into the organization, often accepting unfulfilling work. Contributing to their lack of mobility was the employee's need to service ever increasing personal debt. Purchasing the American Dream, a house, meant combining a 30-year mortgage with a 30-year corporate career.

Ironically, the institutional employee was still eager and willing to take on large financial commitments well into the future, when his or her employment was terminable at will. The reason was an unbridled optimism about the future of Welfare America and an unspoken trust in the Corporation to live up to their bargain. This optimism was part of the American character carved out of an expansionist view of the vast frontiers of the 19th century, and buoyed up by an unprecedented post–World War II economic expansion.

All of this would change.

RESTRUCTURED AMERICA

THE GATHERING STORM

The promise of prosperity was held open to all in Welfare America. The country knew no limits. First, the West, next the world, and then "the wild blue yonder" into space. *All the Right Stuff* epitomized the new pioneering mood that burst from the Kennedy years of the early 60s. Johnson's "guns and butter" reckoned that simultaneous victories could be achieved in a war on poverty and a war in a small remote Southeast Asian nation. Why not in the land of "the best and the brightest"! In the 60s, the American economy was healthy and rapidly growing and American business was a model for the world. "Made in Japan" was a bad joke for inferior quality and workmanship. With the growing popularity of Chevrolet Impalas and RCA color televisions, corporations were upsizing and expanding their managerial staffs at a record pace. And giving rise to a new profession known as MBAs. Opportunity and challenge were the call; job security was for government workers. At-will employment was the oil needed to grease business expansion. Unemployment was a government statistic associated with business cycles which only affected America's disappearing underclass. Job loss—like polio—was cured by a "Salk vaccine" of unprecedented postwar prosperity.

Life changed! The Bay of Pigs . . . November 22, 1963 . . . Tet . . . A Memphis motel balcony . . . A Los Angeles hotel kitchen . . . The Chicago Convention . . . Watergate . . . Middle East Oil Embargo . . . Ho Chi Min City . . . Stagflation . . . Iran. A Growing Malaise! It was not surprising that Americans overwhelming voted out the messenger of that "malaise" message for an actor who symbolized our 19th-century "Death Valley Days" heroes and whose generation came to prominence in a more nostalgic 1940s and 50s. This Noble American would take on an almost mystical quality of invincibility after a foiled assassination attempt. However, it is now the "morning (after) in America"—following the Beirut massacre, the Challenger disaster, Iran–Contra, the October 1987 stock market crash, the S&L crisis, and a 1991 recession which may not be over. According to one news account, "The crash . . . . seems to be taking its place alongside other, very different national traumas that have eaten away at America's boundless postwar optimism and sense of wellbeing."[16] Long before the opening of the Berlin Wall and the break-up of the Soviet Union, there was a growing consciousness that we have come to the end of America's postwar era.[17]

"Made in the USA" has become a *patriotic* symbol as more and more Americans purchase foreign goods of superior quality and workmanship. Protectionism has again become a presidential campaign slogan for 1992 but against whom or how many? What started out as the second Japanese invasion has broadened to other Pacific rim countries—Korea, Taiwan, and a host of rapidly developing Asian nations. In direct contrast to trade of the last generation—foreign goods are being imported and American jobs are being exported. Restructuring of American industry, initially at the plant level, is reaching into every office and service establishment as a stop-gap measure to increase competitiveness by reducing costs. Millions of white-collar employees have been—and are still being—terminated at will by their employers. The cause—good, bad, or none at all—did not matter.

LEARNING THAT SMALL IS BEAUTIFUL

From 1881 to 1970 American business dominated world commerce without even trying, because of its sheer size. These halcyon days are over and the restructuring of the American economy is well under way. And it is predicted that by the end of this century "cars from China, optical products from Eastern Europe, and biotechnology from Brazil will make it even more difficult for U.S. companies to compete."[18]

Bigness rode supreme in Frontier and Welfare America—from big country to big employer. America's massive resources and industry's mass production led to an overemphasis on quantity, rather than quality, thus making American goods less competitive in world markets. In 1987, Tom Peters described "the American penchant for giantism" (at the very core of the American economic system), which is now causing untold harm. He argued that Frontier America's "wide open spaces set it all in motion. Farmers cultivated land and wore it out. Farms are a history lesson told by hulks of rusted cars and agricultural equipment. In contrast, the Europeans and the Japanese have lived within limits for centuries, and had to be more careful with resources."[19]

However, century-old American values do not die quickly, as Peters goes on to observe that: "Size, wanting to be number 1 in market value or in the Fortune 500, remains more on the minds of a number of American chief executive officers."[20] In fact, the only movement to smallness is in the number of people employed in U.S. companies as forced terminations and early retirements inevitably follow America's manufacturing decline, and the skyrocketing rates of mergers and takeovers.

THE SMOKELESS SMOKESTACK

Overall, the proportion of Americans employed in "smokestack" manufacturing industries has dropped significantly from over 50 percent at the outset of Welfare America 50 years ago to less than 25 percent now. And despite glowing reports of "healthy clouds of steam billowing" from "rust belt" factories, manufacturing employment could drop to less than 10 percent by the beginning of the next century. In particular, American employment in traditional manufacturing industries such as metals, rubber, chemicals, steel, and automobiles has fallen rapidly. According to the Bureau of Labor Statistics, manufacturing employment is anticipated to level off to 22 million by 1995.[21]

On the other hand, there is a rise of employment in the *service* sector of the economy which is attributed to the needs of an increasing U.S. population and improved standard of living brought about by an increasing gross national product (GNP) and certain productivity gains in manufacturing and farming. However, with the decline of American manufacturing, there is an increasing alarm about the future quantity and quality of service jobs. Manufacturing jobs have been typically better paying than service jobs and have offered better fringe benefits—health care, life insurance and pension—the underlying foundation of Welfare America. On the other hand, many of the service jobs that are anticipated to be created are considered low-tech or semi-skilled, such as fast-food workers and waiters, leading some to believe the American economy is suffering from a "Big Mac Attack."

There is a lot of disagreement on this point. On one hand, futurist Alvin Toffler believes that the decline in manufacturing employment is characteristic of America's move to a "third wave" service-sector economy based on "knowledge work." He argues "the key questions about a person's work today have to do with how much of the job entails information processing, how routine and programmable it is, what level of abstractions is involved, what access the person has to the central data bank and management information systems, and how much autonomy and responsibility the individual enjoys. ... To describe all this as 'hollowing out' or to write it off as 'hamburger slinging' is ridiculous."[22]

On the other hand, *The Next Century* author David Halberstam is not as optimistic. Halberstam writes, "There are those who believe that America can move from the strongest core industrial economy in the world to essentially a service economy without losing its greatness, its dynamism, and its industrial health. I am absolutely certain that we cannot. I think very few people who go into service jobs will go into what might be called high-service jobs, that is, jobs of value, with leverage and dignity."[23]

THE OUTSOURCING OUTBREAK

A few years ago, the K-Car—the product of federally backed loans, bank loans, bank writeoffs, concessions from suppliers and production workers[24]—was going south to Mexico. As a result, Chrysler workers in Newark, Delaware, and Kenosha, Wisconsin, were laid off. Outsourcing, the shifting of manufacturing to typically a "third world" foreign country where labor rates are cheaper is a common occurrence in Restructured America. The Chrysler example—outrageous on its face—was no different than what is happening across many manufacturing industries caught in a price squeeze on profits.

A major concern to many critics is that through outsourcing America is "voluntarily" giving away its industrial base to foreign countries by moving production offshore. Industrial policy advocates have been arguing for the creation of government-backed institutions to revitalize American industry. Others remain concerned that these and other changes will further alter America's distribution of wealth and will result in a two-tiered society, with the "once solid middle tier of American jobs being undermined."[25]

In large part, the problem stems from what part of our manufacturing base it is that we are giving away. According to *The Washington Post* business reporter Paul Blustein, "Japanese firms avoid the 'hollowing out' problem that is said to afflict U.S. industry, in which functions like design are performed in America while manufacturing is moved overseas. Lower-tech products being shifted to overseas production or phased out, while Japanese plants are constantly upgraded for top-of-the-line production.... For the past three years, Japanese spending on new plants, equipment, and research has risen at double-digit annual rates, reaching an astonishing 28 percent of GNP—roughly twice the comparable U.S. figures."[26]

LIFE IN THE NEW "FORTUNE 100"

Stepped-up worldwide competition has furthermore promoted corporations everywhere to take part in a mania of mergers and takeovers. In 1988, *Business Week* reported that "merger mania has survived poison pills, the 1986 tax-reform law, anti-raider backlash, anti-takeover laws, insider-trading scandals, the crash, the moribund junk-bond market, and the 1987 tax law."[27] In late 1991, *Business Week* again reported:

> In one industry after another, companies are announcing strategic alliances and outright mergers that would have set off the antitrust alarm bells in years past. It's as if the seemingly endless tide of seemingly ever-larger mergers in the 1980s have left us all numb: Almost unnoticed, with little public debate, a sweeping consolidation is transforming a variety of manufacturing and service businesses.[28]

Restructured America is in progress! The motivation has been fingered to be pure Wall Street greed—a classic Frontier America survival-of-the-fittest struggle; the causes have been laid to Welfare America's failure to remain competitive. Corporations are acting by busting up, selling off, swapping, acquiring, and reconfigurating basic business units, from rockets to towels, and cutting "excess" management layers and staffs. There is still concern that this mania will not make corporations better competitors in the United States and the world since 7 out of 10 acquisitions of the 1960s and 1970s have not worked.[29] Even less optimistic about merger mania, Harvard Business School professor and author, Michael Porter, argues that "Much of the drive toward consolidation and mergers is generated out of fear. We're running the risk of making things worse not better."[30] Others believe it is nothing more than "dinosaur mating." Regardless, the wave of takeovers will continue if the determinant is to make companies more efficient.[31]

What this also means is that life will never be the same again for at least one out of three workers in the United States, those whose future employment depends on fewer that 1,000 goliath corporations.

BABY BOOMERS AND MUSICAL CHAIRS

Restructured America's downsizing is out of phase with demographics. Baby boomers have arrived to find America's corporate pie shrinking. *The New York Times* reports: "Record numbers of managers are chomping at the promotional bit at a time when there are very few jobs into which to promote them."[32] *Business Week* tell us that "the management ladder is losing still more rungs as companies ranging from investment banks to computer makers, broadcasters, and airlines take the ax to their work forces."[33] *Fortune* reports that in the 1990s the populous baby boom generation will be pressing for promotion just as the middle ranks are reduced.[34]

The children of Welfare America who grew up in affluent times—now committed to families and mortgage payments—are in for a bad joke. There are estimated to be 76 million persons between the ages of 29 and 43.[35] The sheer size of the baby boom generation ensures that millions of top quality workers will never find places near the apex of the corporate pyramid.[36] Since 1980 the number of candidates for every job has doubled from 10 to 20.[37]

The human toll will be particularly hard for the advance guard of this (mistakenly labeled) "privileged generation." Many of the same people whose consciousness was forged by the scars of the Vietnam War, are again caught up in a situation, not of their own making. Critics, such as Hirsch, argue that "employees in their 40s are especially vulnerable because this is the age when new houses and condominiums are purchased, children's schools are selected, and other major commitments are taken on."[38]

Furthermore, who goes and who stays may very well be a game of Russian roulette as more and more companies are jumping on the bandwagon.

THE EXORCISM BANDWAGON

More than 15 or so years ago, Michael Korda described firing as having a ritual significance with a quality of exorcism about it. Somehow sacrificing one person will cause the gods to smile upon the rest.[39] Have we been experiencing massive human sacrifice over the last decade? Do we need exorcisms and smiling gods to solve America's competitive doldrums? In 1988 *The New York Times* reported that "corporate chiefs are sending out paeans" in speeches, published papers, and annual reports, noting how fat has been cut out of management layers.[40]

The Washington Post reports that "there is a new willingness of employers to dump workers at the first sign of economic trouble."[41] *Downsizing* author Robert Tomasko described a "bandwagon effect" in his criticism of "demassing," a brutal and blunt exorcism of large chunks of managers and professionals. When everyone seems to be doing it, it is harder for some companies to face their corps of investment analysts. And as a result, some top managers publicly show their resolve to keep a short rein on costs by eagerly talking about their staff reductions.[42]

Machoism in the corporate suite? The return of John Wayne as 19th-century American hero, Rooster Cogburn? Or as Attila the Hun? Has the legal doctrine of employment at-will become a barbarian's sword slashing away and choosing its victims arbitrarily. Andrew C. Siglar, chairman of Chapin International, bluntly stated, "Cutting isn't the answer—that can be done by stupid arbitrary judgments."[43] And *The Washington Post* reported that "sometimes the best managers are the ones who lose their jobs."[44]

Because of excessive heavy-handedness, the real hero may turn out to be the victim. The ordinary man or woman hurt by this turmoil—a Jimmy Stewart character right out of *It's A Wonderful Life,* but the movie is still under way and the script is being improvised. In the past, the fired employee was stigmatized. According to Dr. Stephen Cohen, if you are fired people will assume you are to blame, which is their way of protecting their continued membership in the organization.[45] Korda argued on a more mystical level that the person to be fired grows in importance in order "to make them responsible for everything that has gone wrong."[46]

However, the pendulum may be swinging the other way. *The New York Times* reported that it is those who fire who are stigmatized these days and criticized for the overexpansion and overhiring in the first place, that made this decade's widespread downsizing inevitable.[47]

In effect, termination decisions on who goes and who stays are becoming less clear-cut. American legal doctrine with some exception provides wide rein for corporate employers to "fire at will" for good cause, bad cause, or no cause at all. And as the bandwagon has grown, a new consciousness has also grown and it becomes more difficult to identify the victims from the survivors. The earthquake has hit, but the aftershocks remain to be felt!

WINNERS AND LOSERS

In the midst of Restructured America's downsizing, the average total pay for chief executive officers jumped nearly 50 percent. Moreover, in the midst of the current recession, *Time* magazine claims that chiefs of America's largest companies—"already making 160 times what average blue-collar employees receive"—got pay raises of 12 percent to 15 percent as the economy nose-dived.[48] Other reports indicate that the average CEO of a large U.S. company now makes 35 times (and, in some cases, 1,000 times) as much as the average manufacturing employee.[49] Whatever the ratio, it is outrageously high when compared to Japan, where the ratio is only 15 to 1, and Europe where it is 20 to 1.

For instance, Lee Iaccoca, Chrysler's chairman (the highest paid in 1986 and the second-highest in 1987) is heralded year after year as "delivering the least bang for the buck!"[50] Influencing its decision to "outsource K-Cars," Chrysler's 1987 share of the U.S. new car market fell to nearly 10 percent, and 1987 profits fell 7 percent. Iacocca's 1990 pay was $4.8 million while the average autoworker's pay was $34,320. Compare this to 1970 when Lynn Townsend, Chrysler's CEO at that time, made $210,000.[51]

While a fury of critics are questioning "whether they are worth it,"[52] the trend toward higher levels of executive pay does not seem to be abating. Executive compensation expert, Graef S. Crystal, observed that "A cash compensation package of $1 million a year, including bonus, has become the bare minimum wage for the CEOs of most major companies." Crystal goes on to predict that in the year 2001, the pay of Steven J. Ross, cochairman of Time-Warner, will top $1 billion.[53]

The fundamental issue is how can people be rewarded with several million dollars each year when American enterprise in general, and some of their own corporations in particular, are in decline. Skyrocketing executive pay levels may be serving to undermine the credibility of leaders,[54] (such as Iaccoca) with their mid-level managers and unionized employees. Perhaps in response to Iaccoca's $17.9 million earned in 1987, the Chrysler Corporation has been prohibited from giving executives bonuses in any year in which its union's 60,000 members do not receive profit-sharing payments. D. Quinn Mills of the Harvard Business School remarked that this unusual ratified demand of the United Auto Workers is "the first bubble in a wave of public revulsion at top management compensation."[55] Ironically, Crystal has suggested the "ghoulish" possibility that departed middle managers may be providing the food for this feeding frenzy: "It may be financed from the bodies of middle management. By having a leaner, meaner organization with fewer levels, the CEO—on the seventh day he rested—takes half the savings and puts it in his pocket."[56]

On the other end of the spectrum is the "contingent work force" as Restructured America has knocked significant numbers of people from the full-time work force. In 1991, it was reported that "the idea of a permanent full-time work force is becoming little more than a dream for millions of people who are being left with low pay and little or no health or pension protection."[57] *The Philadelphia Inquirer* reported that "at least one in three laid-off managers takes a job that pays less and has less opportunities for advancement than the one left behind."[58]

"Underemployment" in America is a growing problem. Part-time workers are growing nearly twice as fast as the number of full-time workers during the period 1970 to 1987. In 1988, the contingent work force totaled between 29.9 million and 36.6 million, or 25 to 30 percent of the civilian work force of 122 million. And, more importantly, nearly 25 percent of the total part-timers cannot find full-time jobs.[59] Involuntary part-time work is creating a new group of second-class citizens who besides having little job security have virtually no health care, life insurance, or pension benefits. These "underemployed" are up over 125 percent since 1970. *The Washington Post* reported that the census of workers without full-time jobs is sure to keep growing as companies whittle away at labor costs to become more competitive.[60]

And so it goes in Restructured America.

A NEW EPIDEMIC

Peter Drucker once equated the fear of job loss to the fear of polio. According to Drucker, the fear of job loss paralyzed us for exactly the same reason that mothers panic at the thought of polio. "Every case, however rare, was unpredictable, mysterious, and catastrophic."[61] Just as mothers in the 1950s feared for the safety of their children as another isolated case of polio was affecting a neighbor one block away, a student in the same elementary school, or a beloved relative or family member, so too the fear of potential for job loss affects us all as we hear about a neighbor, a fellow worker, or a relative. The new outbreak of job loss which has been occurring, remains unpredictable, mysterious, and catastrophic but is no longer rare.

While more Americans of working age have jobs today than at any time in the postwar period, Restructured America is making many uneasy about their work.[62] With the sense of job security disappearing, most Americans now accept that they will have to work in several companies, not just one, during their careers. As a result, most will concentrate on themselves, working only on the immediate task and not on the welfare of their particular employers of the moment. According to one economist, "In the world of contingent work, neither the worker nor the employer makes any commitment that lasts beyond sundown."[63]

Although uneasy about their employment relationship, many employees are afraid to move because of a spreading phenomena known as "job lock."[64] This is where they fear changing jobs because of a medical history that, in today's more stringent insurance market, would probably prevent a worker's acceptance by a new health plan. Just one more legacy from Welfare America's "entitlement web."

It is widely believed this will make American corporations less competitive and efficient. Ironically, the ultimate victim may turn out to be the American corporation itself and ultimately American worldwide competitiveness and influence. Overemphasis on cost reduction to boost short-term profits because it has been easy for corporations to dispose of at-will employees, may in the long run be counterproductive. Tomasko argues that these cutbacks do not always address the appropriate problems and for some companies the greater danger of demassing is the false sense of security it leaves.[65]

Economists, academicians, and prominent business leaders are concerned that American industry has improved but so have our competitors, and quality problems are alleviated but not solved.[66] At the same time, employees are becoming overly concerned with job security rather than product innovation and risk-taking. In late 1991, *Business Week* ran a cover story entitled "I'm Worried About My Job!"[67] According to a senior vice president of Gannett Co., "Employees are running so scared that there is a whole culture that says don't make waves, don't take risks—just at the time when we need innovation."[68] As a result, a new culture of cynicism is emerging as corporations try to get their employees to buy into their new strategies without providing sufficient assurances as to whether it's in the employee's best interest. Some business thinkers fear that the cost-cutting binge which began in the 1980s may depress corporate creativity and competitiveness for years to come.[69]

In summary, we are in a new stage of employment in Restructured America. A crisis has been created not only for the millions who have lost their jobs but also for the surviving employees and the corporations they work for. In resolving this crisis, life could become even more chaotic as old quick fixes are used to address new problems.

CHAPTER 2

FORSAKING THE PRESENT—
OLD SOLUTIONS FOR
INSOLUBLE PROBLEMS

We are going through a second civil rights revolution for workers in this country. It is a time of great flux and change and a lot of uncertainty as to what you can and cannot do.

Robert Fitzpatrick[1]

The reaction to the beginning of Restructured America is predictably negative: disbelief, defensiveness, and a determination to cling to age-old myths and to increasingly obsolete, but familiar and comfortable employment practices. Rather than understanding the fundamental shifts that are taking place as the new era emerges, most attention and energy are focused in any of four ways:

- Critics are embarked on a witch hunt in a misguided search for villains.
- Employees are dragging their former employers to court, developing modern-day precedents to the last American frontier—its 200-year-old employment laws.
- Corporations are circling their wagons in a schizophrenic defense of their behavior.
- Individuals are singularly packing parachutes rather than focusing on how to collectively restore American's competitive position in the world.

Most of this energy has been focused on the "quick fix" and a lot of the activity has been counterproductive and outright destructive, as the following sections will elaborate.

THE MISGUIDED SEARCH FOR VILLAINS

WORLD WAR II REVISITED

The first target of criticism are the companies of foreign nations such as Germany and Japan. However, there is also a growing number of other European and Asian countries that are outcompeting American firms. The fact that some of these countries have in place national industrial policies—to foster their competitive advantage—has produced a populist groundswell favoring American protectionism. In this regard, Japan has become the enemy of the American autoworker, and driving a Toyota or a Honda automobile is paramount to burning the American flag. "Buy American" and increased protectionist tariffs on foreign-made goods has become a politically popular message. These sentiments have the potential to set off a new round of trade wars without any assurance that the American worker will be any better off.

Most Americans consume foreign-made goods because they believe they are better. Shopping for product quality and superior craftsmanship is not seditious behavior. American companies that increasingly understand (or never forgot) this message, are having no problem in holding onto market share. As noted by *Fortune*, 3M, Johnson & Johnson, Procter & Gamble, and several other companies continue to invest in the research and development needed to be innovative.[2]

The Washington Post reports that although "Japan Inc." deserves criticism for many sins, consider the following: "After slowing its exports and trade surplus due to pressure from the United States in the last five years, Japan is still expanding its global reach while attaining new heights of industrial success at home."[3] Blaming the Japanese misplaces responsibility as Robert Reich believes: "the problem lies not with them, but with us." He contends that American-based companies need to (1) invest in more sophisticated production here in the United States, and (2) develop in our own work force the same basic technological competence and organization experience that Japan is creating among Japanese workers.[4]

A final note, it is even reported that Lee Iacocca—who extols U.S. manufacturing prowess in television ads while accusing the

Japanese auto companies of "wearing a Teflon kimono"—does not always practice what he preaches. In return for up to $300 million in cash and other assistance, it was reported that "Chrysler was ready to give Mitsubishi a *dominant voice* in the design and marketing of many of Chrysler's 1993 models."[5]

WALL STREET BLUES

The second target is the "enemy within" or what some have labeled "Wall Street greed." Some critics have argued that Wall Street bankers and security analysts see the corporation as a "cash cow" whose sole purpose is to produce "the highest share price for its owners."[6] In some respects, this represents a fundamental clash in the values of the Frontier and Welfare America eras. Strong, albeit selfish individuals, the type who founded major corporations, are up against managers who have run these institutions over the past 50 years. What has been called into question is the very purpose of a corporation—its supposed "immortality."

On one hand, the Wall Street view is the classic, but narrow, Frontier America competitive struggle of survival of the fittest—that is, the corporation is strictly there to make money for its owners. On the other hand, the view of conventional Welfare America sees a broader role of institutions, that is, "giant companies are living resources for the long run, requiring and entitled to at least some recognition and protection to enable them to continue making contributions to their markets, employees, and communities."

More than likely, the truth may be somewhere in between, buried under myths. For the past several decades, many corporate CEOs have espoused the virtues of free enterprise, while their lobbyists sought to limit competition through favorable government intervention on the part of regulatory and legislative bodies. As a result, many American companies have prospered and have been able to fatten their payrolls with extra management layers and staffs with high salaries and benefits. It is reported that "during these comfortable years, layers of management at utilities, insurance companies, retail giants, and auto manufacturers swelled in corporate headquarters buildings."[7] Foreign competition in manufacturing and deregulated competition in financial services, transportation, energy, and communication has diminished future earning projections and deflated stock prices. Wall Street, regardless of its motives, is reacting to these underlying changes. On the other hand, the American frontier view of survival of the fittest is perhaps too harsh a remedy and ultimately self-defeating in view of global competition from foreign companies supported by their own governments. Undoubtedly, like the elimination of "junk bond" financing, other forms of Wall Street abuse will become the target for new reforms.

CORPORATE "RIP VAN WINKLES"

A third target is the victim—the fired American worker. The typical argument is: "They were asleep within the corporation. Their dismissal will awaken them to find a more fulfilling and rewarding career. They will look back at this event in a year or two and agree it was the best thing that ever happened to them"—a kind of "death and resurrection" picture fitting into a classic storybook ending ("they lived happily ever after"). Still others are less kind and adopt a "they had it coming" attitude. Carl Icahn in his quest for TWA remarked, "These management need shaking up—they're horrendous."[8] A corporate head hunter interviewed by *Business Week* stated, "Companies are getting rid of "B" and "C" players and hiring "A's."[9]

The reasons for making the victim the scapegoat—whether it's for the terminated employee's own good by "waking him up" or for the good of the corporation—are equally questionable. Moreover, these postmortems are largely irrelevant, serving only to provide some justification to the downsizer or the raider for their actions. The problem may not be the individual's performance or potential but their underutilization in poorly conceived jobs. If employees were "lulled" asleep by Welfare America, it was because career tracks were unduly narrow and compartmentalized, allowing little room for growth. While some affected managers may recognize their dilemma, there is little many can do as individuals to change the organizational structure and personnel systems that caused this. And, the web of entitlements they receive, particularly the years of service they have at stake in corporate-defined benefit retirement plans, makes it nearly impossible for them to leave voluntarily.

So when they are forced to leave involuntarily the pain is ever more great, not only because their employer has changed the ground rules after they have invested some of the best years of life in the company, but also because they are held up to ridicule as being the cause of their predicament.

ATTACKING THE MESSENGER

The last target is the Corporate employer or its agents—consultants who specialize as downsizers. Corporations that cut their long-tenured staff are viewed as short-sighted and with some validity if it is purely to bolster short-term profits. And, while firing an employee is never pleasant, some companies make it more unpleasant by despicable heavy-handedness. Even without these unnecessary incidents, there is no way to tell someone they are no longer needed with convincing reason.

Because of this, there has been an unprecedented rise in the use of outside consultants to assist corporations in deciding where and how to reduce staff. These developments have given rise to charges that some consultants are no more than "hatchet men," who are serving as a foil for management, telling them what they want to hear, by recommending "preordained" staff cuts. In addition, the rapid rise in these services has raised concern about the level of maturity of consulting personnel—many are young MBAs—who do not have the experience and judgment needed for such a sensitive task. Perhaps because of this, some have observed that corporate downsizing is too critical to be left to outside consultants.[10]

Despite the faults of the messenger and how the message is communicated, the basic message is the same. American business must change to regain competitive advantage. Flexibility and quality have become watchwords. Companies must renew their organization strategy, structure, people, culture, and systems to be successful in the years ahead. The era of Restructured America is under way and life will never be the same again. Because of its relative newness, many corporations and their consultants have stumbled, making major strategic and tactical errors at the expense of employees. But in the process these companies and consulting firms have amassed a formidable body of hard-won knowledge of what works and what does not work in a restructuring process.[11] What is becoming clear is that companies are not going to get gung-ho performance from scared, resentful, and mistrustful people,[12] regardless of the message.

PIONEERING THE LAST AMERICAN FRONTIER

POOR MR. COMERFORD

Mr. J. L. Comerford is perhaps best known to labor lawyers as the man who kept his wife but lost his job, and thereby giving an extreme, but firm, precedent to the doctrine of employment at-will. As the story goes, back in 1936; Mr. Comerford, a 20-year employee of International Harvester, worked for Mr. I. B. Dawson, a man smitten by Comerford's wife.

After failing in an attempt to gain the affections of Mrs. Comerford, Dawson "out of a spirit of revenge," "wrongfully, falsely, and maliciously" reported that Comerford's services were no longer satisfactory, causing Comerford's dismissal. Although Comerford sued International Harvester, both the Alabama Trial Court and Supreme Court agreed that these facts did not violate Alabama's common law of employee relations. Since he was an at-will employee, the court held not only that the company had the right to discharge him at anytime but also the company's right was "not wrongful because it was malicious and done for improper reasons."[13]

Although this 1936 ruling may be understatedly unfair, it was used as late as 1983 by the same Supreme Court of Alabama to indicate that the common law doctrine of employment at-will remains alive and well. And this is still the general rule of law throughout the rest of the United States, with a relatively few but growing number of exceptions.

AT-WILL EXCEPTIONS

Because of Mr. Comerford's misfortune and other poor souls like him, the American sense of justice and fair play has slowly awakened over the past 50 years. Congress and state legislatures have been tearing away at the at-will rule by enacting laws that prohibit dismissal for specific reasons. For example, the Society for Human Resource Management reported in its review of the 80s that the doctrine of employment-at-will has been eroded during the decade by state courts.[14] In particular, Montana's unique worker-discharge statute provides nonunion employees with basic protection against arbitrary dismissal but also limits court awards they can win if they are fired and sue their former bosses.[15]

The most widely recognized exceptions are Title VII of the 1964 Civil Rights Act and the 1967 Age Discrimination Employment Act, which together prohibit dismissal of employees on the basis of race, color, religion, sex, national origin, and age (between 40 and 70). These federal statutes are often closely paralleled by state and local laws.

While these legislative exceptions have increased the workload of American courts, judicial exceptions have also emerged, as some state and federal courts have taken the side of modern-day Mr. Comerfords. This new wave of at-will exceptions to American common law are noted below:[16]

Implied contractual agreements. Some courts have decided that it was the "unexpressed" intention of the parties to continue the employment relationship for a definite period of time, say a year, unless there was "good cause" to terminate it earlier. For example, an Illinois court held a memo stating "Here is your salary contract for 1973" to be an employment contract of one year's duration, thus limiting an employer's discretion to terminate at will.

Employer's duty of good faith and fair dealing. Some courts now recognize an implicit contractual obligation of "good faith and fair dealing" should apply to employment. Each party implicitly promises not to interfere with the other party's ability to perform and derive benefits. To illustrate, a Massachusetts court found that a 61-year-old salesman had been discharged in "bad faith" to deny him commissions. If Mr. Comerford was now living in Massachusetts, he would have been able to keep his job as well as his wife.

Retaliation against "legal" employee behavior as defined by specific statutes. Many courts have ruled against employers who terminated at-will employees because they either refused to break a law (e.g., commit perjury) or because they were exercising their rights under a given statute (e.g., serving on a jury). However, the courts have usually rejected this notion unless the circumstances tend to be outrageously convincing, such as when the fired employee refused to participate in illegal activities.

Dismissals that contradict a more general notion of the public interest. Absent of any direct violations of law, some courts have ruled in favor of fired at-will employees by relying on their "own" sense of good employee relations. An Illinois court held it was wrongful to dismiss a manager who participated in a criminal investigation of one of its employees. While no specific statute was involved, the court concluded that "public policy nevertheless favors crime fighters." This interpretation was rare since many courts have not interpreted a valid exception without a specific statute.

Tortious breach of contract. Under some unusual circumstances, a court found that an employer, "acting intentionally and in bad faith, breached an implied understanding with an employee." For example, in Montana, the court held that a company's promise to provide a letter of recommendation was fraudulent and malicious, to induce an employee's resignation so that they would not have to pay unemployment compensation.

Negligence. In a more complicated situation, a court ruled against an employer who had every right to terminate an at-will employee but carried out the termination in a negligent manner. On one hand, a federal district court found that a company had good cause to dismiss an employee. On the other hand, the court found that the company did not use "ordinary care" in conducting annual performance reviews because it failed to warn him about his risk of being terminated.

Promissory estoppel. In some circumstances, employers' right to terminate at-will employees has been excepted if the employer unfairly breaks a promise on which the employee relied. In Minnesota, a court found that an offer of employment which enticed someone to quit another job could not be rescinded. The court reasoned that the prospective employee was not given a good faith chance to demonstrate on-the-job performance.

However, the growing trend away from this 19th-century doctrine has contributed to the uneven legal terrain from state to state and has posed some interesting personnel management issues in the process.

CALIFORNIA, HERE I COME

For nearly two thirds of the American work force, there is a good reason to live in California beyond the sunny skies, the year-round gorgeous climate, and the opportunity to see more than one's share of movie stars. Their employers—on the advice of legal counsel—are more apt to deal fairly and in good faith. If dismissed at-will employees can show that the employer's actions were anything less, they will likely prevail in a California courtroom. At present, the "good faith and fair dealing" exception is the law in California, as well as in Massachusetts and New Hampshire.[17] Although other common-law exceptions have been adopted, at-will employment is still the law of the land in nearly all 50 states.

On the other hand, the state of New York continues to be pro-employer with respect to the issue of employment-at-will. For example, a recent New York state appeals court decision extended the right of companies to dismiss employees, even if the firing deprives the employees of their rights as shareholders in those companies. In the case in point, the employed executive not only lost his job but also lost an opportunity to receive a substantial increase in his investment in the company because he was fired three weeks prematurely. The court ruled narrowly that the individual did not have an employment contract, hence he was employed at-will, ignoring whether as employee/minority investor, he was dealt with in "good faith."

This dichotomy of legal interpretation poses an interesting employment relations ethical challenge to employers operating in more than one state. Does a major employer differentiate in the treatment of its employees in California and New York because the employment laws are different? Would a preventive legal strategy require a California manager to be more sensitive to fairness? Assuming a progressive corporation adopts a "high road image" of uniform treatment to all, would the same company's lawyer advise a "low road defense" in a state where "good faith and fair dealing" had been rejected? To be sure, corporate personnel managers must be wrestling with ethical as well as legal issues because most employee wrongful discharge violations evolve from an alleged ethical violation.

A LEGAL NIGHTMARE

The rise in employees involuntarily discharged in the last decade has given rise to an unprecedented increase in employee wrongful-discharge lawsuits. As a result, state courts are creating new rights for workers, as challenges to the right to fire people indiscriminately have grown with a vengeance.[18] The American Bar Association estimates that between 1984 and 1985 the number of lawsuits brought for wrongful discharge jumped by 85 percent, and this jump does not include suits brought for age discrimination. In 1986, the American Arbitration Association recorded over 300 claims for damages totaling more than $29 million, from executives charging breach of contract.[19] According to the Bureau of National Affairs, more than 25,000 wrongful-discharge cases are pending in state and federal courts.[20]

The basis in law for each new employee complaint is some previously legislated or judicial exception to the general at-will rule. However, in turn, favorable judgments for the dismissed employee produce a new set of precedents, thus paving the way for the next round of fired-employee complaints. In effect, the opposing parties to suits are modern day pioneers in a previously unsettled frontier of American employment law. However, while folklore is nostalgic about the accomplishments of 19th-century settlers, it overlooks the uncertainty, pain, and hardship—many pioneers were buried along the way. Employees who take on their employers may not succeed regardless of the merits of their complaint because they lack the time and resources necessary. Those who are successful may not be that successful and at a price. What manager wants their next employer to fear they would litigate the slightest inequity? Many employees who may want to sue will not because of the uncertainty and the potential stigma. They will instead choose to be airborne, packed with a parachute.

For their part, corporations are attempting to minimize their legal exposure. One outplacement firm reported that over one half of the companies they surveyed required dismissed middle managers to sign a release not to sue if they were going to receive enhanced severance benefits, and over three quarters of their terminated senior executives must sign a similar release. For any suits filed by former employees, employers feel compelled to justify their actions, possibly spending more on a legal defense than necessary if the aggrieved employee had been treated differently. And, while highly unlikely, some corporations are being advised to countersue the employee[21] in recognition that their "best defense may be to go on the offensive," particularly in cases where they believe the suing employee is trying to get something that management feels he or she is not entitled to. More importantly, it will be advised to adopt a cautious arm's length posture with its employees to mitigate the prospect of future claims.

The schizophrenic defense this will produce in corporations, and in turn, the "solo" behavior it will provoke in employees—the next two solutions—will only worsen America's ability to be competitive.

A CASE OF CORPORATE SCHIZOPHRENIA

THE WARNING IS ON THE LABEL

> This guide tells you about our firm, our policies, our procedures, our benefits, and our expectations of you as an employee. It is designed to assist you during your employment by serving as a ready reference source. *It is not a legal document and does not constitute an implied or expressed contract or guarantee of employment.*

A statement like this is now in the opening paragraph of untold numbers of corporate employee handbooks. The highlighted sentence was added in self-defense, probably on advice of a company lawyer. Because personnel manuals and employee guides are often construed by courts as employment contracts, labor lawyers have been spending a lot of time combing through these documents. As a result, disclaimers have been inserted like the one above and self-congratulatory statements have been eliminated, caveated, or watered-down. According to business legal expert Daniel Moskowitz: "Companies have tried to make the changes (in their employee handbooks) with as little fanfare as possible."[22] Take, for example, another self-serving statement which has been revised by the added underlined statement.

> Our high proportion of long-service employees is one measure of the success of our efforts. *Of course, all of our policies and mutual expectations are subject to prevalent business and economic conditions.*

"Long-service employees" and "our policies and mutual expectations"—products of Welfare America's personnel systems—are now "subject to prevalent business and economic conditions" of Restructured America.

What will be the implications of this legal maneuvering on the credibility of corporations with their employees? The underlying message is that Welfare America policies don't mean anything if you take us to court when you lose your job. The American Management Association's Horton believes that corporations are "unwittingly sending out the wrong message" by emphasizing "our freedom to fire people for no good reason."[23] The credibility of responsible employers, already considered low, will plummet further, following the sad example of the tobacco companies,[24] who have been forced to hide further behind their warning labels in each successive case of product liability.

And, what if these legal disclaimers backfire in unintended ways? Can a corporation enforce policies against moonlighting or conflicts of interests if an employee it desperately needs and values refuses to abide by this code of behavior and cites the company's legal disclaimer in his own defense?

THE RUSH TO HALFWAY HOUSES

Beyond the schizophrenic message in corporate communications, employers are doing a double-take with their fired employees—in part to alleviate any guilt but also to lessen the likelihood they would be dragged into court. Once the bad news has been conveyed, the more benevolent terminators belatedly befriend those terminated, and offer assistance in outplacement. In this regard, most major corporations use professional outplacement firms to ease the trauma on the fired American white-collar worker. Many believe these firms provide invaluable counseling as well as temporary office to report to each day, complete with phones, secretarial services, and employment manuals. Revenues have grown from $35 million in 1980 to $350 million in 1988 according to Kennedy Publications of Fitzwilliam, New Hampshire.[25] The growth of outplacement firms, which Hirsch terms "halfway houses,"[26] is believed tied directly to the jump in dismissals resulting from corporate restructuring."

Despite any misconception, outplacement firms do not place their employees in jobs, they mostly counsel and motivate the fired employee to make it their full-time job to find another job. While good outplacement firms can provide many valuable services to the fired workers, they also provide an invaluable service to their other client, the fired employee's company who typically foots the bill. Simply, they focus the fired employee on his future job opportunities, away from the past injustice and rage he may feel about his former employer, thus decreasing the likelihood he will ever sue. According to *Fortune,* "The corporations that pay for outplacement service generally love it; having the outplacers around makes firing people easier."[27]

The quality of outplacement service—while highly regarded under normal circumstances—may not be able to keep pace with the rapid growth in this profession. According to outplacer Louis Masterson, "Outplacement has become a haven for people whose qualifications are suspect, people with a marketing focus."[28] As the number of firings have increased their workload, outplacement firms have taken on more staff. Some staff additions have gained their outplacement expertise by being fired. One critic compares this expertise to a surgeon's claiming expertise in cardiac surgery because he had his own heart operated on.[29]

On top of this, the outplacement specialist constantly faces a fundamental ethical dilemma in serving the fired employee and his ex-company. Are the interests of both parties still the same? What if they are not? What obligation does the outplacer owe the fired worker, a stranger who will never use their services again? What obligation does the outplacer have to the company paying the bill, who probably used their services in the past, and will do so again. As a result, some believe that "outplacement is still an industry trying to find and define itself, mixing opportunism with altruism."[30]

Restructured America has been a boom for outplacement firms. However all booms last for only a fleeting period of time. What will remain however will be the collective experience of the fired employees who received outplacement service—which will help or haunt the outplacement industry in the future.

COMFORTING THE SURVIVORS

A third type of 180-degree behavior is in how corporate employers are acting toward the surviving employees. Will the arm's length employment relationship produce fiercely loyal employees who support new ideas and risk-taking when people are anticipating the second shoe to fall? For example, throughout the "downsized" AT&T system, workers reportedly feel like dominoes. According to Mark E. Notestine, AT&T's vice president for human resources, "There's so much ambiguity, people are very nervous."[31]

What is also making employees nervous is a trend started in sunny California where they try to force their surviving employees to literally "sign away their right to sue."[32] According to some news accounts, employees are being asked to sign a clause which states that their jobs and pay may be terminated at any time, with or without cause, at the sole discretion and option of their employer.

Requiring job applicants to sign sue and coercive statements is, at best, a very questionable business practice. One observer comments that at-will dismissal statements on employment application forms are analogous to the "yellow-dog contracts" of the 1920s, which required job applicants to sign a statement that they would not join a labor union if they were hired. Yellow-dog contracts were later invalidated by labor relations legislation.[33]

Again, human resource practitioners are caught in a bind. While again trying to minimize the corporation's legal exposure, they are sending out the wrong message: that survivors can be fired for no good reason. What a comfort!

WHEN LIGHTNING STRIKES TWICE

A final form of schizophrenia concerns the manner of downsizing. According to many management authorities it is better to cut deep and take the pain all at once, rather than dragging it out, so that those who remain are not in constant fear. In other words, strike all at once so the survivors can find comfort because "lightning does not strike twice in the same place." Many companies apparently initially subscribed to this approach by following a brutal "demassing" strategy. These actions led to wishful thinking as far back as 1988—that the downsizing phase of American management is behind us.[34] At the same time General Motors announced that it will have to slash at least 100,000 jobs by 1992.[35] Most observers—executives, placement agencies, and organizational experts—are more realistic. They believe that "managers should brace for more upheaval and for lasting changes."[36]

So who can be sure? How can anyone suggest that "downsizing is over," given that merger mania is still under way, hence the jobs of potential takeover targets are still "on the chopping block." Moreover, short-sighted demassing in critical areas could be quickly followed by a new hiring surge, and then cutbacks again. In fact, the biggest reported shortcoming has turned out to be that companies "are good at cutting jobs, but less good at cutting out unnecessary work."[37]

"Quick cuts" and "quick rings of the final buzzer" are no more than "quick fixes" to restore corporate credibility and employee loyalty. When asked about future restructuring, we should be reminded of the advice of an old sage when asked by a young man whether he should participate in today's debate: "It's better that people wonder why you didn't speak than wonder why you did."[38]

A CRASH COURSE IN BECOMING AIRBORNE

MIDLIFE SURPRISES

Who does not remember where they were when they heard that President John F. Kennedy was assassinated? And when we heard that the shuttle Challenger had met disaster? And, when there is a personal crisis, who does not vividly remember the event, whether it be the loss of a loved one or a job?

The character of a nation is not forged by prosperity but by crisis—the Great Depression, Vietnam, and the Challenger disaster. The character of the fired at-will employee is shaped by the scars of the event. All of a sudden, they are cast adrift, thrown out of the plane, or overboard to lighten the load in Restructured America. And, because they were nurtured in Welfare America, many are free-falling without a parachute or a life preserver; after all, these entitlements belong to their employer. According to Hirsch, "it often happens at the most likely age to have just celebrated doing well on the job by taking on heavy financial obligations based on the clear sailing many are told they can look forward to at the company."[39]

The wheel of fortune is spinning! Life will never be the same. This new reality, seared into their consciousness, unleashes a whole range of emotions, stresses, and energies. Undoubtedly many will look back and say "Thanks, I needed that!" But most surprisingly, all are being told by their former employer to singularly bear the brunt of Welfare America's misfortunes, and with impunity, because of Frontier America's employment laws. However, these fired at-will employees are in for some additional surprises. The rules of becoming re-employed and staying employed may forever change their outlook on life.

NETWORK OVERLOAD

The first lesson a fired at-will manager learns is to be a modern-day Paul Revere. Get the word out! However, it is not the British who are coming this time. In Restructured America, it is not enough to take away the pay, fringe benefits, and position status of the dispossessed. The fired employees then must proclaim their predicament not only to their own network of friends and business associates but, next, to wider audiences of people they don't know—to extend their outreach for help.

Anyone who has ever been through this situation quickly learns about "the law of large numbers," a fallback to a distant "college 101 class in statistical probability." This is the central message of Carl Boll,[40] who became the father of the "broadcast letter."

While acknowledging the yield is low (about 5 percent), Boll, arguing that the job searcher has nothing to lose (he has already faced the ultimate rejection), recommends sending out literally hundreds of these letters. Boll's thesis has been updated and broadened for all types of job searchers by Richard Bolles. Bolles describes the numbers game: "If you place sufficient bets on enough different numbers, one of them is bound to pay off for you."[41]

So the fired at-will manager learns to swallow his pride and write to dozens of people he knows, and hundreds of people he doesn't know, using quality stationary marked "personal and confidential." On an micro scale, the average job seeker sends out 100 or more such letters, often accompanied by follow-up "are you interested" phone calls. On a macro scale, the number of unsolicited letters increases geometrically as the number of job seekers increase—like an atomic explosion. The secretaries of targeted CEOs who receive these "personal and confidential" letters must spend all of their time deciding which ones their bosses should read.

In the age of unprecedented firings and layoffs, there has got to be a better way.

FREE AGENTS IN A CLOSED SHOP

The next lesson the fired at-will manager learns, once in a new job, is to "look out for No. 1." These modern-day "Robert Ringers"[42] are being told to "pack their own parachutes" or life preserver, depending on their mode of career progression. The mid-life MBAs in their late 30s or 40s are going back to business school, at least to the placement office, so they can relive the fantasy of having multiple job offers and sign-up bonuses. After all, that's how it all started—the happy hunting season of corporate recruiters climbing the walls to see them with lavish offers and career promises. And it continues for the recent graduates—the new kids on the block—who seem to be breaking new thresholds. Why not? Let's do it all again. Just download corporate loyalty, pack a personal computer, and one's own recruiter and lawyer. The MBA Invincible charging at the corporate windmill. The enlightened individual against the dark barbarian forces of evil. It will work, won't it?

Frank Sinatra was a free agent; he did it his way! Joe Namath was a free agent; he did it Jimmy Walsh's way![43] A variety of other entertainment and sports figures are free agents; they did it their way! Very few managers are free agents; most do it the corporation's way. Hirsch believes free agent managers should negotiate with prospective employers to make your responsibilities, perks, and benefits "explicit." However, it is still a rare manager who has enough "clout" to command a full-fledged employment contract—"X" salary for "Y" years. Free Agent Managers need clout to be successful.

What is clout? It all depends. The blacks in their struggle for civil rights realized that no one would give them what should be theirs; they had to demand it and back up their demands with force. Fortunately, Martin Luther King chose to demonstrate the force of his convictions by practicing nonviolence. He and his followers gave new meaning to the 19th-century self-reliant Noble American individual. They were good men against a bad system, and they put the weight of their convictions behind their view. The only free agent managers in this country who will have any clout will have to follow that example, not by protests or sit-ins, but by demonstrating that they are independent of their employer. The others, with their network and their "packaged skills," will be no match.

THE NEW RADICAL

The popularity of presidential candidate Jesse Jackson among middle-class white voters in 1988 stemmed from his message about "economic violence."[44] "Jacksonomics," although drawing favorable attention, would be regarded as radical by most Americans. Reversing Reagan's 1981 tax cut, cutting defense spending, and restoring Great Society social programs appear drastic. Yet Jackson's oratory had driven home the message that we are in the midst of a "high dislocation, with ordinary people being impacted by violent events." *The Wall Street Journal* warned that "further down the road, the decline in middle-management jobs could result in a socially disruptive horde of highly educated and deeply frustrated people."[45] While it is unlikely that the middle class will become "radicalized," many voters—farmers, auto and steel workers, and middle managers—are becoming more concerned about issues of employment security. This growing awareness is affecting not only those directly displaced and the survivors but also the general public, whose consciousness is being raised by events like the October 1987 crash, the trade deficit statistics, and the looming threat of a recession, or worse, in the not-too-distant future.

Again, middle managers are increasingly caught in the "middle"—lacking the job guarantees and severance packages of union workers and the employment contracts and golden parachutes of top management. Some authorities have argued that they may turn to others for help. While it may appear inconceivable, unions may now find a more sympathetic target in their organizing drives—particularly among clusters of lower-level professionals and managers. *Fortune* reported that "managers by the thousand have joined a union called "Me-First."[46] Further, as Jackson's "economic violence" message has started to grab hold, Congress and state legislatures—increasingly sensitive to middle-class unemployment—enact more statutory exceptions, causing further erosion to the at-will employment doctrine. Commentator Richard Reeves has argued that millions of Americans, when they find that "there is nothing left for them in the 1990s," will turn to "government, if history is any guide."[47]

Closing on a somber note, it is not beyond imagination that if the situation deteriorates further, history will repeat itself with a major depression. If a depression is so unimaginable, just consider what Eliot Janeway said in the spring of 1991 as federal government 1991 unemployment statistics suggest the economy is on the path to recovery.

> The real problem isn't consumers but the financial system, which is so weak that comparisons to the early 1930s are not inappropriate. If you look at the broader picture of tottering debt structures, falling incomes and prices, it suggests we might be exposed to a danger that we thought had passed from history half a century ago—a depression.[48]

If this happens, more radical measures may become popular. In this regard, consider the wide popularity of Dr. Ravi Batra's predictions of another depression in the 1990s. A closer reading reveals that Batra recommends fundamental reforms of American enterprise under the "Proutist system" by:[49]

- Placing a cap on executive salaries (for example, maximum salary can be no more than 10 times the minimum wage).
- Breaking up certain industries and redistributing ownership and control of major corporations to its employees.

Although Japan's leading automotive executives only get about six to eight times as much as their employees (compared to 12 to 18 times in the United States),[50] such drastic surgery may be an over-reaction from people who are "mad as hell and not going to take it anymore."

What's really needed is to blend employment law and personnel policies to fit today's realities, the subject of the next part of this book.

CHAPTER 3

VISIONING THE FUTURE—
NEW WORKPLACE TRENDS
AND OPPORTUNITIES

As Peter Drucker often says, "Don't solve problems. Pursue opportunities." That's the highest wisdom.

George Gilder[1]

Is this another "doom and gloom" book? Looking at the glass as being "half empty" rather than "half full." With all this talk about the "end of America's postwar optimism," why not mention our overwhelming success in the Persian Gulf? The success of those Patriot missiles and "nintendo-like" bombs certainly attest to America's technological prowess. And this hinting about a depression in the 1990s is just negative thinking—after all aren't we now in full economic recovery from the recession?

You may be right. The last two chapters are certainly a "linear" depiction of the past and the present. And somehow the handling of the Persian Gulf crisis does not fit neatly into this discussion. Despite the tragedy of the Kurds and reported disarray among "the Commanders," this was a remarkable success—demonstrating to the world community what is great about American resolve, knowhow, sacrifice, and plain guts. However, what was most remarkable in this writer's eyes are two things. First, our leadership's outright disdain for "bottom line" numbers (e.g., daily score cards and body counts) and their obvious loyalty to their "human beings at work" over in the Gulf. Second, and because of their predisposition for people rather than numbers, they were not "linear thinkers" when it came to winning the war. They were opportunistic! Holistic! Inventive! Because they cared about the lives of people under them. Remember our soldiers in the Saudia Arabian desert saying that "the fastest way back to the United States was through Kuwait"? A straight line. They were wrong! The fastest way was not a straight-line frontal attack; it was "around" Kuwait. Schwarzkopf and his team pursued an opportunity, they did not react to or try to solve the problem as defined to them.

The military's "workplace" was in the desert; American corporations have a different workplace but no less of an important challenge and opportunity with respect to the lives of the people under them. How many corporate chief executives and their management want to feel, think, and behave like the commanders of Desert Storm? Probably all would do so if they were not under the constant day-to-day pressures of "running a railroad" with foreign competitors, corporate raiders, and investors breathing down their neck.

Well, stop riding down the same "linear" railroad tracks and start looking for ways "around" these problems. In the process, consider 10 workplace trends so that you can pursue opportunities in managing your human beings at work.

A SPROUTING SPIRITUALISM

BEYOND THE "IS GOD DEAD?" ERA

All the news about Yuppies, the "me-decade," and "the money society" makes it difficult to see that something seems to be happening in America. People are increasingly searching for something inside and beyond themselves. The pendulum seems to be swinging back to the spiritual, or at least it is not moving more to the material. Perhaps, this is because America is "graying." Or because of many traumas that remind us of our material limits. *Time* recently reported that "the past decade brought growth, avarice, and an anything-goes attitude. But the 90s will be a time to fix up, clean up, and pay up."[2] Some social observers have already dubbed the 1990s as the "We-decade."[3]

At the heart of this spiritual revival is a fundamental drive to restore a sense of moral values. Allan Bloom has hit a raw nerve in his criticism of "the dreariness of the family's spiritual land-scape."[4] Bloom reminds us that religious teaching, "attending church or synagogue, and praying at the table were a way of life, inseparable from moral education."[5] Even liberal theologian Rabbi Neil Kushan argues that moral teachings raise our consciousness toward certain absolutes "to be truthful, not to steal, not to hurt others, and to be kind and helpful."[6] And Soviet commentators, like George Arbatov, say there are changes in America's moral atmosphere with the fading out of the spree of greed and corruption.[7] This growing spiritual renewal—whether New Age or established religion—will likely be as real at the turn of the next century as it was proclaimed to be dead nearly 20 years ago.

It may be a sign of a changing time that people are no longer questioning whether "God is dead?" but whether "greed is dead?" In an article whose title asks the same question, *Fortune* reports that three out of four working Americans age 25 to 49 would like "to see our country return to a simpler lifestyle, with less emphasis on material success."[8] *Time* reports that "in place of materialism, many Americans are embracing simpler pleasures and homier values. They've been thinking hard about what really matters in their lives, and they've decided to make some changes. What really matters is having time for family and friends, rest and recreation, good deeds and spirituality."[9]

One of Naisbitt and Aburdene's "megatrends 2000" is "religious belief," which they believe is intensifying worldwide, for no other reason than the gravitational pull of the millennium.[10] What does this have to do with American employment relations today? Everything!

THE POWER OF ETHICS

Around the same time that the Beatles were declaring "God to be dead," Antony Jay was critical of corporate "duplicity" and of loyalty that flowed in one direction only: up, not down.[11] Probably referring to employment at-will, he argued that it is duplicitous to say that people can always leave, while they are encouraged to commit themselves to the organization for life.

The "duplicitous face" of Corporation Man is in most cases a conditioned response of managers or professionals who were "only doing their jobs." This person, according to Charles Reich, is one without absolute or transcendental values who disdains personal responsibility for what an organization does. *The New York Times* recently reported that for at least 25 years Americans "have failed to instill basic values in our children, in the workplace, and in many other parts of our society. We are simply not getting across such basic ideas as decency, fair play, courtesy, hard work, scholarship, perserverence, self-confidence, teamwork, discipline, and a host of other character traits. We have been traveling a path of ethical relativism."[12]

Gary Edwards, executive director of the Ethics Research Center, argues that "Companies are increasingly concerned about ethics ... because the cost of behaving unethically can be great.... They hope their efforts will prevent misconduct but also bind people to the company and that has implications for productivity and quality." As these ethicists report, "Johnson & Johnson, IBM, and Xerox have made ethics and operations indivisible not so much by telling employees how to behave but by grounding the entire company in values such as good customer service, respect for employees, and high customer service."[13]

As a case in point, Alcoa's chairman, Paul H. O'Neill, and its former president, C. Fred Fetterolf, believe that "biblical principles of truthfulness, compassion, and stewardship should not stop at the factory gate."[14]

THE BORN-AGAIN INSTITUTION

So many American employers are starting to get this message—and some have always understood it. For every Tenneco whose outrageous behavior in laying off their employees was vividly documented in the *Houston Business Journal*[15] there was an IBM. Many restructured companies have found it less a matter of human decency than hard-nose pragmatism to treat fired employees with "respect, kindness, and even solicitude." Furthermore, there are reports that a "new corporate philosophy is slowly gaining favor in boardrooms across the country," that is, people are more than just employees, they are "individuals who are inextricably attached to a family."[16] While the focus of philosophy right now is only on creating a "family-friendly workplace" by providing "family-friendly benefits," such as day-care assistance, it still represents a move in the right direction. As one example, work-and-family job positions are cropping up in such companies as Time-Warner Inc., Bank of America, AT&T, Marriot Corp., IBM, and at the *St. Petersburg Times* Company.[17]

Furthermore, through vehicles, such as Employer Stock Option Plans (ESOPs), at-will employees are beginning to have more control over their employer. While employee ownership is not the same as "employee management," employees generally have the right to vote on major issues such as a merger or reorganization. The ESOP is an American version of a century-old Western European tradition of workers' cooperatives, encouraging employees to own shares in their companies. In the past 15 years, nearly 9,000 corporations have enrolled almost 9 million employees in ESOPs.[18]

The values of these born-again institutions will no doubt take some of the fire out of the employment-at-will doctrine.

THE GLOBAL GLUE

THE TRANSNATIONAL CORPORATION

Nearly 20 years ago, Peter Drucker proclaimed that the world has become a "global shopping center" where every business, even purely local ones operating in northern Michigan, will have to understand the world economy.[19] What was true in 1974 is even more true in 1992. Because of the global competition, southern Michigan is no longer the automobile capital of the world. And even more real today is Drucker's "transnational corporation."[20] Unlike the "multinational"—a 19th-century structure which makes products or furnishes services for its own discrete national markets—the transnational corporation integrates manufacturing plants in several different countries to sell products in any number of countries. It is not only based on Drucker's global shopping center—a world common market with no national boundaries but also a global manufacturing plant, due to outsourcing. Why else were the aftershocks of the 1987 stock market crash instantly felt around the world?

Drucker's transnational corporation—boundless in its global market—remains bounded, however, in the political realities and employment customs of each host country. One of the primary challenges of companies operating in Europe or the Pacific Rim has been to seek cultural understanding and to find ways to motivate and retain employees of different races, nationalities, languages, and cultures. This was the key message of a conference of international personnel managers.[21]

One of the keys has been fitting together the employees of the transnational corporation—expatriates, host country nationals, and third country nationals.

EXPATRIATES, HOST COUNTRY, AND THIRD COUNTRY NATIONALS

A transnational human resource strategy must fit three types of people:[22]

- **Expatriates**—Citizens of the country of the parent corporation assigned to a "foreign country" location (for example, Japanese employees of Sony working in another Pacific Rim country).
- **Host country nationals**—Local employees who are citizens of the foreign country in which the transnational corporation is doing business (for example, American employees of Sony working in the United States).
- **Third country nationals**—Employees who are neither citizens of the country in which they are working nor citizens of the country in which the corporation is headquartered (for example, a French citizen assigned by a U.S. multinational corporation to a plant in Belgium).

Far more complex than problems of a purely domestic corporation, the problems of integrating these three types of people are enormous, given their different cultures, languages, customs, and laws. Yet, for the transnational corporation to add any value beyond the sum of its component parts, it must strive to be transcultural. As such, the largest companies, in order to provide opportunities for their best people, attempt to build an international service corps without regard to national origin to fill key positions at corporate headquarters or in "overseas" affiliates.

And for many American-owned companies, there is a growing trend toward international service as management development programs are being redesigned to include international assignments. *The New York Times* reported that "slowly but surely, hands-on international experience is moving out of the nice but necessary category and into the 'must have' for those on the corporate fast track."[23]

This has the benefit of blurring the "we–they" cultural differences of expatriates, host country nationals, and third country nationals as well as blurring the geographic boundaries of national employment laws.

BLURRING OF NATIONAL EMPLOYMENT LAWS

What happens if an American expatriate employee is discharged overseas? Or, a third country national from Belgium working for an American corporation is fired in Canada? What if the American expatriate and third country national decide to sue under a combination of domestic and foreign employment statutes? What laws would apply? Most likely, more than just the American employment-at-will doctrine. For example, U.S. antidiscrimination laws remain fraught with peril for international employers.[24] What foreign businesses may not be ready for is the complex array of U.S. laws and regulations designed to balance the rights of individuals and the rights of business owners.[25]

Daniel Kendall of Rohm and Hoss, found that "the most significant American 'import' in the area of employee rights has been the growing body of court cases that challenge the doctrine of employment at-will. Unlike in the United States, the courts in many foreign countries have established over a long evolutionary period, the rights of individual employees to be protected from wrongful, or unfair, dismissal."[26] For example, from *Fear of Firing:*[27]

- In the United Kingdom, the 1972 Contracts of Employment Act and the 1974 Trade Union and Labor Relations Act afford British workers considerable protection against the threat of unjust discharge.

- In West Germany, the "Kundigungssrutzgesetz" (a mouthful!) requires employers to provide a valid reason for dismissal, in other words, to show cause.
- In Belgium, perhaps the most developed of all countries in employment relations, high termination indemnities are required, not only for situations where an individual discharge is disputed, but even where terminations are based on economic considerations.
- In Japan, the land of lifetime employment, most companies provide large lump-sum indemnities by paying one year's current wages for each year of service.

This "extraterritorial" application of both U.S. and foreign labor laws is but a logical next step in Marshall McLuhan's "global village" and as Kendall concluded, "there is no reason to suspect that these cases will do anything other than grow!"

THE FICKLE FUTURE

THE OBSOLESCENCE OF TOMORROW

On Thursday morning, April 14, 1988, Merv Griffin—an old radio-show crooner ("I've got a lovely bunch of coconuts") and TV talk-show host—was standing in the Lawrenceville lobby of the New Jersey Casino Control Commission. He was there dictating to waiting reporters a new chapter to *Trump—The Art of the Deal.* And in the process, he had thrown the Atlantic City casino industry and its regulators into a new "numbers game." All of a sudden, controlling ownership of Resorts International had switched from Donald Trump to Griffin and the number of casinos had increased.[28] Joe Papp, the Commission's budget officer, had to tear up his 1989 projections.

While certainly not the reason Restructured America has been labeled "the Casino Society," Tom Peters and others argue that "predictability is a thing of the past."[29] Yesterday's excellent companies are no longer excellent! Gulf Oil is Chevron, and United Airlines is Allegis is United Airlines! Once-depressed Boston has been booming, and oil-rich Houston has been a bust (but that

is changing, too!). The new "Walt Disneys" of the boomer generation—George Lucas and Stephen Spielberg—have lost some of
their magic, while the old Walt Disney magic is back and rated
"PG" and "R." Fat people in high school are thin at high school re-
unions. On Wednesday, May 11, 1988, Trump backed out of his
deal with Griffin—perhaps because only Trump can write his
book.

What is true today may be false tomorrow. As noted earlier,
most of our projections into the future tend to be linear extrapola-
tions from yesterday to tomorrow. Just as we are comforted by holding on to our 19th-century folklore, a high degree of statistical
"confidence" comes from projecting yesterday's numbers into the
future. While these projections are no doubt necessary, we are wise
not to be fooled by high statistical correlations of past events. And
on Friday, May 27, 1988, Trump and Griffin issued "a joint statement" that they had reached an agreement;[30] perhaps as a prelude to
writing "a joint book." Because of people like Griffin—and of
course, Trump—Papp and others need to go back to the drawing
board.

Because of our fast-moving environment, corporations now go
back to the drawing board a lot more often than even before. Business survival in Restructured America's new economy will depend
on management's ability to thrive on the tides of change or face the
possibly of being swept away by them. And for employees, the labor
market has become a place of "churning dislocation," with companies changing and jobs being redefined.[31]

It is three years later and counting. Griffin and Trump still
have their casinos but both nearly became bankrupt because of this
deal, and Joe Papp got a promotion. Nothing stays the same for
very long.

ROUTINIZED RESTRUCTURING

"Restructured America" or "Restructuring America"? "Restructured" implies a one-time event or "a problem to get around." Regrettably, many organizations that have opted for large-scale
demassing, with large one-time layoffs to improve short-term profits, are reacting to a "problem to get around."

For those familiar with the "right brain/left brain" concept, these have been left brain management approaches—cold, mechanical, and unimaginative solutions, based on quantitative deductions from internally generated cost statistics and bottom-line projections. Companies that thrive on change are more likely to have a penchant for the right brain, with its emotional sensing devices for customer satisfaction and employee loyalty—criteria which constantly escape quantification. These managements are guided by a "holistic" vision, not bureaucratic rules and memoranda.

"Restructuring" may actually be a more fitting term because it refers to a continuous adaptation of organizational forms, procedures, and systems to gain market advantage, particularly in an era of "telescoping technology." John Stepp, former U.S. deputy undersecretary of labor, said "Today's technology has telescoped product and process life cycles so much that skills are becoming obsolete at a breathtaking pace. Instead of paying for jobs, employers are now paying for a variety of skills that workers acquire."[32] In this regard, Robert Waterman differentiates among "renewing companies in the degree and rapidity of people moving from job to job."[33]

However, employees "nurtured" on Welfare America entitlements and "nervous" about job security will not willingly adapt to a continuous renewal process.

THE DYNAMIC JOB DESCRIPTION

The reluctance of employees to adapt to changing markets and customer needs will become more, not less, of a problem for large corporations. Ross Perot's continued criticism of General Motors' inertia due to its committee-driven structure and bloated management layers is one visible reminder of America's latest malaise. Narrowly defined management roles cast into concrete by "job descriptions," career ladders, and pay ranges has long been the principal root cause of this dilemma. According to Waterman, job descriptions are one of the "staples of management control," "stamping in distinctions and rigidity rather than stamping them out."[34]

However, job security of at-will employees, fueled by either past or anticipated layoffs, has quickly become an equally formidable obstacle. The new "arm's-length" climate makes people adverse to risk, questioning, "what's in it for me?" The solution that Waterman sees in continuously renewing companies is to provide a policy of job (but not position) security. The personnel management implications of such a policy will undoubtedly favor "rank in person" rather than "rank in position" compensation and career development schemes, such as are found in the military service or in some large companies such as AT&T, with its levels of district manager. The danger, however, is in replacing one compartmentalized bureaucratic structure with another highly layered one. The successful firm of the future will have fewer organization levels, with more responsive, autonomous units, of highly trained and flexible people.

THE QUALITY QUEST

THE SEARCH FOR SNOW WHITE

"Disney's Folly" was on the drawing boards in 1937 for three years and by the time it was produced in 1937 it was 10 times over budget, putting its creator further in debt. Over 750 artists made at least 1 million drawings, with only 250,000 being used in the film. Studio chemists spent months of research mixing 1,500 paint colors and shades to determine final hues for painting characters and backgrounds for the Technicolor film. A multiplane camera invented by Disney technicians provided the animated scenes with a three-dimension depth-of-field quality. In turn, Disney staff composers interweaved eight songs and underscoring to match perfectly with the animated action on the screen. In the end, *Snow White and the Seven Dwarfs,* after more than 50 years, is without question one of the true marvels of the motion-picture screen. First released in 1938, it has been reissued six times—in 1944, 1952, 1958, 1967, 1975, and 1987—each time surpassing its previous attendance record.[35]

The success of *Snow White* is due to the creative genius and business showmanship of Walter Elias Disney, as everyone knows.

But a good part of his genius was in building a unique organization of dedicated, creative people, most notably his famous team of animators but also all the other technicians, composers, writers, character voices, and other staff. The magic of Walt Disney is alive again. Michael Eisner's magic[36] has transformed Disney into a money-making kingdom with earnings heading toward one billion dollars a year.[37] While a remarkable feat, it still is a sign of the times that Eisner's "Duck Tales," TV's number one syndicated cartoon show, is made in Japan.

Although computer technology and labor cost considerations have played a role in the disappearance of Disney's craftsmen, something—beyond our nostalgia for the past—appears wanting. Maurice Sendak, in a tribute to Disney's animation, knows what it is. He has stated, "Over the past few decades, there has been a collapse of the sense of pride in craftsmanship, of the sense of excellence. Usually this has nothing to do with money."[38]

And while we wax nostalgic, consider the renewed popularity of Lionel trains, as parents yearn to pass on childhood joys to their children. These remarkable model trains of post– and pre–World War II American vintage are again being replicated by newer editions, but not nearly as intricately crafted. Moreover, these uniquely American-created toys often are "outsourced" to places such as Korea and Taiwan.

While hardly monumental, these are but simple illustrations of what Tom Peters describes as "the crushing quality problem" which has "contributed to America's decline in the steel, autos, semiconductors, construction, and financial services."[39] For example, Japan's automakers have continued to race ahead in quality, which has led to attaining almost a 30 percent share of the U.S. market in 1990 compared to 23 percent in 1986.[40] The quality issue remains the sharpest thorn in American industry's side, with many companies just realizing that they are in a "quality race," with some just scrambling to try to catch up.[41] Peters observed that the quality of Made in America goods and services perhaps "stinks" and that many companies ignore that "quality equals profit."[42] *Snow White*, which cost $1.5 million to make in 1937, has returned literally hundreds of times that amount since its initial release.

But "a quality improvement revolution" requires at-will employees to be "eating, sleeping, and breathing" quality,[43] a commitment that "free agent managers" in today's arm's-length climate may find difficult.

FOLLOWING THE CALL

Some believe you can gauge a worker's effectiveness depending on whether they are "following their call." Despite that both wear uniforms and have military-type ranks, the allegiance that police officers and firefighters profess differs because their work is so different. All professions have different callings, whether in public safety, a religious order, management consulting, medicine, law, or engineering.

In this regard, there is a definite imbalance response to callings between the United States and Japan, as evidenced by the shortage of Americans entering the manufacturing and engineering professions. This no doubt bears some dependence on the financial rewards and social status of these professions to each country. However, times change! A 1990 headline "Business Graduates: Shying Away from Wall Street" reported that after the market crashed in 1987, MBA "interest in Wall Street crashed along with it."[44] Other polls are finding that a growing number of MBA students, worried about the stability of investment banking, are opting for manufacturing jobs instead.[45] Perhaps there is hope.

Apart from the monetary and social attraction of any profession, the call really takes on a moral and aesthetic dimension of having pride in one's work and delighting in the results when adding subtle extra touches. As a case in point, *The Washington Post* reports that "Alcoa executives focus on the 'morality of quality'— giving a customer a product that is as good as claimed is in fact a moral decision."[46]

Just as sure as Walt Disney's team of animators and film technicians were the building blocks of his remarkable success, modern-day corporations will be no more than empty shells without real people who are willing to work "above and beyond their call." Yet what is their allegiance in today's shaky, arm's-length environment?

THE OATH OF ALLEGIANCE

Allegiance is defined as devotion or loyalty to a person, group, or cause. It sounds strained when the term is used in connection with the relationship of employees to their employer. Just imagine, employees standing up like school children with their hands over their hearts making the pledge. Foolish stuff! Yet, most "company men" did just that, and not by empty words but by actions and deeds. It was part of their "call." And if there were words to the corporate pledge, they probably still exist in the employee handbook dealing with subjects of personnel conduct, company expectations, and so on. But as pounded home already, the oath proved to be a one-way street, as implied employment bargains were ignored and expressed "warnings" were added to employment manuals.

W. Edward Deming, "American industry's new cult hero," credited with helping transfer Japanese manufactured goods from schlock to high quality, is a proponent of tight allegiance between employees and employers. He believes that a company has to be run on "team work between workers and managers." In a meeting of the Greater Philadelphia Chamber of Commerce, he warned that companies cannot function properly unless they "wipe out the fear that keeps employees from pointing out bottlenecks and suggesting improvements."[47] Look at USAA, a prosperous insurance and investment management company, which has managed to remove "bottlenecks" in processing paper and has become more effective in providing service to its customers. USAA's productivity is reportedly enhanced by keeping its employees "loyal, comfortable, fit, and smart—beginning with a 69-year policy of no layoffs"![48]

Because of Deming's message, the pledge will no doubt return, to provide the "glue" needed to marry "corporate needs for quality obsessiveness" and the "individual's calling to a higher purpose" beyond having a paid job. How the oath will be worked out will vary. But it will have to be there, if product quality is going to be improved. As Robert Reich has contended, for America-based companies to develop a base of technical competence similar to Japan, "requires broad sacrifices and commitment of the sort we are not accustomed to making or demand of one another."[49]

THE DOWNSIZED DEMOGRAPHICS

BOOMERS, BUSTERS, AND BOOMETS

Three things are happening to shape the American work force: (1) people are living longer, (2) they are generally having fewer children, and (3) they (at least yuppie households) are taking longer to have fewer children. The so-called baby boom generation (a media-coined misnomer) owes more to wartime abstinence than to increased fertility. After all, the size of Welfare America families could be counted with one hand, while the size of Frontier America families needed at least two. The boom was caused by timing—couples producing children all at once—a phenomenon reproduced in miniature one night in New York City thanks to Con Ed.

The baby boom generation, people born from 1946 to 1964, are swelling up the American work force and some are having a rough time staying on because of labor surpluses. However, many argue that the "baby bust generation" will lead to labor shortages by the middle of the next decade. Who are these "busters" anyway! Certainly they are not the next generation, the descendents of the boomers—born 30 years later (the average time between generations). Rather, they are the "in-between" group, the offspring of the people who still had children "after the lights came back on" in Welfare America. This "in-between generation" will create an hourglass in America's work force at the sunset of this century, because they are relatively few in number.

And what about the next "real generation," sons and daughters of the boomers—the "boomets"? Because boomers are reportedly having only about half as many children as their parents did, as the boomets enter the labor force by the end of this century it will drop by at least 10 percent from present level. In the past, Welfare America, with almost actuarial precision, facilitated the flow of people through the world of work. While self-proprietorship was dead, the 30-year mortgage or "credited service" of a retirement plan allowed parents to literally get out of the way of their sons and daughters. Any overlap was incidental and momentary. Florida—the growth state—and the retirement payoff were waiting.

Welfare America is over! Who goes and who stays in the work force is one big question. Another question may be how long one stays in the work force. In a human resource article entitled, "Retirement Should Be Obsolete," the authors predict that "the problem of unemployment for the aging is only beginning to surface as a social dilemma and will be felt much more strongly as we approach the 21st century."[50] Consider these statistics reported by *The New York Times:* In 1930, two out of every three men 60 years or over were in the work force. In 1950, half worked, and by 1980, the figure had dropped to one in three. Furthermore, the Bureau of Labor Statistics has estimated that by the year 2000 only one in four men 60 and over will be working. And, although there has been a surge of women in the work force, most women still leave the work force before they turn 60. Another legacy of the downsizing dilemma? The paper also reports that many people in their 50s and 60s who were forced out of their jobs or who chose early retirement still hold little hope of making it back into what they see as the mainstream of working life.[51]

But these are only straight-line predictions.

THE SUNSET OF SOCIAL SECURITY

Social security, the bedrock of Welfare America, is in trouble. However, it is not a catastrophe waiting to happen to its current beneficiaries. Rather, it is in danger of becoming increasingly irrelevant to the retirement planning of future beneficiaries now footing the bill. Because of politically popular, "pay as you go" financing, social security has become nothing more than an "income transfer" from the working generation to their retired parents. The myth of a social security "trust fund" has become an explosive political issue as "boomers" are being made aware by Senator Patrick Moynihan that their payroll contributions are used to mask the real size of the growing federal deficit.

Because of this arrangement, *Fortune* reported that social security is nothing more than a "chain-letter arrangement by which the young support the old."[52] Horror stories have already been put forth of future "generational warfare," as the buster generation revolts against the burden of supporting boomer retirees. Whether it's funding social security or simply buying a house, the boomers have always been on the wrong side of the curve. Paul Hewitt, executive director of the Retirement Policy Institute, has said: "The baby boom generation has been its own worst enemy. Whenever we wanted anything the price went up, and when we sold, the price went down."[53]

Because of the difficulty in funding social security for the boomer generation, alternative vehicles, such as IRS-qualified IRAs and company-sponsored savings plans, began sprouting up as a way of forcing the working generation to put more money aside for their retirement. Unfortunately, these government-sponsored plans have become less attractive since the 1986 Tax Reform Act. What remains of these "deferred income plans" will come under more scrutiny as Congress searches for ways to balance the federal budget.

Furthermore, because of the turbulence in Restructured America, at-will employees who are participating in corporate "defined-benefit" retirement plans have good reason to worry whether they will stay employed to their normal retirement date. Even though many are vested (meaning they own whatever corporate contributions were made on their behalf), they realize that this amount will not be enough to survive on for very long. Furthermore, even those who stay may find that they are victims of a disturbing new trend. An increasing number of employers with "overfunded plans have revoked their promise, terminated the pension plan, and made a minimum payment to workers and kept the rest."[54] And the unprecedented growth of the contingency work force, whose members lack these fundamental benefits, makes this problem even more acute.

This points to the inescapable conclusion that an increasing percentage of boomers will need to be working well beyond their 65th birthday. Most of these people will probably *want to* as well.

SELECTING SUCCESSIVE CAREERS

We have all seen McDonald's commercials that feature senior citizens as well as teenagers behind the counter. Or, if you have flown to Ft. Lauderdale, you may have noticed that an increasing number of employees makes the airport look like a senior citizen's home. Rather than any planned career strategy, this phenomena has perhaps more to do with the shrinking labor supply of "buster generation" teenagers and young adults, requiring "back filling" by their grandparents. In fact, quite a few economists foresee a worker shortage so severe that at retirement age boomers will be able to cut a deal to continue to work on their own terms.[55]

Ronald Pilenzo, the retired president of the Society for Human Resource Management has pointed out that the "graying" American work force poses great challenges in the years ahead. But in this process, he is also pointing to a myth of corporate employment policy, that older people must shift from becoming "contributors" to "beneficiaries." Just look at George Burns, or for that matter, Ronald Reagan, George Bush, Bob Hope, and Richard Nixon! There are many people whose real contribution comes once they turn 60 or 70 years old.

Professor Joseph F. Quinn, an economics professor at Boston College, argues: "It is clear that it doesn't make sense to set up a system where people go from working all the time to working not at all. And yet that's how the workplace has been structured. One week you work 40 hours and the next week you retire and have no work."[56] This is no doubt why so many people pushed into Welfare America's retirement have difficult adjustments to make despite all the financial security. Surveys by the American Association of Retired Persons (AARP) have found that from a quarter to a half of older workers and retirees would delay retirement if they could work fewer hours.

Increasingly, middle-age baby boomers are looking beyond the psychological challenge of their "golden years" to their plan for future financial security. A Merrill Lynch survey of people aged 45 to 64 found that 52 percent expect to work at least part time in retirement.[57] Beyond waiting to sign up for McDonald's in the year 2010, many will no doubt give increasing thought now to second careers to supplement their retirement earnings. For many, it will be an opportunity to do what they always wanted to do as an avocation, by answering their call, whether it's opening up a bed-and-breakfast inn at Cape May or Cape Cod or becoming a concert violinist. Upper-right brain people, now caught in lower-left brain jobs because of the pay, fringe benefits, and status, may eventually become liberated. And, many will find themselves preferring to pay into social security long after they are 65 rather than taking money out, thus sharing the burden with their sons and daughters.

THE HIGH-TECH HOUSEHOLD

THE ILLITERATE Ph.D.

DOS 5.0 . . . . Wordwrap . . . . Cursor . . . . Boot . . . . A>copy file 1. Txt + File 2 + File 3. Txt File. All/IV . . . . WP5.1 . . . . Quicken . . . . Qquit.

Literacy, the ability to read and write, while growing in importance in Frontier America, became a prerequisite for success in Welfare America. In Restructured America the definition of literacy is being broadened to the language of personal computers. In all walks of life! Needless to say, many professionals, highly educated in the age of punch cards and slide rules are now playing catch-up. For some of us, "1 2 3" used to mean something you said to the school doctor.

Since the early 1980s, the personal computer has revolutionized the top of one's desk—whether at the office or in the home. Over the decade 1977–87, the world market for personal computers increased in value from a few million dollars to $27 billion.[58] Tom Forrester argues that the meteoric rise of personal computers is likely to eliminate its distinction with other types of computers such as "mainframes" and "minicomputers."[59] And *Fortune* predicts that there could be "ten times as much progress" by the year 2000 as there was in the past 12 years.[60]

The advent of personal computers has been accompanied by a "software revolution," as new programming languages have sprung up. While most personal computers were originally purchased for video-game entertainment, their ever increasing "affordability" and wider application to sophisticated "word processing" and "spreadsheet" calculations have made for a significant market. This is particularly true among adults who don't want themselves or their children to fall behind in this "literacy revolution." And in the process, they have given rise to "telecommuting" and "home-working." Telecommuting is considered the natural result of an explosion in the number of personal computers at home.[61]

REZONED RESIDENCES

It is the afternoon of June 7, 1999, in Montgomery County, Maryland. A zoning inspector, armed with a citation is about ready to make his move on his target, a "telecommuter" who has clearly "stepped over the line." After nearly a week of surveillance, the zoning inspector is certain that Dagwood Boomster's "homeworking" business has been exceeding the threshold criteria, requiring an R-C (residential-commercial) rating. The R-C distinction was approved two years ago by the Montgomery County Council as a means of increasing its rateables due to a revenue shortfall in taxing commercial establishments as more people opt to work at home. To be sure of his position, the zoning inspector is armed with Boomster's tax returns of his telecommuting income and recent telephone charges indicating the level of digital transmissions. Poor Boomster is about to receive not only a new tax assessment but a stiff fine for not reporting his new R-C status.

While this is only fictional, sometimes reality imitates art. A Montgomery County zoning change affecting home offices may be an omen of what is coming. According to Montgomery County: "If you intend to use your office for income-producing work ... it would be good to check first with local zoning authorities to see what type of work is permitted and under what circumstances."[62] The rise of homeworkers calls into question a fundamental assumption of conventional zoning theory and practice.[63] More significantly, and relevant to the subject at hand, it calls into question the fundamental assumption about "conventional employment practice"!

Futurists are among the most enthusiastic supporters of the idea of home-based work.[64] Alvin Toffler, the father of the "electronic cottage," remarked that "the numbers (of homeworkers) today are vastly greater than the largest numbers we allowed ourselves to imagine. The homeworkers are not just flakes and corporate misfits, and the trend is not a passing fad. The rise in the home office reflects changes in corporate culture at the deepest levels."[65]

A survey found that more than 25 percent of the estimated 17 million who work at home use a personal computer to run their business.[66] According to Forrester, "homeworkers" now comprise 10 percent of the entire U.S. work force, with some 200 companies having initiated a telecommunicating experiment.[67] The Society for Human Resource Management (SHRM) argues that "after many years of unfulfilled promise, telecommuting is becoming more widely accepted for a number of reasons, ranging from family responsibility to air pollution" and predicts that in the next few years 'flexiplace' arrangements are expected to finally reach the critical mass necessary to be considered a legitimate work option."[68]

There are many types of homeworkers: computer programmers, data entry clerks, word processors, various professionals, and executives. In fact, the concept of "knowledge worker" is not bounded by the spatial constraints of an office the way that industrial workers needed to work in the factory. Today, many professionals—with or without telecomputing capacity—occasionally split their time between home and office. A 1989 survey of 521 of the nation's largest companies found that 40 percent of their employees who work at home are men, and that 88 percent of them are managers.[69]

A lot of good has come out of homeworking: savings in daily commuting time, money, and stress; opportunities to homemakers and the handicapped; and increases in productivity by an estimated 35 percent. The concern, however, is that homeworkers will end up (1) isolated from their employer (lacking Naisbitt's "hightouch,"[70] they will likely be overlooked for promotion), (2) exploited in computerized sweatshops, and (3) becoming second-class citizens with respect to job tenure, pay, and benefits. Perhaps another annoying concern of working at home is that no one believes you actually do work. Managers need to look at flexiplace opportunities for their companies as well as themselves and not focus on whether they can watch what their subordinates are doing.

PICKING PARALLEL POSITIONS

Flexiplace work arrangements will result in a new breed of employee—more independent than imaginable. Once the home—rather than the office—becomes the locus for work, why does the homeworker need to work for just one employer? Just as technology of the industrial revolution destroyed self-proprietorship and turned America into a nation of employees, the new technology could lead to a rise in new "cottage" businesses. In fact, a National Association for Cottage Industry has been formed to promote homeworkers' interests. These "cottage businesses," like many small companies, have emerged as the engine of the American economy, fueling much of the job creation and technological innovation in the United States. In fact, small business has generated a great majority of the 20 million of jobs added to the economy.[71]

When working at home, the traditional ties that bind a worker to a single employer become less important. Work-a-day concepts like "9 to 5," "coffee breaks," "1st line supervision," "attendance," and "appearance," no longer have any meaning when an employee is 50 miles from the "office." It also demonstrates that much of Welfare America's "office work" was managed like "plant work," which is one of the reasons restructuring may have been sorely needed.

"Homework" is defined in terms of discrete tasks or projects, not on "the amount of time spent" or how the employee "behaves." As such, enterprising workers need not be employees of any one company, but could "free lance" their skills to several organizations—in effect, go into business for themselves. SHRM predicts that "as cost drops on essential equipment like fax machines, a fully equipped home office is within reach of many otherwise office-bound (and hence employer-bound) workers."[72] High-tech tools are becoming so affordable that the average family now has the computing, teleprocessing, fax equipment, graphics, and desktop publishing power of an Exxon or General Motors two decades ago. And in two-income families, couples now have the working capital necessary to get started. Toffler argues that "today's resurgence of family business is not just a passing phenomenon. We are entering a 'post bureaucratic' era in which the family firm is one of many alternatives to bureaucracy and the power it embodies."[73]

This is already happening but still too much in its infancy for many to take serious notice. It will no doubt be fueled by Hirsch's free agent managers due to the arm's-length climate of employee relations in Restructured America. Working simultaneously for several employers still has some formidable hurdles to overcome. Corporate policies against moonlighting will need to be revised. And, at least one professional society may have ethical questions about potential conflicts of interests. In particular, the American Bar Association (ABA) is concerned about the growing reliance on "lawyer temps," that allows temporary lawyers to work for many firms in a short period, possibly learning the secrets of a myriad of clients.[74] Robert Silverberg, a partner with a Washington law firm, believes that the trend in hiring "temporary" lawyers will likely grow because many law firms are now faced with the need to downsize their staffs. However, Silverberg cautions that firms which hire "lawyer temps" will need to carefully review the lawyer's experience to ensure that the interests of the temps' other clients are not in conflict with the firm's clients.[75]

Perhaps this is even more reason that this new breed of self-proprietor—whether free lancer or contingent worker—will need a "home away from home" to provide benefits, employment information, and negotiating clout so that they will not be exploited by large corporations. And they will need to develop a "code of ethics" to avoid conflicts of interest with their part-time employer of the moment. Toward this end, many may turn to their professional association. However as ABC correspondent Brit Hume points out: "If their numbers keep swelling at the current rate, there soon will be an organization called something like the National Association of Home-Office Professionals. It will have a newsletter, an annual convention, and, of course, a Washington office."[76]

THE PROFESSIONALIZATION PUSH

SOCIETIES OF PROFESSIONALS

The Educational Testing Service (ETS) is not as well known as the series of admission exams it produces for its major client—The College Board. However, ETS is increasingly becoming known for the wide range of tests it produces for its other clients (professional societies and licensing and certifying boards) to measure fitness in all occupational walks of life from mechanic to minister. Work force professionalization is not a new reality. Twenty years ago, Toffler observed "the professionalization of industry,"[77] and John Gardner declared "the loyalty of the professional man is to his profession and not the organization that may house him at any given moment."[78] However, it is even more true today, as evidenced by the growth in number, membership size, and clout of professional societies. And, more professions are increasingly regulating their membership through certification exams produced by sophisticated testing services such as ETS.

While everyone takes for granted that a professional engineer needs to be registered and a public accountant has to be certified, today there are also "certified management consultants," "accredited personnel managers," a variety of other "licensed practitioners." As technological advance has led to further work force specialization, these societies have grown to promote "professionalism" and the "professional interests" of their members. In this process, many professional organizations have become like big businesses, employing large national staffs headquartered in major cities such as New York, Washington, or Chicago and supporting a confederation of state and regional offices.

The rapid growth of professional societies has led some, such as the American Institute of Architects and the Society for Human Resource Management, to undertake major studies to determine their future strategic direction. Supported almost entirely on the dues from individual members, the future viability of these societies is now linked to the continued job growth of their membership—many of whom are at-will employees of major corporations.

LATERAL WELFARE WEBS

As they have grown in size, professional societies have expanded their services into a variety of "welfare" interests of their members, often overlapping with the welfare systems of the member's employer. For example, the International City Management Association (ICMA) is in the business of providing retirement protection by offering a "defined contribution" program to its members. Because of their lack of job security and high turnover, the city management profession has had difficulty in accumulating retirement benefits. In similar fashion, other professional societies may offer group life, accidental death, long-term disability, or health insurance plans to round out their members' level of coverage. Just as Welfare America employers could offer their workers "group benefit protection," professional societies can offer some levels of protection to several thousand members. It is unlikely, however, that there will be a mass exodus of at-will employees from corporate-sponsored benefit plans because those are subsidized by employers and the federal government. Under these corporate plans, employees receive tax-free benefits worth about $300 to $400 above and beyond every $1,000 of salary they receive, only costing their employer one-half that benefit, thanks to Uncle Sam. Professional societies cannot match that kind of arithmetic but they can provide a safety net where job security is threatened.

However, in Restructured America where staff accountants, personnel specialists, and other laid-off middle managers are without these benefits, the potential role for professional societies becomes very large indeed. Group coverage against a major medical emergency or some other catastrophic event becomes very important to the growing number of displaced and contingency workers. Such coverage also becomes important to the free lancer or free agent who chooses to work with tools of their high-tech household. Any further reshaping of our tax code may need to give these professionals tied to their professional societies a more "equal playing field" such as is now enjoyed by large private employers.

FUNCTIONAL REPRESENTATION

Restructured America's upheaval at the workplace is starting to affect the mission and role of the concerned professional's surrogate. Professional societies, while always providing newsletter updates on "jobs available" and "jobs wanted" are in some cases instituting "hot lines" and other job placement services for their affected membership. Some have even gone as far as protecting the membership status of those fired or laid off by suspending dues requirements until members can get back on their feet.

As of yet, however, most societies have taken a less visible and more low-keyed approach in protecting the interests of their members—not wanting to appear like a union at odds with corporate management. The International City Management Association (ICMA), in furthering the interests of the city management profession, has recognized that the best approach in dealing with political bodies (who often fire a good number of city managers) is conciliation, not antagonism. Still, the ICMA provides a "home away from home" for their members by supplying them with model employment agreements and other information necessary to negotiate with feisty city councils. Because of this, some city managers have closer ties to the ICMA than to the city where they work.

While most professional societies follow the model of the ICMA, increasingly some will also look at the role of the National Education Association (NEA) which "proactively" promotes teachers' interests in many of the nation's public school systems. For whatever reasons, the NEA—one of the societies of the teaching professional—has not been "shy" in presenting its views and looking after the interest of its large membership. Whether such militancy has been good or bad is irrelevant. Such functional representation is possible and may be growing if professional societies feel that members' interests are becoming markedly different from employers' interests.

This is particularly relevant to societies which represent the wide variety of homeworking professionals who, lacking "collective bargaining," will become, as direly predicted, second-class citizens, without competitive pay, fringe benefits, and job security. In these situations, professional societies may find a role by—passively or actively—helping their members hammer out explicit employment agreements, thus further eroding employment at-will.

THE GRASS-ROOTS GRIP

THE STAKES FOR STATES

The venerable Tip O'Neill once said that "all politics is local." Equally true in this Republic, "all employment is local." Stated a familiar way "if your friend loses his job, it's a recession, if you lose your job it's a depression!" To put it one other way, some states are viewing Restructured America as a boom, whereas other states see it as a depression.

The fallacy of capsulated terms such as *Frontier, Welfare,* and *Restructured America* glosses over the remarkable and vast geography of this country and the unique cultural and economic diversity of the "rust belt," "sun belt," and other regions. It is reported that the "immense diversity of the United States is mirrored in the nation's labor market."[79] While Corporate America's economy is merely "threatened" by foreign competition, state and local economies are actually ruined by plant closings and industry stagnation. Just remember one of the 10 most critically acclaimed motion pictures of 1989 was *Roger & Me,* a low-budget satire about filmmaker Michael Moore's quest to get General Motors Chairman Roger B. Smith to visit Flint, Michigan, to see the devastation wrought by GM plant shutdowns.

And as one drives across the American landscape, pockets of agricultural-based Frontier America can be seen in the dwindling rural towns and villages of southern New Jersey or southern Illinois, as well as in many other regions. Just as Alvin Toffler argued that America's Civil War was fought between southern "agricultural-dependent first-wave" and northern "industrial-dependent second-wave" economies, the problems of most state legislatures tend now to be of either rural Frontier America and of urban Welfare America. And the emergence of Restructured America will produce a new breed of reactionary, protectionist coalitions of local political forces against the outsider-transnational corporations and the Wall Street invaders, whose outsourcing and dismantling policies threaten the viability of their communities.

And because the stakes are bigger locally, Naisbitt may be right in predicting that future political movements will be from the "bottom up."[80]

"CARROTS" AND "STICKS"

When William Donald Schaefer, Baltimore's irrepressible mayor became governor of Maryland, he was immediately faced with a crisis. A major employer in western Maryland, was about to pull up and close its plant, leaving many without jobs and putting the area in an economic depression. Schaefer, long known for his "do it now" style immediately sprang into action and saved the day, at least for awhile. Schaefer's negotiating tactics may never be completely known, but he apparently made them "an offer they couldn't refuse."

Economic development is an important subject for the nation's governors. For a while, Michael Dukakis almost made a successful campaign on the "Massachusetts Economic Miracle."[81] Whether it is to promote the introduction of high-tech industrial parks in northern Virginia or the preservation of smokestack industries in Ohio or Pennsylvania, governors and their legislatures have made economic development their number one concern. *The Washington Post* reports that "while the federal government remains gridlocked in a sterile debate about taxing and spending, state governments are developing not only a new economic policy agenda but the radically new methods of governance necessary to bring it to life."[82]

For the most part, states have focused on economic development "front end," that is, finding ways to attract investment in building new plants or office complexes through favorable tax treatment and other economic incentives. Little attention so far has been focused on economic development's "rear end," the closing of a plant and abandoning workers to the rolls of the unemployed.

And there is good reason for this! States trying to attract new industry would be hard-pressed to explain penalties they attach to industry disinvestment. But Restructured America's turmoil produced such a requirement in the Worker Adjustment and Retraining Notification Act. And, reportedly, many believe that states will take matters into their own hands and pass mandatory provisions because of the overwhelming popularity of "60-day advance notice."[83] For example, The Massachusetts Mature Industries Act encouraged employers to:[84]

- Give workers 90 days' notice or severance pay.
- Continue to offer health insurance during that period.
- Provide retraining.
- Help some companies keep their doors open.

All of a sudden, "sticks" are supplementing, if not substituting, the "carrots" of economic development. And once enough state legislatures jointly move in this direction, the focus of economic development "incentives" may change.

In fact, we are already seeing many states stepping into the void created by federal deregulation and laxity in enforcing antitrust laws. According to news reports, states are "throwing blocks in the path of corporate raiders,"[85] state attorney generals are "flexing their muscles,"[86] and are constructing a "fast spreading patchwork of state barriers to hostile bids."[87]

GEOGRAPHIC REPRESENTATION

Major transnational corporations know how difficult it is to close a plant in Belgium, but what about closing a plant in Wisconsin or New Jersey, or for that matter any state in the nation? These are issues that have not been important in the past and, if current wisdom prevails, they may continue not to be so in the future. There are already protests that "fifty different states" can't all set antitrust policy.[88] Or can they? A bill on this subject was passed overwhelmingly by the Pennsylvania state Senate with broad bipartisan support, as well as support from an unlikely alliance of many of the state's major corporations and its most powerful labor unions. Among the key provisions are guarantees of severance pay and labor contracts if the takeover bid succeeds. And while 23 states have already adopted anti-takeover restrictions, the Pennsylvania bill compels the transfer of raider profits to the target company if the takeover bid fails.[89]

Rural America legislators remind us constantly of Frontier America's roots and love affair with the family farm, but what about the next wave of "populist" legislators? Will they remind us of the destruction of Welfare America's industrial families—who comprise a larger percentage of the voting population? Halberstam contends that "the people on Wall Street who today make such horrendous decisions to close down plants in small towns do it readily because they have never known the people they are damaging."[90]

The unemployed, the underemployed, and the remaining at-will employed are growing in numbers. Spiro Agnew's "silent middle class" are now the Vietnam veterans, the Chicago demonstrators, and "the new poor." Their wrath will no doubt turn on the leaders of institutions in government and large corporations and the people who have garnered all the wealth for the sake of "having it all." As *Business Week* reported, the "real villain(s)" of *Roger & Me* was not Smith but CEOs of every American company[91] (including Lee "Kenosha, Wisconsin" Iaccoca: "remember the K-Car") who not only close down factories but also close down America's cities. Like the people of Flint, the people in Kenosha still have not recovered.

Politicians will undoubtedly lash out at the Smiths, the Iaccocas, and the "people on Wall Street," as well as "faceless" transnational corporations. No doubt, as a result, a bandwagon of reforms will be enacted to protect the voters at home from "job loss." A likely target will be employment at-will.

THE INFORMATION IMPLOSION

FEEDING THE MUSHROOMS

Back in 1985, a noted Harvard professor addressing a retreat of consulting firm partners, observed that some firms treat their employees like "mushrooms." "Keep them in the dark, feed them [expletive deleted] and when they get too big, cut off their heads." While most corporations hardly treat their employees like mushrooms, many critics believe that we are a far distance from full disclosure. Even before middle managers became an endangered species, Antony Jay criticized corporations as experts at concealment who employ further experts to burnish the corporate image, by selective disclosure of favorable information."[92] In the mid-1970s, the American Compensation Association found that a vast majority of corporations did not provide their employees with basic information about their salary grade, the maximum salary they could receive, and related salary advancement and promotional opportunities—information that is widely shared and understood by employees in governmental institutions. In today's business climate, it is a safe bet that most corporations who are adding legal disclaimers to employee handbooks are doing so without fanfare, in essence, keeping their employees "in the dark."

On the other hand, many large corporations spend hundreds of thousands of dollars each year on "internal communications" efforts to facilitate a two-way dialogue with their employees as a way of improving morale and instilling a climate of trust. These efforts range from publishing periodic newsletters to regular visits by senior corporate executives practicing "MBWA" (management-by-walking-around), as well as special one-time consultant-led sophisticated attitude surveys and "focus-group" discussions among the "rank and file." These efforts, in turn, often lead to glossy reports and videotaped messages aimed at gaining employee cooperation and commitment to some new strategic thrust.

Despite these internal public relations drives—with the Madison Avenue flair of a product or presidential campaign, the "spin" on the message appears to be increasingly meeting with a certain cynicism, as employees, according to Jay, "contrast these glowing self-portraits with actual behavior."[93]

KNOWLEDGE WORKER UNREST

Why? Why not? At the Saturday morning, June 8, 1968, funeral mass at St. Patrick's Cathedral, Senator Edward F. Kennedy moved everyone by his eulogy for his brother. Bobby Kennedy represented the pugnacious, crusading, and questioning zeal of the students of the late 60s—challenging the moralities and moral authority of their parents, their universities, and government institutions. Given his résumé, Bobby, even more than his older brother John, was a "knowledge worker."

Today, American institutions employ the most highly educated generation of workers in the history of the world. And, it is this generation of knowledge workers which has produced the high-tech revolution, biotech discoveries, space age exploration, and related advances. It is also this generation which grew up distrustful of large corporate organizations, heeding the concerns of William Whyte and Charles Reich. Yet, once beyond academia, many accepted the corporate promise of career advancement because it was "the only game in town." But not without some misgivings and a lot of questions.

"Comparable worth" or "pay equity"—the movement of the 1980s is mistakenly considered a "women's issue" when it is really a "knowledge worker's issue." Nurses, social workers, librarians, and secretaries are questioning where they belong on the pay scales of their employers. Regardless of one's view on the importance of "market forces" or "the fallacies of job evaluation," we are witnessing a phenomenon. A segment of "knowledge workers" are sophisticated enough to be asking the right questions and demanding straight answers from their employers. According to one labor lawyer, there is a realignment of power in the employment setting and of being up-front with employees, where employers have to "decide the relationship they want with their employees, honestly disclose it, and then live by it."[94] In this regard, backroom pay strategies and black-box methods are being exposed to the light of day in ways unheard of during Bobby Kennedy's civil rights crusade.

The late Hedley Donovan, former managing editor of *Time,* provides a clue of what we are in for when he describes "intellectuals," which are hard to differentiate from today's "knowledge workers." Donovan states that "Intellectuals tend to be skeptical, little given to hero worship. They need to know that their boss practices loyalty down."[95] Because Restructured America's downsizing has weaned many baby boomers from Welfare America's mammary gland, they are, of necessity, more independent and autonomous. Toffler, perhaps somewhat professorial, notes this powershift when he remarks "as the work force (that's all of us) is ceded more autonomy, it (we) will demand increased access to information."[96] On a more gut level, Ilene Gochman, a vice president of Opinion Research, says, "The days when management could say, 'Trust us, this is for your own good,' are over."[97]

THE CORPORATE SUNSHINE LAW

Anyone who has had any dealings with political bodies in Florida finds another reason "it is the sunshine state." City councils cannot meet as a body without telling the public in advance. The power of sunlight was drilled home to the New Jersey Highway Authority, which, to its belated embarrassment, voted in "closed session" to raise the long-standing 25-cent parkway toll to 50 cents. Needless to say, the public's (and their press's) "right to know in advance" were violated, and as a result, today, a parkway motorist heading to Park Ridge or Cape May only needs 35 cents per toll.

We know that ghoulish characters from Hungarian villages in Europe "don't like sunlight." Yet Europe, rather than the United States, has been more of a pioneer in allowing employees access to sensitive information about an employer's financial condition, and ensuring that they are, at least, informed in advance about decisions on plant closings, acquisitions, and other "life threatening" actions. Kendall reports there is a substantial legacy in the practice overseas:[98]

- The United Kingdom: Employers are supposed to notify unions and employees in advance where layoffs are planned.
- France: The employee representatives of the *comité d'entreprise* have access to large quantities of information on company operations.
- Germany: "Co-determination" is firmly established, dating back to the 1920 Works Council Act, with worker and union officials sitting on "supervisory boards" of companies.

The pendulum is swinging toward more, not less, information to employees. And, as the trend continues, the details of implicit at-will employment bargains will no doubt be further fleshed out. It will no doubt require explicit no-layoff policies in employee personnel guides, thus further eroding the 19th-century employment at-will. As employers seek to regain or hold on to employee trust and loyalty, they will need to give their employees more information in choosing the most appropriate employment strategy. And, as Toffler notes, "the more educated a population, the more democracy it seems to demand."[99]

THE CONSTITUTIONALIZED COMPANY

CORPORATE CITIZENSHIP

It was the morning of another mild September day in the late 1980s, perhaps not unlike September 25, 1789, when the first U.S. Congress approved the Bill of Rights. However, on this particular morning a middle-aged vice president of a company that he had been with almost 15 years would begin to learn about his employment "rights." Within the space of 30 minutes he would hear statements like the following: "it may be fair or foul, we are in a situation where there is a lot of pressure to encourage you to leave ... the pressure is coming from ... elsewhere in the organization ... it might be true that you were like the bastard son that reminds them of their mistakes ... it might not be fair but ... you better accept it and deal with it." In effect, they told him he was being fired, it probably wasn't fair, and there was nothing he could do about it.

Well, they were wrong. There was something he could do about it. He sued the company for wrongful discharge. However, this "corporate citizen" would learn that whatever rights he thought he had as an employee would be disputed by his employer. Although the company admitted to the above remarks, as well as saying to the employee that "there wasn't anything you could have done differently. You were the victim of bad management practices that were outside your control," they argued that they had good cause to fire him.

But, they also argued that they did not need any cause, because this vice president was, in their opinion, an at-will employee. Although this specific case was eventually settled out of court, what was not settled was the following question: Did this employer have the right to fire this long-term employee for no cause or bad cause?

Lewis Matby of the American Civil Liberties Union probably would believe they did. Matby, the ACLU's coordinator of a Taskforce on Civil Liberties in the Workplace, launched in 1990, argues that the Bill of Rights does not apply to the workplace: "you can work for a company for 20 years and lose your salary, your health benefits, your pension—lose it all and never be able to tell your side of the story. And there is nothing you can do about it." In an article reported in *The Philadelphia Inquirer,* Matby goes on to say "that about half of the 50,000 or so complaints the ACLU or its affiliates receive are workplace-related. He argues that exceptions to the common law doctrine of employment-at-will are so few that they are of little use to most workers."[100]

THE "BILL" OF RIGHTS

Matby, as reported, believes that "people can enjoy greater rights at the workplace without disrupting efficient business operations." He argues that the idea is not to keep lazy workers from being fired, but to assure that no one loses his or her job without a good reason."[101] But others would argue just the opposite; it would be the "lazy workers" who would hide behind any rights that in anyway protect their job. One could easily point to the federal government's bureaucratic "civil service system" of employee rights. Because of this, civil service reform was instituted over a decade ago to make it less burdensome for managers to get rid of lazy and incompetent federal workers.

The clash between the rights of employers and the rights of employees is heating up today and it extends over a wide playing field—from subjects such as employee rights to privacy versus employers' rights to a drug-free workplace and on to the pros and cons of employment at-will. At this point, it appears that employee rights advocates are gaining ground. In this regard, there is now a Business Integrity Institute which is dedicated to protecting employer's eroding rights.[102]

The Society for Human Resource Management envisions more and more of the Constitution being applied in the workplace when it states:

> One of the attitudes the Baby Boomers brought with them into the workplace was a broad, legalistic conception of justice. "Constitutionalization" of workplace justice has been largely responsible for the erosion of the traditional employment-at-will doctrine. It is clear today's workers have a different sense of employment rights and responsibilities than did their predecessors, and until some new "social contract" has been agreed to by both sides, we will continue to see friction in this area evinced in antibusiness legislation and courtroom battles.[103]

The major reasons for employer/employee battles over rights has to do with who gets stuck with the "bill." Employment at-will is first and always an economic issue. And economically, employees always have been "labor units of production"; for the past 200 hundred years, these labor units have been a "variable" cost terminable at the will of the employer. But times are indeed changing and "workplace power" is changing too.

THE AUTONOMOUS EMPLOYEE

In completing his "future shock" trilogy, Toffler writes about what he terms "the powershift"—which he defines as a shift in the very nature of power from wealth to knowledge, or more accurately "knowledge of knowledge." He argues that knowledge now provides the key raw material for wealth creation and it more likely the employee, not the employer, who owns this raw material. Toffler cites that:

> Today we are living through the next power shift in the workplace ... a new autonomous employee is emerging who, in fact, does own the means of production ... crackling inside the employee's cranium.[104]

This "new autonomous employee" poses an enormous human resource challenge to employers, as well as an unprecedented opportunity. The challenge is to throw out all the "linear thinking" personnel guides and rule books and start with a blank sheet of paper because the old solutions (legal caveats in handbooks, explicit "employment at-will" application forms, "position" evaluation plans, demassing strategies, "executive-only" compensation plans, etc.) are not going to work in managing this "human" resource. The reason is not new. What is new is its importance today. It boils down to this—employees, like citizens, do have voting rights. Remember the old saying, "If you don't like it here, you can vote with your feet!" Well, a lot of knowledge workers will exercise this "constitutional right," taking with them "their new means of production," because "by-the-numbers" management are not convincingly demonstrating "what's in it for them to stay there."

On the other hand, the opportunities which can be pursued by offering employees the rights to a clearer measure of "loyalty-up, loyalty down" are unlimited. Unlike capital wealth, the new knowledge-wealth is self-renewable and limitless. Firms which are able to win the "hearts" of autonomous employees will reap the un-limited benefit of their "crackling minds."

To do this, it will be necessary to empower the autonomous employee to make choices, by first understanding—from their point of view, not management's—the choices they face.

CHAPTER 4

EMPOWERING THE AUTONOMOUS EMPLOYEE— A TIME OF CHOICES

Now, for the first time in human experience, we have a chance to shape our work to suit the way we live instead of our lives to fit our work.

Charles Handy[1]

Restructured America demands flexible employees. Well, what will (or should) employees demand of Restructured America? We know that employees want flextime arrangements and now they are increasingly seeking "flexi-place" arrangements by literally taking their jobs outside of what used to be the physical boundaries of the workplace. But what happens when they start to demand other things such as flexi-roles, flexi-profession, flexi-commitment, flexi-career, and of course, a flexi-employer.

What subjects are on employees' minds these days? What is crackling in those craniums? What do (or should) they care about? What "choices" do they have to shape their work to fit their lives? Who is leading and shaping the discussion? Employers? Or employees? Are the CEOs on top of this "bottom-up" movement? Assuming they are trying to be, they are (or should be) looking for leadership from their Human Resource people who are on the front line of this employment revolution. What should the HR practitioner tell their CEO to tell their employees?

Andrew Grove, the CEO of Intel Corp, answers workers' questions about workplace concerns in a weekly syndicated column called "On the Job." Many corporate CEOs, relying on their human resource experts, are (or should be) having similar "fireside" chats with their employees about what they can expect "on the job." What should they tell their employees about their job choices? Here is one script to consider.

LONG-TERM VERSUS SHORT-TERM EMPLOYMENT

IN THE LONG RUN WE ARE ALL DEAD!

What is the difference between long-term and short-term employment? *Time!* Just as every journey begins with a single step, the long term is no more than a series of short-term steps. And for most employers and employees, long-term employment is retrospectively defined by the tenure of people who have been there over the years. Employer statements inviting employees to a "career" with the company are "best case" scenarios extrapolating the 1940s' and 1950s' "organization man" into an unpredictable future. According to Dan Lacey, author of *The Paycheck Disruption,* "The very concept of a job is changing. We are, in fact, on the front edge of a grand disruption of the Industrial Era—the only economic system that most Americans alive today have ever known." Lacey's thesis is that "job disruptions—and the stresses they create—are no longer limited to any one class or category of worker."[2] According to various authorities, people no longer work 50 years for a gold watch and it is expected that working men and women may make seven or eight significant job changes in a lifetime, nearly a 50 percent increase from the standards of the 40s and the 50s.[3]

Why not have lifetime employment like the Japanese do? After spending 30 years with one employer, this could indeed become a relevant question to pose. Even in Japan, where the concept of lifetime employment was popularized, it remains a misnomer. In that country, only 30 percent of the work force (almost all are men!) are considered lifetime employees.[4] The balance are temporary, short-term workers. Proponents of Japanese employment practices overlook the cultural differences. Women are second-class citizens! Men need only apply for lifetime employment where organizational rank is based on seniority. What is more important than adopting other "foreign customs" is for the United States to use (rather than confuse) what we already have, or are about to experience.

And so what we already have is a short-term employment culture as framed in our 200-year-old employment laws, confused by long-term employment personnel systems of the past 50 years, and "painfully" rediscovered in Restructured America. The key is to build on that culture so that it works for all of us.

FIFTY WAYS TO LEAVE YOUR LOVER

How long should the employment relationship last? *As long as it works!* Despite the simplicity of this response, it is fundamentally true. But fundamental truths can get complicated pretty fast as they are applied to real-world situations. "Works" for whom? The employer or the employee? What does "works" mean and how do you measure it? Over what time period?

In expanding Welfare America, the relationship could be easily terminated during the initial years of employment—a "dating period"—when position status and fringe benefit entitlements were not worth very much to the employee. And the employee's worth to the employer—characterized by accumulated knowledge and experience—was minimal. Once beyond this dating period it could last a career. And like lifetime marriages before no-fault divorce became popular, no one questioned how long the employment marriage would last since the parties were committed to make it work, by accepting a lot of give-and-take over the years.

However, in Restructured America, "as long as it works" takes on much more immediacy! Just as Mayor Koch would frequently ask New Yorkers "How am I doing?", employers and employees are looking for more frequent feedback on whether their relationship is still working for them. The popular question, "What have you done for me lately?" is being overtaken by, "What can you do for me today and more importantly, tomorrow?" In other words, my commitment to you (that is, my willingness to invest future dollars to finance your future compensation cost) is based on your projected (not past) return on investment.

For an employer concerned with price/earnings ratios and short-term profits, the question of "how long the employment relationship should last" is being painfully reviewed on a closely watched basis. Many employees, settled in the midst of a career characterized by "years of service" in a defined benefits plan, are finding out, just like Mayor Koch, that it can be hazardous to find out "how well I am doing."

The focus on the past has been on the two or three good reasons to stay with one employer—job security, loyalty and commitment—as opposed to the 50 or more reasons to leave the relationship ... better opportunity, more money, promotion, different life-style, change. And as we work our way out of Welfare America entanglements, more attention will be focused on "how well am I doing today?" and "what can you do for me tomorrow?" Now we finally get to the point. *All future employment relationships will be short-term in outlook, focusing on, and protecting against the 50 ways to leave. And, in the process, this short-term focus will provide a stronger building block for the longer-term relationships that survive.* How am I doing? How do I fit into the company's future? What are my options? And if I don't have any options, why not? These questions are part of every person's employment survival kit.

ONE SMALL STEP FOR MAN

How do you determine whether short-or long-term employment with one company is better for you? By the alternatives! Just as the voters of the United States decide whether a president should be elected for one or two terms by considering whether they would be better off with the opposition candidate, employees (as well as employers) need to look at the alternatives. Again, the logic seems straight and simple but sometimes the real world seems to get in the way. Alternatives are opportunities, which, are unpredictable, nonrecurring, and not easily quantified. For example, we may receive an attractive job offer which we must decide to accept or reject before we find out if we won that long-deserved promotion.

The past solution of getting some kind of commitment from your employer about your chances for the promotion and in turn the amount of "clear sailing" that advancement will provide, may be less bankable in today's arm's-length atmosphere of broken bargains. The free-agent prescription, regardless of whether you accept the new job or wait on the commitment for promotion, is to negotiate and get it in writing. How practical a solution this really is remains questionable to the majority of middle executives in large corporations.

The alternative and the direction that America seems to be heading in is to further erode the doctrine of employment at-will. For example: the Federal Courts Study Committee, created by Congress in December 1988 to examine problems facing the U.S. judicial system. The Study Committee released its report calling for a greatly expanded role for the Equal Employment Opportunity Commission in handling wrongful discharge cases. This would give EEOC oversight of wrongful discharge claims and, in essence, create a federal wrongful discharge statute.[5] More revolutionary, a Model Employment Termination Act (META) has been developed which would allow termination only for "just cause" while limiting damage awards to employees. META is to be proposed to the states as legislation they could adopt or modify as they see fit. Adoption of META would eliminate the common law doctrine of employment at will.[6] This small step would be a giant step for mankind by providing a fundamental building block for constructing "meaningful" longer term employment relationships.

KNOWING WHEN TO STAY

What do you want from your employer? Fill in the blanks! The $64,000 question, yet most people have $64 or $64 million answers. On one hand, we answer this question only on the margin in $64 increments of "more time off," a "raise," a "promotion," or more "autonomy to do our own thing." Very few of us "zero base" our employment relationship until it's too late! If we happen to lose our job, then our prior salary, title, and fringe benefits become our reference point in trying to find another job. On the other hand, we fantasize $64 million answers in the everyday lottery of making it to the top and striking it rich. Both our micromanagement and megalomanic tendencies miss the point of how we can get in better touch with the one relationship that consumes most of our time and energy.

- Do you like what you are doing? Do you understand why you are doing it?
- Are you active and creative in your work? Are you controlled and passive?
- Do you value and respect the people you work with? What about the people you work for?
- Can you see the results of your efforts? How is the organization better off because of your work?
- What does the future look like? Are your advancement opportunities unlimited? Or is your career too narrowly defined?
- Do you only stay at your job because of the money, fringe benefits, and accumulated retirement credit?
- What milestones have you crossed over in your career? What check points remain? Have you already "peaked-out"?
- What else would you rather be doing? Why are you not doing it?

What are you willing to give up in return? Fill in the blanks! This is the cost side of the question of "What's in it for me to stay?" Beyond the actual cost of time and effort spent, the daily little tyrannies and petty humiliations, the stress and the pressure and other "observable inputs" (the birthdays missed, the roses ignored, and of course, the fabulous jobs obtained by your peer group).

What is important to have is not only how much it costs you, but how that cost is translated into value for your employer, and in turn, how have you been recognized and rewarded in return.

KNOWING WHEN TO LEAVE

How can you determine when it's time to leave? Easily. When your employer tells you! Sometimes when a question (like the one above) is easy to answer, the answer may be harder to question.

So back to the same question, when do you (rather than your employer) know it's time for you to leave? *The answer is: We do not know when it is time to leave, we only know when it's time to "prepare" to leave.* It doesn't pay to jump out of an engine-stalled plane until we have our parachute ready. How long that will take depends on how quickly we react, which we hope won't be too long.

In determining when it is time to prepare to leave your employer, consider:

- Has your company recently been merged or taken-over?
- Are you in an "overhead" staff position?
- If you are a "manager," do you supervise less than three employees? Are you stuck in the "middle" of a hierarchy of more than six layers?
- Is your department being "studied" by outside consultants? Are your activities being "analyzed"?
- Who are your "allies" in the organization? More importantly, who are your "enemies"?
- How much "grapevine" information do you get? Is it less than what you used to get?
- Have your raises been borderline? Have promotions been elusive?
- Do you find yourself talking more about your past accomplishments than your future challenges?
- How hard is it to come to work each day?

If you decide it's time to leave, what are you doing to increase your visibility outside the company, and do you network not only to your business acquaintances and friends but also to their business acquaintances and friends? Have you picked out some organizations that you would like to join and figured out a way of getting introductions into these organizations?

And, when you are ready to leave, with one or more offers in hand, take one more look before you make the "jump." Are you jumping out of the "frying pan" into the "fire"? Be realistic about yourself and your prospective employer's reasons for hiring you. Have you "oversold" yourself? Sometimes it is better to wait around—even at the risk of being fired—than to voluntarily change jobs and get fired a year later by your new employer. The "implicit" likelihood of a severance package from your old employer will be a lot better if you have not worked out an "expressed agreement" with your new employer.

EXPRESSED VERSUS IMPLIED BARGAINS

GOOD FENCES AND BAD NEIGHBORS

When should contractual terms and conditions be applied to an employment relationship? All the time! In its simplest form a contract is no more than an agreement between two parties—an employer and an employee—to exchange something they mutually value—money for personal services. Remember Frontier Americans' bargaining: "You help me take my cattle to market and I'll pay you 'X' dollars." Each got something, known as consideration, from the other. In Welfare America you may remember, this simple employment bargain got a good deal more complicated. The employee's "consideration" included noncash fringe benefits, "assurances" of future advancement opportunities, and most importantly, future job security and position status in the organization. The employer's consideration, in return, was the person's hard work, dedication, and willingness to forgo immediate cash payments in wages for future rewards. Given the complicated nature of this arrangement, there was a lot of give-and-take. In Restructured America, however, it is becoming increasingly clear that the "give" and the "take" will need to balance out much more often. So contractual terms and conditions—price, quantity, time period, duration of the agreement, nonperformance penalties, and "settlement clauses"—will need to be understood by each party.

Remember the old cliché that "good fences make good neighbors"? Don't believe it, particularly if the next bit of wisdom is to compare a "good fence" to a contract, particularly an employment contract. Another viewpoint: *Good fences don't make good neighbors; good neighbors only make good neighbors, and "good fences" only protect your property from bad neighbors!* In other words, a contract—whether it's an employment agreement or some other bargain or deal—will not ensure that the parties are willing and able to perform; it will only set conditions which minimize your exposure and risk. In management consulting there has never been a contract written that can protect a client from a bad consultant, or a bad consulting study. Only a good consultant can do that, regardless of whether there was any contract in the first place. And as only Donald Trump can state, "a contract is the starting point to sue someone!"[7]

Still it is important in today's arm's-length employment environment to build a fence in order to protect your "property rights" in your job from bad neighbors who break bargains.

THE DOWNSIDE OF INSTITUTIONAL MEMORY

When is an "implied agreement" sufficient? When you are sure that your employer is "committed" to keeping their word to you. And when you are willing to risk the consequences?

In an arm's-length employment environment, "commitments" need to be explicit; implied understandings only work in a climate of trust and intimacy that build up over a long period of time. However, this does not mean that every aspect of the employment relationship needs to be spelled out in endless detail, resulting in inflexible bureaucratic rules. Just spell out what is important to you. Your future!

- What amount of job security can I expect? Is the term of my employment "defined" in renewable time blocks of a year (or more, or less) or is it indefinite?
- What do I have to do to keep my job? Are there preset, objective standards that I have to meet?
- What do I have to do to receive salary increases, bonuses, and promotions? When am I "eligible" and what are the competitive standards?
- What amount of "due process" can I expect? If my performance is rated "unsatisfactory," what opportunity do I have to improve or to appeal the rating?
- How much "advance notice" will I be given if I am fired or laid off?

In Welfare America, employment relations in private corporations were hardly ever spelled out in this level of detail because large paternalistic employers were expected to take care of their "loyal" employees. This level of "formality, distance, and contractualism" was more characteristic of the United States federal bureaucracy. In private sector organizations it was normally sufficient for a manager to informally promise to their employees, "you have a career here," "I will see that you get that salary raise or promotion," "keep up the good work and you will never have to worry about losing your job."

But all this has changed! The manager who may have made these commitments may no longer be there—a victim of downsizing or a hostile takeover. Past promises and subtle understandings have fallen victim to a "corporate Alzheimer's disease" as corporate managerial layoffs have also killed off a lot of institutional memory cells.

Are "explicit" employment agreements really necessary? Not if there are "truthful" employee handbooks!

THE UPSIDE OF TRUTH-IN-ADVERTISING

What to look for in employee handbooks? Everything!

First, read the "fine print." Most large corporations produce glossy employee handbooks or "guides," as the more sophisticated corporations are calling them. After all a guide is a less definitive expression of the employer's position on matters pertaining to your future; it is . . . a guide. Where is the fine print? Several places. The "introduction" or opening paragraphs will undoubtedly contain a statement that the handbook or guide is not a "legal document," but what that really means is that it is not an employment contract. So beware from now on. Next, it will probably go on to state that the guide does not in any way "guarantee" employment, which probably means that following the policies and procedures in the guide will not assure you that you will keep your job. Lastly, sprinkled throughout the entire book will be "qualifiers"—sentences starting with words such as "however" or "although"—words which water down or disclaim a previous statement.

Next, carefully read the sections pertaining to "performance appraisal," "salary review," "promotions," "corrective action," and "termination." Unfortunately, the presence of any "legal disclaimers" as noted above may make this a futile exercise. Nevertheless, it is important to know whether these subjects are covered at all and how much is said. For example, if there is a performance appraisal process, are the procedures and standards spelled out somewhere? Is there an appeal process and are there "corrective action" procedures outlined before someone is dismissed? The likelihood is that these processes are not spelled out, particularly for the more highly paid employees.

Unfortunately most of us never spent much time looking at these guides until we had a problem. In the past, these problems were mostly related to the "fringe" benefit areas pertaining to collecting on a medical claim or worrying about how much vacation time we were eligible for. Now it is as important for employees to spend as much time "combing" through these guides as it is for our employers' lawyers. And we should be prepared to start asking some tough questions.

Of course that's easy to say but it is much harder to do, depending on our relative bargaining position. But that is the point. If we are in arm's-length position, where we are able to ask "what's in it for me to stay" or "what's in it for me to join this company," then we can ask these questions as a prelude to negotiating an explicit employment contract. Everything is negotiable!

And the more frequently this happens will corporations find it administratively less burdensome to have truth-in-advertising as part of its corporate communications.

GOOD FAITH AND "FEAR" DEALING

What employment relationships can exist entirely on "good faith"? Religious vocations! Unfortunately ever since Adam and Eve, we mortals have had to live with original sin, as well as with laws and lawyers, to protect ourselves from ourselves. And as a one-time Nixon adviser reasoned, our "hearts and minds" are led by controlling other parts of our anatomy. So employment bargains based entirely on good faith are no longer "bankable" without a few "sticks" to ensure everyone gets their fair share of "carrots." And this requires that the employment relationship be based in part on "fear." Yes, F-E-A-R, *fear*!

"Fear of Firing," an authoritative legal and personnel analysis on the growing number of exceptions to the at-will employment doctrine,[8] makes this point. This monograph by the Society for Human Resource Management (SHRM) tells employers to show caution in firing employees who have a basis for dragging them into court for "breach of contract" or some other at-will exception. This statement represents an "about face" or a "reverse of the pendulum." We have always thought that it was the employee who was afraid of being fired. Can you imagine Mr. Dithers having to consult a lawyer in the midst of a fit of anger as he is about to shout those immortal two words to Dagwood Bumstead, "You're ____!"

There will be many who will argue that this "fear" on the part of employers is not good for this country's economy. Remember Alfred Sloan of General Motors saying, "What's good for General Motors is good for the country"? This is the same argument, but in reverse. They will point to the tough anti-layoff laws in Europe and how that is contributing to high unemployment. They will say that potential shareholders will be unwilling to invest in a company that has high "fixed" labor costs because of penalties associated with "questionable" employee terminations. What they probably will *not* say is that this will make it *harder* for "raiders" to dump unprotected at-will employees and to minimize or eliminate their pension costs. And they will not see the value of employee agreements as a potential "poison pill" against hostile takeovers.

And they will point to the cost of litigating "frivolous" claims without seeing the value of settling these in a new "people's court."

THE PEOPLE'S COURT

Why should employment disputes be handled quickly in a new people's court? To cut down on the volume! Peter Drucker argues that the United States is leading the movement to convert the employee's job into a "property right" and the "vehicle for this transformation" is the "lawsuit." And he says that "as few managements are yet to realize, in practically every suit the plaintiff wins and the employer loses."[9] What Drucker does not say is that few employees have yet to realize these odds. Once they do—as many are beginning to—we will watch the floodgates of lawsuits open wide. As we all know, the United States is not in short supply of lawyers—in fact there are more lawyers in the State of New Jersey than in all of Japan—and the lawsuit is as American as apple pie. Just imagine television ads showing "You have my word on it" selling legal counsel for "wrongful discharge claims" at affordable, bargain-basement rates. And imagine the "volume discounts" for class action suits by groups of laid-off employees because of downsizing.

Drucker rightly argues that employers can protect against this by providing: (1) objective and equal performance standards, (2) due process, and (3) the right of appeal to a disinterested third party[10]—items that should be part of the "explicit" employment bargain whether in a "legalized" employee handbook or individually negotiated employment contracts. However, assuming there is no one totally disinterested within the company, the use of independent arbitrators is a logical next step before going to court. Generally, impartial complaint mechanisms pay off in many ways: they are cheaper and faster and build employee morale because there is a feeling that management power will not be used capriciously.[11] As a result, the use of outside arbitrators is on the rise and represents a swift vehicle of dealing out justice based on the facts of the case applied to the law, while weeding out frivolous claims.[12] It is also less costly to the parties by avoiding a protracted legal battle where the outcome is less certain, the amount of "damaging" publicity potentially unlimited, and the size of a "jury award" for actual and punitive damages likely to be much greater. One lawyer, who specializes in labor and employment law, argues that arbitration is "quick, much less expensive for everyone concerned (including taxpayers), more consistent, and more likely to facilitate settlement."[13] Because of this, IBM, Federal Express Corp., and a growing number of employers have set up internal impartial review boards or mediators to handle wrongful discharge cases. Some, such as Northrop Corp., go even further and submit the dismissal decision to an outside neutral arbitrator.[14]

And through this process, employers and employees will become more equal bargaining parties in their employment relationship.

BIG VERSUS SMALL EMPLOYERS

DOES EMPLOYER SIZE REALLY MATTER?

Another major decision we face is whether it is better to work for a large company or a small one. What difference should employer size mean to you? Not as much as we have been led to believe in

Welfare America, where working for a large corporation often meant better pay and fringe benefits, more "development" opportunities, and of course, employment security. In Restructured America, the decision to work for a "big" company these days can often be as hazardous as if you had invested in a high-priced stock on the eve of the October 1987 stock market crash. It is usually a good idea to first understand why a company is big, or why a stock is priced high, before jumping on the bandwagon.

What can you still expect from a large company? While not as much as before the days of the "legal disclaimer," you still have access to a lot of capital—financial, intellectual, firm reputation, and "good will," and internal and external people networks. For example, Xerox or IBM employees, and even their alumni, are empowered with the sense of having been (1) accepted into "world class" organizations, (2) received "first class" training and development, and (3) built up a network of future personal contacts among fellow employees, customers, suppliers, and, yes, even competitors. And, if you "wrongfully" lose your job, a larger employer provides a better, or at least bigger, target to sue.

Historically, prior experience with a big corporation can be an invaluable way to obtain the tools and know-how to eventually start your own business. Many of the most successful business entrepreneurs started at what they are doing after working for a large company for several years. And some of these individuals, like Ray Kroch, the founder of McDonald's, started in middle age after they had been fired elsewhere. This proves that failing or making mistakes is never the end if you are willing and able to learn from the experience. Furthermore, studies indicate that the more successful entrepreneurs benefitted from making "asinine mistakes" somewhere else. *So if you have to learn by "trial and error," it is better to do so on a large company's payroll than on your own.*

What are you willing to put up with if you work for a large company? You need to be willing to tolerate a lot more bureaucracy, "turf battles," and impersonal communication and leadership. However, as large companies are "restructured" and "downsized" there is the intent to eliminate "excessive management layers," "unnecessary duplication," and "bureaucratic red tape," and to make top management more aware of their employees and responsive to their needs.

What you have to determine for yourself is whether the organization is still too large and whether you are part of the reason that the organization is too large!

WHEN IS BIG "TOO BIG"?

Can a company be too large? Peter Drucker was asking this question long before downsizing became popularized and years before we started "in search of excellence" by trying to get closer to customers and employees. In 1974 Drucker was critical of "the unmanageable service institution"—the Department of Defense, the 3,000-to 4,000-bed hospital, and the 5,000-to 6,000-person management consulting firm spread over 100 offices in 50 or 60 countries around the world. He was right on target when he concluded that the top people cannot lead by personal example or even know what is really going on in 400 or 500 different consulting assignments where the quality of the service is of paramount importance to each of the 400 or 500 clients.[15]

Yet, even today, the "penchant for giantism," as observed by Tom Peters,[16] has inflicted the management consulting industry with a vengeance. "Scale" has become the driving slogan, as these firms are "gobbling" each other up in an unprecedented race of mergers and acquisitions in order to achieve the worldwide position[17] that Drucker criticized. In fact, many suggest that consolidation in the consulting industry is inevitable. Ten years hence, 75 percent of the world's management-consulting business may be handled by fewer than 20 firms, compared with about 40 firms today. At the same time, most observers say that most failed mergers founder on the "people" factor.[18] So it remains to be seen whether the merged customers and employees will be any better off as a result of the changes.

What are the real economies of scale? When is it more profitable to be bigger? It all depends on what goods and services the company sells and what is considered an "economical unit of production." If you are a manufacturer of automobiles, you have to be of sufficient size to produce enough cars at prices consumers can afford while covering your design, engineering, production, normal inventory, distribution, advertising, and selling costs. So a certain amount of "bigness" is taken for granted in the automobile industry. If, on the other hand, you are in the management consulting business, you can operate as a "solo practitioner" or as a firm with 15 to 100 employees; you do not need to have 5,000 employees.

Once an organization gets well beyond its "right size," the management starts to exhibit any number of "diseconomies" from being too big. Most notably, there is a propensity for excessive "internalization." This means people are more concerned about what goes on inside the corporation—office "politics," the over reliance on committees, and a myopic view of the customer—than on what goes on in the outside world. As a result, (1) headquarters' "staff" jobs become more important where you are more visible than if you are out in the field, (2) the number of people supervised, office size, and other "perquisites" become symbols of organizational status, and (3) your political connections and placement in the "pecking order" or in the organization's "layers" become ends in themselves. Peter G. Keen, chairman of the International Center for Information Technologies, believes that "Your company is too big when your people spend more time infighting over turf than paying attention to overall mission."[19] In Restructured America, many who are internalizing are finding it as perilous as investing in the stock market.

WHEN IS SMALL "TOO SMALL"?

The alternative is to work for a smaller, or even a medium-sized, company rather than a "Fortune 1000" corporation. What you should look out for when you work for a small company: Your present—and future—position within the organization. And by *position*, we are not referring to your current job title and duties, which are hardly ever written down or formalized, but rather your individual *positioning* in the management, control, and—ultimately—the ownership of the firm.

Why is this important? In a small company you are not going to have the same access to the financial, intellectual, people, and reputation "capital" of a large transnational firm. You will probably not even have very good fringe benefits. But this does not mean your employer is not going to expect as much from you; they are even more dependent on your contribution, simply because they do not have that many other employees. And while they are dependent on your contribution, they will not give up ownership or control unless they are convinced you will go somewhere else. Which gets to the point: *All organizations—big or small—are built around people, but small organizations are the people.* When people like Iaccoca or other corporate "leaders" in their television ads talk about their 100,000 or so employees as being the company, they fail to mention all the corporate policies, procedures, and other bureaucratic rules and memoranda that provide the "glue." If you have any doubts about this just remember the last time an employee of a large company quoted you a company policy but then did not solve your problem. On the other hand, a small "struggling" company is much closer to and dependent on the customer as well as on your services. Do not forget this as you "expressly" negotiate your future. After all, one alternative you may have is to become your small employer's "competitor."

When is small "too small"? When you do not have the "critical mass" to be profitable and be positioned to grow. After all, if you are in an "ownership" position in obviously your own, or in someone else's company—remember, now part of it belongs to you— why do you want to lose money, or not grow? There is nothing wrong with growth, and, ultimately, being "big" is good if you are the one who is on top. What this requires is that you establish a "market niche."

Why is "market niche" important? Because it differentiates you from other potential sellers of the same product or service and thereby gives you a competitive advantage. Acquiring this niche requires, above all, concentration and focus. And the position can be obtained by leadership in a distinctive market which can be defined by geography as well as by consumer tastes and values. Or it could be in mastery of a particular function or technology.

Or it could be from becoming a "satellite" to a "mothership"!

MOTHERSHIPS AND SATELLITES

What is a "mothership"? You guessed it! It is a large, but "rightsized," corporation that you will want to work for from the moment you put down this book. Now, what is a "satellite"? You guessed it again! It is that small business you joined, or started, after leaving a large, but "wrong-sized," corporation for one reason or another. In the 21st century, we are going to see a lot of "motherships and satellites" down here on earth quite like those we have read about that travel among the stars. So jump on board— one or the other—and let's go for a ride!

Remember that in Restructured America large mothership corporations are "casting off" good, long-service employees— economists, accountants, middle managers, and other staff positions—to lighten the load. Rather than packing "parachutes," some fired at-will employees are getting wise and going "high tech." They are constructing their own satellites! And in the process finding their orbital niche to service the "downsized" mothership which will still need a lot of "specialized" goods and services that they will have to purchase on the open market. With all the "busting up" of companies and the "selling off" of assets that is now going on, large corporations will need to buy back a lot of the staff support and in-house expertise that they are now getting rid of. Hirsch, in discussing managers in the 1990s, makes this very point. "To retrieve many of the in-house activities they threw out, companies that restructured will be heavy users of consultants and more frequent customers of companies marketing the very services that these clients just axed."[20]

So where and how do you fit in to this faster-paced "intergalactic" employment environment? You will have to first recognize that life will never be the same again, and that we are all in some way on our own—in orbit—needing to connect somewhere with a mothership. But we also must recognize that "paternalism"—or more appropriately (and no more sexist) "maternalism"—is dead. We "employees" are no longer in our adolescence; we are now in a matured American economy. So this means that we no longer march lock-step, like the average high school home-room class where the students all follow a standard curriculum. Because of the "high tech household," many new ventures and freestanding services will emerge outside of, but supportive of, the large corporations. No longer locked into narrowly defined work, we are now in a university where we are on our own with a lot more freedom to pick the classes (type of work) we want as long as we accumulate the right amount of credit (money) to graduate (survive). For all the employees who graduated from college only to find themselves forced into, and thereafter stuck, in lock-step corporate jobs, it's about time! How do you make this new environment work for you to prevent a collision? Hold on to your seat and stay tuned!

THE "NETWORKED" ORGANIZATION

Most new jobs created in the American economy have, and will continue to be, with small, growing companies, not large corporations. In fact, most of the highly publicized mergers of large corporations over the past several years—sometimes referred to as "dinosaur mating"—have resulted in a net reduction of jobs in the American economy. So, in the years ahead, we will likely see a lot more new business ventures in the wide variety of service industries where "front-end" financing requirements and other barriers to entry are minimal. For example, *The New York Times* reported that corporations are already "clamoring" for outside help from consultants as they "reduce their size, restructure, and try to cope with a rapidly changing business environment."[21] And Hirsch predicts that a wide range of professional services (public relations, advertising, law, research, and engineering) and other activities (maintenance, repair work, and food service) will expand to support these large corporations after "downsizing."[22]

The problem is that our working careers will become more risky as we move from the "safety" of a large corporation to starting our own business venture. Then possibly later we move back to another large corporation, and so on, as we "orbit" a totally new navigational course. Because we can expect that there will be a lot of motherships and satellites competing for the same "airspace," we will need to fine-tune our "radar" to avoid a collision by finding our "orbital" niche. Among the questions we should ask are:

What are the potential gains? What is unique and valuable about your skills and expertise? How can your prior experience be more broadly applied to benefit not only your present employer more so, but also other potential employers? What is the market need that is not being met? And who are your potential competitors?

What are the potential losses? How much of your own money, time, and energy are you willing to invest in starting your own business or joining someone else's business? Do you really trust and want to rely on the "business savvy" of someone else? What about your own business judgment? Do you have a plan to succeed, or is this just a whimsical, egotistical idea? Do you have a plan if you fail? How and when will you cut your losses? What will you do next? How much cash do you have in reserve to stay solvent?

Who is in your network? What are the names of the 50 to 100 people to whom you intend to market your new product and service? What are their positions, budgets, purchasing authority, and organizational and personal needs? Do they know of you and your business and are they likely to "beat a path" to your door? Who are your suppliers and competitors? How can your professional society help you? How will your network either ensure your success in your new venture or help you move on to your next job if all else fails?

Remember that just because you are not part of a large corporate organization does not mean that you cannot create your own "networked" organization.

EMPLOYER VERSUS PROFESSION

WHY DO YOU "CUT STONES"?

What type of work do you do and why do you do it? How often do you think about this? And, what do you say when someone to whom you have just been introduced asks you, "What do you for a living?" Assuming you were a "stonecutter," would you respond by saying: "I am a certified stonecutter and have been recognized by my profession, because of my articles and speeches, as one of the leading authorities on quartz in the country." Or would you simply respond to the same question by saying: "I build cathedrals!"

Stated another way, are you more concerned with "professional workmanship" and therefore more likely to identify with the type of "specialized work" you do? Or, are you more concerned about how your and others' "functional specialties" are related to your employer's business strategy and vision, whether it's to build cathedrals or to sell toothpaste? We are encouraged to believe that—as an organizational team—we should be mutually concerned about: (1) being the best stonecutter, tax accountant, procurement specialist, or bottle washer, and (2) "building cathedrals." Although this "win–win" strategy makes good sense, these mutual concerns for, and identity with, our "profession" and our employer are rarely ever equal at 50/50; the balance is more likely to be 75/25, 33/67, or 51/49.

In early Welfare America, the "organizational" men or women, whether they were accountants, clerks, or engineers, identified 90 percent with their "career employer" and only 10 percent with the function they were doing at the time—because over a career with their large employer they probably moved across a number of functional specialties. However, this was before the advent of Drucker's "knowledge worker,"[23] before "functions" became "professions," before "professionals" needed to be "certified," and before the explosive growth of "professional societies." And it was before Restructured America's arm's-length employment.

In Restructured America, the weights in the balance between employer and profession are likely to change sides more frequently over your career, depending on how you are able to answer the following questions:

1. **What is your "profession"?** What body of knowledge do you use in your work? Is it industry-or employer-specific (e.g., unique plant/process/product experience)? Or is your experience broadly applicable and potentially valuable to a wide variety of employers in several industries?

2. **What is your employer like?** Does your employer really care about you and the "other human beings" who work there? Do you have a future there in terms of developmental opportunities and reasonable job security? Is there truth-in-advertising? Is your employer and your industry profitable and growing?

How you answer these questions may determine whether you want to climb the corporate ladder at Cathedral Builders Unlimited or "cut stones" for somebody else!

THE "OCCUPATIONAL CORE"

Another way to determine whether your primary allegiance should be to your employer or to your profession is to find out whether you are part of the "occupational core" of the company. What is the occupational core? The professionals who are "on the line" and whose work "drives" the business. Every organization has an occupational core:

- In primitive tribes, these professionals were hunters, not base campers.
- In the U.S. Army, the core is in the combat branches—the infantry, armor, and artillery.
- In a public accounting firm, the core is still made up of the CPAs, even though the management advisory profession is increasingly becoming more important.[24]
- In your "electronic cottage" business, the core is *you*.

However, in a large transnational corporation that operates a diversity of businesses in many countries, pinpointing the occupational core(s) is never quite as simple because it often has many dimensions, including:

- **Business units:** For example, the seven baby bells hunt used to be in just the telecommunications "business" but are now focusing their hunters on the "information processing" business as traditional industry boundaries continue to blur.
- **Geographic markets and production centers:** For example, American companies have discovered the Pacific basin, while Pacific basin companies have known about America for some time, and both have each employed "mercenaries"—first, second, and third country nationals—to take part in the "hunt."
- **Functional expertise:** Unlike its role in Frontier America— or, for that matter, "Prehistoric America"—the "hunt" has gone high-tech, mass market, and into a litigious environment so the hunters need the direct support of research and design engineers, product managers, advertising people, and lawyers.

- **Headquarters command and control:** And with the hunt going after a variety of prey, spread out all over the world, and using an arsenal of weapons, the "base camp" has had to become a command and control center.

So the occupational core of a major corporation can include a variety of professions. And, the professionals who make up the occupational core are typically treated like first-class citizens because their role is critical to the hunt. As first-class citizens, these employees are the first to share in the spoils of the hunt (by getting larger salary increases and bonuses) and to advance to leadership positions (by getting the lion's share of the promotions). It is no wonder why many career Army officers would jump at the opportunity for combat duty over assignment to a Pentagon desk job in order to "get their ticket punched" for their next promotion.

In any organization, however, the occupational core never remains fixed in place but moves on to include new professions, while discarding or de-emphasizing others. For example in the 1960s the Defense Department embraced the "systems analysis" profession—known as McNamara's "whiz kids"—only to de-emphasize their role later on. And in the tobacco industry, the lawyers have taken over "command and control" of the "smoking and health" controversy by carefully screening all corporate communications to avoid any claims that smoking is beneficial, thus contradicting the "health warnings," and opening up the probability of a new wave of lawsuits. And so, as you seek a balance between your employer and your "profession," you will need to make a continuing judgment if Cathedral Builders Unlimited thinks "redwood and glass cathedrals" are the wave of the future.

THE SHAKY STAFF BRANCHES

Still another way to determine whether your primary allegiance should be to your employer or your profession is to know what are the "shaky limbs and branches" and whether you are already "out on a limb." What are the shaky limbs and branches? Consider the following examples:

- **The "head shed":** Are you on a large corporate headquarters staff that has to get "lean and mean"?
- **The "groupie":** Are you part of a headquarters staff group which was considered "in" yesterday but is "out" today?
- **The "excess baggage":** Are you in a staff function that here-after will be performed by the company which just acquired your firm?
- **The "out-housed":** Do you provide a "specialized" service that can be purchased on the open market and at a lower cost?
- **The "assistant to (whom it may concern)":** Are you staff to someone who is about to retire or otherwise be terminated from the company?
- **The "Lone Ranger":** Are you in a job in which no one "of importance" in your company either knows what you do or cares whether it gets done?
- **The "leaderless":** Are you a "manager" with no one to manage except your secretary, who also reports to five other people?
- **The "middle" manager:** Are you a manager "layered" on both sides, whose main job is to provide a "management messenger service"?
- **The "clientless" consultant:** Are you: (1) a planner whose plans are not followed, (2) a policy developer whose policies are ignored, or (3) a "deep thinker" whose thoughts are forgotten?
- **The "fractured functionary":** Are you "sharing" a job with someone but both of you are getting paid "full time" for it?
- **The "uninvited" and "uninformed":** Are you finding that you are missing out on important meetings and that there are no more "grapes" on the office grapevine?
- **The "symbolic sacrifice":** Is it possible that your "departure" is one way of atoning for the "sins of the world"?

If any of this may be troubling you, then think "profession" and start to look for a new home!

BEFORE THE BOUGH BREAKS

We all find ourselves "out-on-a-limb" from time to time in our professional careers. When this happens, we need to be ready "before the bough breaks" in our employment relationship.

To avoid unexpected "free falls," you need to ask yourselves:

"What does my profession do for my employer?" How does the "body of knowledge" that you apply at your work improve your company's product or service, increase shareholder value, company revenues and profits, and/or minimize costs, liability, and other potential losses? What new ideas, innovative approaches, technological advances, and information about what works and what doesn't work elsewhere can you bring to your employer? How does your employer rely on the quality of your advice and your workmanship? Are you considered the final authority in your area of expertise? Do you provide your employer with good advice and finished staff work? Despite the fact that you are "certified," are you really a "professional"in the eyes of your employer? How does membership in your professional society help your company?

According to some experts, people are beginning to think of *career* as associated with a particular function or profession as opposed to being associated with a particular organization.[25] Before you invest the best years of your professional career, only to have the "bough break" when you least expect it and can afford it, you also need to ask yourself:

"What does my employer do for my profession?" How does the work you do for your company advance your professional "body of knowledge" and your "skills" at what you do best? Do you get enough "practice" and is there a large enough "playing field"? Does your company's philosophy dismiss the importance of your functional contribution? If, for example, you are a human resources professional, does your company not believe that people are their most important asset? Does your company consider your profession part of the "occupational core" of its businesses? How much are they willing to invest in your future?

Depending on your answers to these questions, now may be the time to start shopping for either a new company or a new profession.

PEOPLE MAKE ALL THE DIFFERENCE

Finally, it is important that one critical item does not get overlooked in deciding whether your primary allegiance is to your employer or your profession. People! *Corporations do not fire professionals. Corporations do not even fire people. People fire people!* Remember, people in corporations also help "their" people by hiring them in the first place, making them into a "professional" buyer, compensation specialist, or even a "stonecutter," through on-the-job training and experience, and they protect the jobs of "their" people to the extent possible. So, if you are on a shaky bough about to break, it is because you are not "connected" to the "right" people!

Why has this lesson been lost on American corporations? It really has not been lost; it has only been confused. *The "absence of loyalty" in major corporations is the absence of "institutional loyalty," not "people loyalty."* In fact "people loyalty" has probably increased to fill the void, as you and your co-workers and "professional" acquaintances in other companies have tried to help your "outplaced" friends find other jobs.

Remember the story of *The Godfather*. It really was not about the Mafia or even about a family of Italian immigrants trying to realize the "American dream"; that was only the setting of the story. The real story was about a "networked organization" built on the relationships between people based on the "exchange of favors"— remember the undertaker in the opening scene—and reinforced by a "code of loyalty." Successful politicians have known this all along.

In the age of the "legal disclaimer," we are finding it necessary to have a "godfather" somewhere and some of us are even assuming that role. So, in determining whether your primary loyalty is to your employer or somewhere else, first consider whether you have—or are—a "godfather":

Who is your "consigleone" within the corporation? Do you have more than one? It's better if you do. Do they feel this way about you? How do you know? What favors have you done for them lately, or, more importantly, could do tomorrow? And, most important, are they in a position to return a favor when it really counts?

Are you a godfather or a godmother? Do people think of you this way? Someone's got to do it! How can you continue to help "your" people and will you be in a position to do so? Who are your people? Are they other employees in your company? Are they business acquaintances and members of your professional society? How can they ever return the favor?

What if you find that you are coming up short with answers to these questions. Do not panic or despair. We all have to start someplace, so start by building your network inside and outside your company. And in the meantime look for a "player representative" outside of your company.

What is a "player rep"? *A player rep is any person or organization that can help you either keep your current job or find a new one.* Who is *your* player rep? Since you are not part of a union, it could be your professional society or it could be an executive recruiter or a labor attorney. Most importantly, your player rep is a person (or persons) who can, and is willing to, be of help either as a favor or for a fee.

So in deciding on whether your primary loyalty is to your employer or to your chosen profession, just make sure that you are not alone in that choice!

FULL-TIME VERSUS PART-TIME EMPLOYMENT

WHAT "TIME" IS IT?

What does "full-time" mean? Does it include "quality" as well as "quantity" time? In Welfare America, the "company men and women" never needed to ask this question because they worked at their jobs "full-time." Their "hearts and minds" and their "bodies and souls" were committed to their employers. After all, that was their part of the bargain; their employers would take care of the rest. And if you were handed an unexpected assignment at five o'clock that needed to be done by the morning, well, that was to be expected if you were going to demonstrate that you had what it takes to get ahead in the company. And, of course, it was out of the question for you to have any "outside obligations" aside from your family and some outside courses you might be enrolled in at the local community college. This was company policy even for people stuck in nonchallenging, "dead-end" jobs but who would have had plenty of time, energy, and intellect to devote to a sideline business on nights and weekends. In effect, all your "eggs" were in one "basket."

However, since the beginning of Restructured America, a lot of baskets are proving to be only as strong as the "implied employment bargain," and "nest eggs" are being destroyed all over the place. And in the new arm's length employment climate, some people will seek a clearer understanding of what "full-time" means by asking their employer some straightforward, but tough questions:

- What do you really expect of me in this job? What specific goals, objectives, and tasks do I need to accomplish?
- How much say do I have as to how and when the job gets done? And if I can finish my work ahead of schedule, do you know what you want me to do next?
- What other duties do you expect me to perform? Are these activities meaningful to the business? Or are they just to consume my time so that I appear "busy"? Would these activities—as well as my job—be cut in a downsizing?

What does your job require of you? If you work in a full-time, salaried position, when are you off duty? Is it after five o'clock until nine the next morning? Or if your work consists of projects and tasks, are you off duty when you complete the project or the task, regardless of what time it is? Unfortunately, many employers either do not know the answer, or worse, they will not answer this question because they are too used to "minding" their employees, in what amounts to an "adult day care center." In this regard, *The New York Times* reports that "many companies refuse to allow executives to work at home because of the belief that if you're not watching your executives, they're not working."[26] *The Washington Post* adds that "many human resource executives believe that corporate rules about how and where work should be performed may slow the spread of telecommuting."[27]

Given the rise of telecommuting, who will decide (and on what information) when you are done "working" at your "full-time" job? You may ask:

- What do you really expect of me in this job? What specific goals, objectives, and tasks do I need to accomplish?
- How much say do I have as to how and when the job gets done? And if I can finish my work ahead of schedule, do you know what you want me to do next?
- Assuming I am able to get my job done, may I be allowed to pursue other outside business interests which do not compete or conflict with the company's?
- What is the company's policy toward moonlighting? Why am I not allowed to work at another job or my own sideline business on my off-duty hours? What is wrong with "moonlit" nights and weekends as a way of not keeping all my eggs in one basket?

Marvin Bower, in his widely cited book *The Will To Manage,* argues for this freedom when he states that "doctors, ministers, teachers, artists, authors, and other individual *professional men (and women)* (italics and "women" added for emphasis and political correctness) are necessarily self-governing, and they succeed or fail accordingly."[28]

So as future implicit and explicit employment bargains are worked out, it is worth not only knowing the "correct time," but also "managing" it well.

PART-TIME EMPLOYEES OR EMPLOYERS

And what does "part-time" really mean? Does part-time employment refer to the employee or the employer? The employee, of course. Who ever heard of a "part-time employer"—in Welfare America? A long time ago there were some very intelligent and influential people—the "opinion leaders" of their day—who were convinced that the "sun orbited around the earth" and wrote books professing that the "earth was the center of the universe." We probably all know some people alive today who may act as if they are the center of the universe.

Most large corporate employers in their handbook discussions about part-time employment create the impression that it is the employer—not the employee—who is the center of the universe. However, it really depends on your "vantage point" (which affects your point of view) which of the two parties is the real "part-timer." In this regard, Frank Doyle, a General Electric senior executive, predicts that the "power of the 90s will be people power" and it "will go to people with adaptable minds, flexible skills, and portable pensions."[29] These people will view their employers-of-the-moment quite differently than in the past and may work for more than one at a time.

In Restructured America, nearly 20 percent of the American work force are "contingency workers" and the number is growing. While a number of contingency workers work "full-time" when they can, their hold on a job is extremely tenuous at best. More so than any other group in American society, contingency workers not only understand what arm's-length means but can measure the full length of the arm that makes them "second-class" citizens. Why should this growing segment of Americans—whether part-time or "full-time for the moment"—put all their eggs in one employer's basket? And what about the "downsized survivors" if their full-time job takes only part of their time? Why not work for more than one employer? If you fit this category, why not just call your employer a customer or a client and manage *your* time and *your* "revenue sources" carefully.

What is wrong with having "parallel positions" with two or more employers? Many of us have already experienced having more than one boss if we have ever been managed by a "matrix" where we report "functionally" to one person and "geographically" to another. And we may also read one of the many "success" articles that the best way to get ahead is to "manage your boss(es)." So carefully decide: Can you afford not to have a second income source (besides your spouse)—whether you are considered to be full-time or part-time in someone else's vision of the universe?

Just remember a man or a woman's "electronic cottage" is not only their castle but it is also the "center of their universe," particularly when they work for part-time employers!

WHO OWNS THE REST OF ME?

America is on a "quality quest," remember. Quality is "in," quantity or "bigness" is "out." In a "knowledge-worker" society, quality improvements come about because of the applied "knowledge" of the "worker," whether they work in small "quality circles" or whether they work alone. Peters and Waterman saw the most "innovative" knowledge workers as pioneers who resided in their now-famous "skunk works." These "champions," about "eight to ten people ... located in a dingy second-floor loft six miles from the corporate headquarters" had the support of senior corporate management.[30] What else did they have, or could they expect, in return for their pioneering efforts?

A good deal—a promotion, a good bonus, and salary advancement, some equity, and a lot of recognition—but not nearly as much as they contributed, and for good reason. They were employees first, innovators second. They were not entitled to patent or copyright their work. If these "knowledge workers" produced a new "computer language," a manual, or even a best-selling book which just might happen to be titled *In Search of Excellence*, it could legally be considered a "work made for hire," that is, "a work prepared by an employee within the scope of his or her employment." And there was nothing wrong with this arrangement—when these employees were assured a good degree of "job security."

But a lot has changed in the last several years. Best-selling authors—in this case, Tom Peters and Robert Waterman—continue to be best-selling authors; however, they no longer work for that employer. Legal disclaimers as expository (or, more appropriately, non-expository) prose in employee handbooks are the new "literary product." And people are not willing to invest their "intellectual capital" in a corporation that will "fire at-will" at the first sign of bad times.

Who owns the "intellectual capital" created by the knowledge worker in the full-time employ of a major corporation or even a small company? The employer! The employee is working in their facilities (whether a second-story loft, a laboratory, or a high-rise office building), using their supplies, equipment, and people, and working on their "time." Despite the dogged dedication and technical genius of Disney's animators 50 years ago, remember who owns *Snow White*. And it has to be this way for American business to be willing to invest in innovative people in restoring quality to American-made goods and services that can compete in worldwide markets. But at the same time, these corporations are obligated to provide their "full-time" employees with more than an "arm's-length pat-on-the-back" for doing a good job.

However, a more perplexing issue will need to be resolved in the coming years. *Who owns the "intellectual capital" of the knowledge worker who works "full-time," but for more than one employer?* For example, management consulting firms often produce innovative approaches, methodologies and techniques to "job evaluation," "materials management," and other client problems, as a direct result of a major client assignment. Who owns the "intellectual product" produced by the consultant but paid for by the client? Who has the "copyright"? It is not always clear. Was the "intellectual product" a culmination of prior work for many clients and other research? Is it only a "by-product" of the client assignment? Does the client or the consultant care who owns the copyright? What future value is it worth and to which party?

Nevertheless, owners of "satellite businesses" in coming years will undoubtedly be concerned about who owns their "intellectual capital" because it may be what they need to create their "orbital niche."

THE DISAPPEARANCE OF LEISURE TIME

Remember the predictions in the 50s and early 60s that Americans, because of their growing "affluence," would increasingly become a "leisure society" with lots of "free time" and "disposable earnings." To a large measure these predictions have been realized by some segments of American society, but not by all. Many middle-age and middle-class families struggling on one, or even two, paychecks to support a family and a mortgage are constantly searching for ways to make "productive" use of their "free time." And as Alvin Toffler commented nearly a decade ago, "This casts the whole question of leisure into a new light."[31]

Toffler, however, was only referring to his concept of "prosuming," that is where we spend our free time refinishing antique furniture, building a redwood deck, or "working" at some other "Harry or Harriet Homeowner do-it-yourself project." We are performing "unpaid" work for ourselves to cut back on the cost of using some outside service. And in the process, as Toffler stated then, "the distinction between work and leisure falls apart." So the struggling family has followed Rule #1 of the two cardinal rules to becoming "rich." Rule #1 is to "save money" by "prosuming" or any other means possible. *And since this book is about improving employment opportunities, it is focused on Rule #2, which is to "earn more" by: first, staying employed, and second, getting "paid" for work in your "free time."*

How you go about accomplishing this can vary all over the map. There are pamphlets, books, seminars, audio and visual materials, and people with plenty of wisdom and advice to offer anyone. What is important for employers and employees to recognize and to reach agreement on in their employment bargain is that American workers will need more options. Not necessarily to get rich, but just to protect the financial stability of their family—by not having all their eggs in one employer's basket if they ever get fired.

Work in your free time is still "work," whether you receive money or barter, or a compliment—as opposed to a complaint— from your spouse when you finally fix that leaky faucet. Blanket opposition by large corporate employers to any form of "moonlighting" because these "additional physical and mental demands could significantly lower your performance level at work" does not give you enough credit to manage your own affairs properly. According to Professor Frank Schuller of Dartmouth's Amos Tuck business school, "If someone is still getting his job done and his sidelines cause no conflict of interest, why not let him do his own thing in the great American phrase? He'll probably be a happier, more confident, and possibly a more creative worker."[32] Even *Business Week* is now editorializing that "companies might consider the unthinkable—permitting employees to moonlight in order to develop the kinds of entrepreneurial skills, self-confidence, and direct contacts with customers needed to begin their own businesses if the day of reckoning comes."[33] To survive in Restructured America, people should be "empowered" to make productive use of their leisure time as long as it does not conflict or compete with their full-time employer.

And it is entirely possible that employees who are not restricted from making productive use of their leisure time—either to save or to earn more money—will be "energized" to be even more productive at their normal work.

AFTER ALL, IT IS ABOUT "TIME"!

Charles, our son, will graduate from high school in the year 2000. It is also about time for American workers to "graduate" to a "new time" full of unlimited options and opportunities. Restructured America is not only about dislocation of unsuspecting, innocent people caught in a wave of turmoil. It is also about the hope that these wrenching changes will ultimately revolutionize American employment relations to make employers and employees equal bargaining partners at last. Soon my wife, Tricia, and I will painfully discover that our child will no longer be a "child" and will demand to be treated like an adult. Soon American employees will demand to be treated as "adults" in their employment relationships. They will demand fair, ethical treatment by management; they will raise more questions and insist on straightforward answers; they will sue when necessary, and they will gain better control over "their time."

Time! I remember the words of an 80-year-old man, now deceased, who had no regrets about his life. Except, he wished he had more "time"! In many ways time is all we really have—to play, to love, to raise a family, and to work at a career. Remembering an old saying: We need to "spend" our time wisely. And as everyone knows, our employment relationships consume most of the scarce and precious time we have left on this earth.

Restructured America provides the opportunity for working Americans to regain control of their time. At-will employees who have been fired can wake up to a world of new possibilities and realize their true potential. Surviving at-will employees in an arm's-length relationship now have the opportunity—and the right—to question their employer on "what is in it for me to stay here." And full-time employees have the opportunity—and the right—to question "moonlighting" prohibitions that treat employees like "children." *And lastly, employers have the opportunity—and the obligation—to redesign their "Welfare America" employment systems to meet the needs of "human beings at work" in Restructured America.*

The next two parts of this book suggest how this can happen.

CHAPTER 5

HUMAN BEINGS AT WORK—A VOYAGE BACK TO THE FUTURE

The future is no longer a simple extrapolation of the past; it's an incredibly rich array of stories waiting to be told.

Michael Schrage[1]

Five hundred years ago, Christopher Columbus undertook a voyage in pursuit of an opportunity. The linear thinkers of his day no doubt reckoned that Columbus's "number" would soon be up. He and his crew of "employees" or whatever they were called in those days did not fall off the earth. They sailed into history.

Today it is easy to envision the world's shape; it is not easy to envision the shape of future corporations. Walter Kiechel laments that all the organizational restructuring "which just seems to go on and on . . . [why] can't these behemoth [corporations] get the drill right." In his article on the merits of the "learning organization," he goes on to say that "what Corporate America needs is a new model company that builds in the capacity to change."[2] One could very well envision that the "new model" of a right-shaped and right-sized company would have no one shape or size but will be continuously adapting its organizational structure and employees to sail into a nonlinear and fickle future.

And if future corporations are in a continuous state of "reshaping" and "resizing" perhaps it is also about time that we redefine what a corporation—or for that matter any employment enterprise—will be in the future. Throughout this century, our understanding of organizations has been "framed" by static dimensions—numbers of employees, organizational "lines and boxes," and of course, organizational "roles." Career expectations have always been based on advancing people through a pyramidal structure. And now even that shape is changing and the pyramid, unlike the world, has become flat. However, people still expect the new shape to be cast in concrete so that they can construct other ladders. In short, everyone—managers, human resource practitioners, and rank-and-file employees—frames his or her expectations about future career possibilities based on a linear extrapolation of a static view of their organization. And, human resource policies, practices, systems, and programs have provided the "glue" to marry the expectations of everyone.

Now the old glue is no longer working because business conditions are changing too rapidly. And employers have been getting a "no-fault" divorce because of the employment-at-will doctrine. This is also not working. What is needed now are "reframed" human resource policies, practices, systems, and programs. Charles Handy defines "reframing" as the:

> Ability to see things, problems, situations, or people in other ways, to look at them sideways, or upside-down; to put them in another perspective or another context; to think of them as opportunities not problems.[3]

The "problems" have been unanticipated and change in business conditions unrelenting. The "opportunities" are to define organizations and their human resource practices in reframed terms of the dynamic elements of change.

How can this be done? One way is to try and fill up a lot of pages with a lot of expository prose about what steps individual companies have been taking to adapt their personnel practices to changing business conditions. The problem, as Kiechel suggests, is that there are no model companies. And while there may be model practices, they appear more as "piecemeal" changes rather than any reframed plan to address the issues we are wrestling with in this book. The most serious concern is that this type of exposition would also be a "linear extrapolation" of the past.

To escape this bind, this chapter will tell a fable. It is the story of a fictional conversation which occurs between two people about 15 or so years out in the future. It could very easily be any two people—a father and a daughter, a mother and a son, an elder and a pupil, or as in this case, a corporate CEO and a cub reporter. The conversation occurs during a "tour" through a 21st-century corporation. The purpose of the tour is to define this company in dynamic, rather than static, terms, focusing not on structure and shape but, instead, on how "employees" (1) move into, (2) work in, (3) get rewarded, (4) move through, and (5) get out of this organization in a humanly way. In other words, forget form! How does this new model function?

To tell this story, the form (or mode) of writing also changes to person-to-person dialogue. Why? To break out of the linear pattern of this book! To put a CEO on the "hot seat." (How many CEOs today can explain and justify the inner workings of their organization to the press?) To communicate! By changing the writing mode, this author runs a risk that some of you who have read this far may not appreciate the change. I will regret this. However, I would regret it more if the book's message was lost because we were wedded to one form of writing. The message is this: Employment bargains of tomorrow will not be one-way conversations, regardless of how good the expository prose; they will be based on two-way (point/counterpoint) conversation—the only way real agreements can be hammered out between adults. With this introduction behind us, let's get on with the story.

The Time:	The turn of the 21st century.
The Place:	The executive offices of a transnational corporation somewhere in the United States.
The People:	A CEO and a reporter.
The Purpose:	An interview about one model company.

The reporter, beginning the interview: "The President and Chief Executive Officer of Columbus Industries has agreed to discuss the inner workings of his company in light of all that we have recently read about the turmoil of Restructured America's *arm's-length employment,* as we enter what many believe is the 'Pacific Century.' . . . Mr. President."

The president, looking a little annoyed, said, "First, I believe it is important that I clear up any misunderstanding that you have about me, this company, and some other misinformation you apparently have. First, I am the Chief *Ethics* Officer because that is the challenge I face in doing my job."

The reporter seemed puzzled, "But, I thought your major challenge was to make profits for your shareholders and to increase the price of Columbus Industries' stock so that your company won't get taken over by hostile raiders."

The president responded, "Well, all that is true, but as I said, it is my *challenge* to do this 'ethically.' As the chief ethics officer it is my responsibility to see that all the other officers and employees of Columbus Industries follow my example. Fortunately, my job in protecting the company against hostile takeovers is now a lot easier, thanks to the new 'National Master Employment Contract as Dictated by Law,' which was predicted over 15 years ago.[4] This federal law, which has replaced the 'historic at-will relationship,'—along with some other antitakeover amendments—has provided a 'poison pill.' If only poor Mr. Comerford was around to see this."

"Who?"

"Never mind," the president smiled. "Next, it is not my company. The company has been 'born again' and now belongs to a wide range of groups—the shareholders, the employees, our customers and suppliers, and even the communities where we are located—because of that old political movement called . . . uh . . . I can't seem to recall the name."

"The 'Grass-Roots Grip'!"

"That's it," replied the president.

"I certainly can see that," said the young reporter. "Anyway, you said I had some other misinformation."

The president looked at the young reporter, "You use the terms *Restructured America* and the *Pacific Century.* First, there is no *Restructured America* anymore, the term is now obsolete, even though it may have been useful a decade ago to explain some fundamental changes taking place and how employment law, personnel systems, and business conditions were all out of whack. But all that has changed. That's why we are having this tour of the 'mothership'."

"I understand what you are saying," replied the reporter, "but what do we call *America* these days? Please, I need some kind of a handle for my story."

"How about, *Competitive America*?"

The reporter really looked puzzled, "But I don't understand, I thought America was being outcompeted by all these Asian countries as well as by a bunch of other developing nations."

"A lot has changed in the past 15 years," said the president, proudly. "We are now holding our own in world markets. After all, America is now the leading producer of digital high-definition televisions (HDTVs). And, as I was going to say, people are starting to realize that it is not the 'Pacific' or the 'Atlantic' Century. It's just the *Twenty-First Century*."

"Okay, but you can't deny that we still live in an arm's-length employment environment," the reporter, now very confused, shot back.

"I'm not sure what you call it anymore. All I know is that it works, and that is why I invited you along for this tour—to let you see how employees are treated as they move through this ship."

"When do we start?"

"As soon as we have 'rightsized' for the voyage!"

COMING ON BOARD

RIGHTSIZING AVOIDS DOWNSIZING

"One of my jobs as CEO is to determine how many people we can carry on this ship. Think of how Christopher Columbus had to staff his ships to ensure that he had enough of a crew to sail—but not too many if he was to remain afloat. This is called 'rightsizing'! And in the previous century's 'jet age,' it was the reason that airlines chose to 'bump' passengers before—rather than after—takeoff. Unfortunately, many employers at that time did not understand this or did not care because they could 'fire at-will'—and I guess that is why many employees started 'packing parachutes'. Did you know at one point parachutes became so in demand and fashionable that an annual survey tried to determine how many 'colors' these parachutes were made in?"

"No, I didn't know," said the reporter, "but it's easy to rightsize a sailing vessel or a plane, but how do you rightsize a large corporation?"

"You start at 'the bottom'."

"But that's crazy! Most of the books I've read always start at the top by trying to make headquarters staff lean and more productive and by getting rid of excess organizational levels!"

"Young man, you are still referring to 'downsizing.' I'm talking about 'rightsizing'! In fact we found that, too often, downsizing is narrowly focused on cost cutting which may only marginally boost 'productivity.'[5] Let's get back to some basics. As Peter Drucker noted, 'In all the hundreds of books, articles, and speeches on American competitiveness—or lack thereof—work rules and job restrictions are seldom mentioned.' Yet Drucker contended that many of these 'rules' and 'restrictions' resulted in poor work scheduling, oversized work crews, the lack of labor-saving equipment and the wrong deployment.[6] Before these books you've read were written and before there were 'organizations' to be 'downsized,' human beings were performing work. Take, for example, police officers and firefighters. Everybody knows what they do. And they have been around a lot longer than many corporations. If you were going to rightsize a police department, you start by determining the number of police officers you need to quickly respond to a citizen's call for help and to solve the crimes that occur, in order to catch crooks. Once you know how many police officers you need on the beat to protect the community, then you decide how many leaders—sergeants, lieutenants, captains, and chiefs—are needed to 'organize' and 'manage' their work. It's that simple!"

"Pardon my curiosity, Mr. President, how do you know so much about cops?"

"Oh well, you see, in my next career I intend to go into law enforcement."

"What?"

"Young man, you will understand by the end of this tour."

"Okay. For the moment, Mr. CEO, let's assume you do know how to upsize your ship. But how do you keep it that way?"

"Through 'negative management points.'"

NEGATIVE MANAGEMENT POINTS

The reporter looked puzzled, "Do you mean that you reward managers who are negative to their employees? As chief ethics officer of this company, I thought you, of all people, would believe in 'positive management' practices where employees are motivated by rewards for doing the right thing instead of being penalized for doing the wrong things. Why do you give 'points' to negative managers?"

"I don't give points to negative managers. I tell them what I expect of them and help them to discover their shortcomings, and help them to improve their relations with their employees. I am referring instead to our job evaluation system."

"'Negative management points' in a job evaluation plan? Mr. President, my readers are not going to understand this."

"I'll try to explain. Since you appear to be familiar with the management literature, you may recall that Robert Tomasko in *Downsizing* reported that job evaluation plans have a 'pro-management bias.'[7] Simply, a position with management responsibility for the supervision of others will be rated higher on the job evaluation plan than a position with no management responsibility. This will translate to the management position receiving a higher salary grade and therefore a higher salary. And it is likely that the salary grade and salary will increase, depending on:

- **The number of employees supervised:** An employee who manages a staff of 50 will likely receive more job evaluation points and a higher salary than an employee who only supervises 5 people. This will naturally create pressure to upsize the organization.

- **The number of reporting levels 'below':** An employee who is higher in the 'pecking' order of the organization—for example, a 'Level 5 District Manager'—will receive more management points than a 'Level 1 District Manager.' This will create a 'bottom-up push' for more salary grade levels and organizational layers.

- **The fewer reporting levels to the 'top':** An employee—in a management staff position—who works in a corporate headquarters, as opposed to a field office, will likely receive more job evaluation points. This will attract more people to headquarters' jobs, which will naturally swell as corporate managers try to increase the number of people they supervise so that they also get more management points.

"As I'm sure you are aware, job evaluation has been a very useful tool to provide a measure of fairness and 'internal consistency' in how we pay our people. It was the single, most often used way—although controversial—for women to obtain 'pay equity' during the 1980s and 1990s. However, while the job evaluation plan was designed to fit the organization structure, many times the reverse would inevitably take place—the organization would evolve to fit the job evaluation plan."

"But I don't understand."

"Don't worry young man, many managers did not understand this either. It has to do with 'reward systems,' 'human behavior,' and 'capacity to change.' A job evaluation plan is a reward system. Employees are rewarded with more salary money when they receive more evaluation points. In time they realize that the only way to get more points is: (1) supervise more people, (2) climb higher in the pecking order, and/or (3) get into a staff position closer to someone at the top. Employees are 'human beings at work.' It is human behavior to seek ways to better your position by trying to change your job, or at least have your job description be rated higher in the job evaluation plan. Most organizations are continually changing—departments are reorganized, staffs are increased as managers find ways to increase the scope of their responsibilities, and employees seek ways to gravitate to the top. Job evaluation plans—for example, the U.S. federal government's position classification plan—tended to remain static for several years. So naturally it is only human nature to redesign the organization to maximize the payout from the reward system—which does not have the capacity to adjust that quickly. Do you understand now why Tomasko believed that the 'management bias' in job evaluation systems resulted in a 'midriff bulge' in the organizations of many corporations?"[8]

"Yes, I understand what the problem is, but what is your solution for it? How will negative management points make a difference?"

"Excuse me, it has already made a difference! In any year my managers know that the sum total of all job evaluation points are fixed at some ceiling amount. To illustrate, we have 20,000 employees with an average job evaluation score of 200, which means that we have a total of 4 million points for the company (20,000 × 200). If managers want to reevaluate a job upward we let them, as long as they have the additional points in their budget. If they don't, they can deduct the points from their own job. That's where we get the term *negative management points*."

"But isn't this administratively complicated?"

"Not in the age of 'pocket computers'!"

"But isn't this control too restrictive on the organization?"

"No, each year we adjust the ceiling upward—as well as downward—to reflect our growth, and changes in our business conditions. It simply recognizes that our payroll is at any one time a 'zero-sum game,' and our employees believe it is better to be stuck with some negative management points, which at worst only affect a small percentage of their salary dollars, than to lose it all through layoffs and firings. If Restructured America taught us anything, it was that."

"But I'm sure your 'professional' employees don't like this control, because the ceiling on points also affects their occupational promotions. They are not even part of management and they are being restricted in their advancement opportunities. How are you going to explain this?"

"You were not around in the late 1980s, so you don't realize that many professional employees who were topped-out in 'dead-ended' jobs were the first to be let go when times got rough. We go out of our way to prevent this from ever happening again. And by the way, young man, all our employees are professionals at their jobs and many are finally starting to believe once more that they are company employees again."

"How come?"

"Because we have changed our philosophy away from 'fire at-will' to 'hire at-will'!"

"I guess that's what's next."

HIRING AT-WILL

"As you can see, rightsized corporations that use negative management points to stay that way, have no need to lay off at-will employees."

"You made that quite clear, Mr. CEO. I remember reading that it started to become obvious to a lot of people in the late 1980s that the at-will employment doctrine was being used like a 'barbarian's sword' to cut the fat out of many corporations—by firing long-term at-will employees who had no job security protection. It was shown that this type of downsizing never proved very effective because—once the pressure was off—the same companies started staffing-up again, only this time with more-expensive, but less-experienced, 'free agent managers,' who cared only about their own careers, not the company. Under this arm's-length employment climate, product quality and service really went down and America's worldwide competitive position only got worse. And when our competitive situation continued to deteriorate, these same companies started to downsize again after promising the survivors 'lightning wouldn't strike twice.' After that, the number of 'wrongful discharge' lawsuits exploded and they had to start a 'people's court' to cut down on the volume because of a remark that Peter Drucker made in one of his books. It was like going from 'crisis to chaos.' It's because of all the turmoil in Restructured America that I am interviewing you about your rightsizing remedy."

"I understand, young man. So you see why we build our organization around the number of people needed 'at the bottom' to do the work required, not to fit the job evaluation plan."

The reporter, starting to get impatient again, said, "Look, you made that clear, and why the emphasis is away from fire at-will, but I don't know why the emphasis has switched to *hire at-will,* or even what the term means. Would you start to explain before we waste an entire page!"

"Certainly, but a little background sometimes helps. Well, to start off, 'hire at-will' means pretty much the same as 'fire at-will.'"

"That doesn't make sense! How can hiring someone be the same as firing a person. It is like equating marriage to divorce."

"That's the point. If you recall the American tradition of employment at-will stems from the notion that people have free wills and can enter—and leave—employment (and marital) relationships, freely, for any reason—good, bad, or none at all. The difference is that it takes two willing parties to form the relationship but only one party to break it. And that has been a problem for the 'jilted' party, which was only made worse when he or she had no recourse because of the 'no-fault' nature of the separation. What is required is 'front-end protection.'"

"What does hiring at-will have to do with front-end protection?"

"The at-will employment theory is based on the contractuarian nature of American law. Contracts are negotiated at the front-end of a relationship between two parties, to protect their interests during the term of performance. When we hire someone these days we believe that we are entering into a contract with them to compensate them for their services. We have two basic forms of agreements:

- **Endable enlistments:** A short-term employment agreement that is very specific, and the terms are 'negotiated' with the prospective employee. Some of these employees are 'homeworkers' who work for us part-time. Others are professional consultants who have agreements with us about such things as 'intellectual capital.' Still others are new employees who are still obsessed with 'fifty ways to leave' and are not ready for a longer-term commitment. The 'endable enlistments' provide us a lot of flexibility in the short-term for cost cutting needed due to unexpected changes in business conditions.

- **Continuing commissions:** A longer-term employment agreement that is based more on implicit assurances of good faith and the very clear provisions of our straightforward employee handbook. The employee handbook has been rated as a model for 'truth-in-advertising,' which I suspect is the reason you are here interviewing me. These employees are considered part of the 'core' of our company, and there is more of a mutual commitment to work together for more than a year or two. The 'continuing commissions' provide us the needed stability to launch a quality revolution for the longer term. You will hear more about endable enlistments and continuing commissions later on in our tour."

"But I still don't understand why you call it *hiring at-will*."

"Because both parties have the free will to enter—or not to enter—into either of these agreements. And they have a better idea of exactly what they can expect in return. This is more of an 'adult–adult' relationship than the 'parent–child' ways of doing things in the past."

"I think I understand now, but doesn't all this honesty affect your ability to recruit, if other less ethical companies make false promises and glowing statements to attract qualified employees?"

"Well, not really, young man, these companies are normally only looking for the 'quantified' candidates. All we want are the 'qualified' ones."

"Here we go again, more double-talk."

QUALIFIED VERSUS QUANTIFIED CANDIDATES

"An equally important ingredient of our hire at-will philosophy is to allow our managers almost absolute freedom to recruit and hire anyone they want. Simply, they are free to hire at-will for any reason they choose! Our only requirement is that the person be qualified."

"Wait a minute, Mr. President. This is worse than double-talk! You just said two conflicting points. How can they be free to hire for any reason when you expect them to hire only qualified people. Isn't this the only reason you allow them to hire candidates?"

"Yes! You are right when you say that our managers would not be free to hire at-will if we made them prove to us that they hired a 'qualified' candidate. If every time they hired someone we made them prove the person was qualified, then they would only hire 'quantified' candidates! We do not second-guess our managers. We expect them to make decisions on their own and decision making involves taking risks. We try to train and guide them to make the right decisions. Sometimes it is difficult to know exactly what the right decision is when you can only know after the fact. If they find that a person that they thought was qualified is not working out, well that is the beauty of an 'endable enlistment.' The candidates and our managers both realize that the relationship is easily terminable, almost like breaking a wedding engagement if one or both parties realize that the marriage would probably not work."

"But what does this have to do with quantified candidates? What is a 'quantified candidate'?"

"A quantified candidate is a person who looks good on paper. A *Mr. Right* of the marketplace. The person has just the *right* amount of experience—not too little and never too much—from the *right* places. He has the *right* education from the *right* schools. Overall, the person's qualifications are *just right* for the position. The *right* package that will fit *right* into our mold."

"What is *wrong* with that, Mr. President?"

"Nothing is *wrong*! Everything is *right*! That is my point."

"But hiring your so-called quantified candidate would be the right decision, wouldn't it?"

"It is not the right decision; it is no decision at all. It *appears* on paper to be the right thing to do. It is safe. There are no risks. If Mr. Right later does not live up to expectations and does not perform in the job, there is no one who can question or second-guess the manager for hiring him in the first place. The manager has covered himself, because he was following the specific, quantifiable selection criteria for the job laid out by corporate headquarters. It reminds me of my experience in working with the U.S. federal government, where there was this tendency to only hire the 'low bidder' because it quantified the decision, making it harder to second-guess. In situations like this I wonder what value that manager is providing that could not be done more inexpensively by a clerk with a cookbook."

"Has this ever been a problem?"

"It used to be a big problem before I got here. In the midst of Restructured America's downsizing, a lot of people in large corporations became very adverse to making decisions that would in any way put their job at risk. Everything had an immediate quantifiable, bottom-line implication to it. Company men and women were laid off because their long years of experience no longer seemed right; loyalty couldn't be quantified. When Columbus Industries started hiring again, the market was ready for us with these 'free agent managers' and their 'packaged and quantifiable skills.' Once hired, these managers quickly made the problem even worse because the arm's-length climate was such that they were afraid to make any decisions that might be second-guessed. Hiring someone took a lot of approvals in advance so that sometimes the candidate had already taken another job by the time we were ready to hire him. At one point, every employer was after Mr. Right so that we found ourselves in a bidding war over a very small group of quantified candidates."

"How were you able to solve this problem?"

"It was about this time that I and some other senior managers discovered the 'contingency work force,' which was swelling with otherwise qualified people laid off from important positions, who wanted to work but were having difficulty 'packaging' their experience in a quantifiable way. We took a chance on hiring some of these people, even though many were overqualified or did not fit into our mold, because they truly wanted to work and they seemed to possess something we had missed for a long time."

"What was that?"

"Commitment and loyalty!"

"How did the job market react to your decision?"

"Just as any market would react, marginally!"

THE MARGINAL MARKETPLACE

"Are you telling me, Mr. CEO, that the market is only of marginal concern to you?"

"Yes, any 'market' is based on literally millions of marginal decisions—whether it is the stock market, the housing market, or the job market. When you buy a stock, you pay the least amount you have to, which is set by the number of buyers and sellers who are currently trading in the stock. If you are the only buyer, then you are the market and the value of the stock is whatever you are willing to pay. When this happens we know it is called a 'buyer's market.' Furthermore, you may have been too young to remember 'the Crash of 1987,' but that once again proved that markets are based on investor psychology as to the value of what they are buying."

"But I don't understand what that has to do with the job market and why you believe it is marginal."

"The job market is no different. The problem that I have is that we are bombarded all the time with 'market surveys'—with all these statistics on what we need to pay to hire quantified candidates. While I am not criticizing the reliability of the information, I am not sure how useful the information is when we take a chance and hire the candidates whose qualifications are not easily quantified and may be worth more or less than this 'market data' would suggest."

"Well, what do you do?"

"We tell our managers to hire the most qualified candidates they can find at the lowest rate they have to pay and to not be intimidated by all the scientific data in these surveys. After all, the survey, if it is valid, is just a measure of the market. We should not be putting the cart before the horse."

"I am not sure I totally understand. Can you give me an example of what you mean?"

"Certainly. For a long while in the 1970s and 1980s there was this market for MBAs, particularly MBAs from the Ivy League schools. Each year the market rate for graduating MBAs would jump significantly, fueled at first by the starting salaries offered by strategy consulting firms and then even more so by investment banking houses in the midst of all the merger and acquisition activity happening in Restructured America. At one point, the bidding for new MBAs got so out of hand that firms were offering 'sign-up bonuses,' 'exploding bonuses,' and a variety of other gimmicks. In effect there was this market psychology that made the market for MBAs a 'seller's market.' Managers were looking for Mr. Right, the 'quantified candidate,' and would pay whatever the surveys showed because they were making the right decision which would not be questioned by their leaders."

"What happened to change this psychology?"

"A number of things. The Crash of 1987. An increasing awareness that paying skyrocketing MBA salaries—like the outrageously high, top executive compensation—was no guarantee that product quality or service would be any better. This led Robert Samuelson to observe that between 1963 and 1987 the annual number of MBA graduates rose from 5,787 to 67,496 and by 1990 there were more than a million MBAs. He posed the following question and gave his own answer:

> If (MBAs) were improving the quality of U.S. management, the results ought to be obvious by now. They aren't. Indeed the MBA explosion has coincided with a deterioration in the performance and status of corporate America.[9]

He concluded that the elite business schools were expensive employment agencies and that the MBA boom had gone beyond its initial impetus and was feeding on itself. Old MBAs were hiring new MBAs and the degree was often a de facto job requirement. The MBA was the classic Mr. Right, which led to a corresponding supply of 'Ms. Rights' as women also got on the MBA bandwagon. Unfortunately, many people who followed this MBA boom found themselves overpriced and out-of-work. Many MBAs who were subsequently laid off quickly realized that their high salaries made them highly visible targets in a cost-cutting exercise. So they reasoned what good is a high initial salary if you don't stay employed long enough to earn it."

"So finally then what happened?"

"A lot of senior managers like myself started hiring more MBAs from less-well-known schools as well as older workers—middle-age MBAs who were laid off or just older experienced people, regardless of their degree. Since there were no surveys to look at, we found that we had to hire these people by making seat-of-the-pants decisions on their qualifications and their worth. In the process we found that all of our individual decisions, while considered marginal, became the basis for future surveys about the job market. The more things change the more they stay the same."

"I guess this is the end of the first part of the tour, Mr. CEO?"

"That's right, it's time to get down to 'work'!"

GOING TO WORK

WHAT'S MY LINE?

"Well, Mr. CEO, I think I understand how you decide how many people to bring on board your vessel and how you select the passengers. Now I want to know what happens to them next. What do you have them do?"

"Nothing . . ."

"What!"

"We have them do nothing until we classify their position with us. However, in most instances this happens when they are hired if they are a quantified candidate, because they will fit right into our mold. But if they are an otherwise qualified candidate there is only a rough fit, so we may have to come up with a new classification to capitalize on their background."

"By the way, your quantified candidates are called Mr. Right. What do you call your qualified candidates?"

"Mr. Rough!"

"I should have known better than to ask. What is a 'classification'?"

"I can see some people have never worked in government. A classification is nothing more than the title of Mr. Rough's position and a description of his duties; in other words, his line of work for us. And once we have entered the title of each Mr. and Ms. Rough and Mr. and Ms. Right, we have our 'classification structure.'"

"What does that do for you? Sure seems like a bureaucratic paper exercise to me."

"It tells our employees what we expect of them and what they can expect from us for their career development. We don't see providing our workers with some explicit measure of our mutual expectations as 'bureaucratic.' Our managers are trained to keep these descriptions short and adaptable to our continually changing environment. And lastly, we don't use 'paper' anymore, only electronic messages."

"Whether there is paper or not, your classification structure still seems bureaucratic."

"Not really, young man, but you have to understand the difference between a 'structure' and a 'process.' A structure is a 'static picture of our organization,' like a snapshot taken with a still camera. The 'snapshot'—whether it is an organization chart or a list of position titles and duties—provides all our employees with a common frame of reference. However, just as parents take snapshots of their children from time to time to record the changes in their physical development, we regularly take new snapshots of Columbus Industries to reflect changes in our organizational development. I guess that's where they got the term *Restructured America,* because it was necessary to change everybody's frame of reference about employment relations. Structures are not 'bureaucratic,' however. Structures can quickly become out-of-date, like last year's snapshots of my 10-year-old son."

"Please tell me what you mean about process."

"A process is a moving picture of an organization, like film or videotape taken with a motion picture camera or a VCR. It is a dynamic reflection of human behavior. A process can quickly become bureaucratic if people are controlled by the structure rather than merely guided by it. A position description—a frame of reference which defines mutual expectations—is merely a launching point for the job. Position descriptions are never bureaucratic, only people are bureaucratic—when they hide behind their position descriptions or the organization structure. And why do they behave this way? Fear! A lack of trust that the institution will act in good faith and deal fairly with them. In situations like this, people will not make controversial decisions, they will not take risks, they will only do the right thing, which will have to be written down somewhere in a cookbook, a memo, or a position description. We call this 'management-by-precedent' where the process is 'acted out' like the script to a motion picture. There is no spontaneity. Everything is backward-looking, everyone is looking behind their back, and everyone knows—and sticks to—their lines!"

"But how do you change this?"

"By changing the emphasis to 'how now'!"

HOW NOW, BROWN COW!

"What does one of the flavors of Sealtest ice cream in the 1950s have to do with what we are talking about?"

"Well, it was the only way I could think of to introduce the 'how now' philosophy we follow in this company. And I thought you might want some refreshment. Boy, were they good!"

"What?"

"The 'how now' philosophy is 'bureaucracy bashing' by cutting through red tape rather than getting all caught up in it. A process becomes bureaucratic when people act out a 'script,' for example, a recruitment process—as to how the scene should be played. For example, the recruitment script requires hiring Mr. Right over Mr. Rough. The how-now philosophy is improvising the roles to meet constantly changing business conditions. There is no script. There are few, if any, controls as to how the job should be done. There are, however, explicit statements of what needs to get done and the results expected. And because of the information revolution that took place, Tom Peters accurately predicted we would destroy most of our hierarchy because now our employees have much of the same information that used to be restricted to our managers.[10] As such, they are empowered to change a procedure or a process if that will simplify how the work gets done, or better enable us to respond to some unanticipated development."

"Why did you come up with the how-now philosophy?"

"To meet the challenge of 'the fickle future.'"

"But wait a minute, I read that piece about 'the fickle future.' It called for a dynamic job description. Yet you just got through telling me that your position descriptions are 'structural' and all structures are 'static.' What am I missing?"

"My young reporter, you are missing an understanding of the difference between a 'position' and a 'job.' You see, all of our employees have job security in Columbus Industries. Even our employees who have 'endable enlistments' are secure in their jobs during the term of their enlistment. We only fire our employees for good cause. And even in those situations, we afford the fired employee with the opportunity to appeal the decision in the people's court. However, none of our employees, including myself, have 'position security.'"

"Oh! Please continue."

"As I was saying, our how-now business philosophy in dealing with a fickle future requires constant improvisation to make sure our way of doing business works today even though it may be obsolete by tomorrow . . . or tomorrow may be obsolete . . . ah, I'm not sure which it is, but I do know in the long run we are all dead, so we better 'watch our time.' Boy, I could sure go for a brown cow right about now. Being a CEO with nearly 200 people directly reporting to me is not easy. Sometimes I feel like I am conducting a symphony orchestra.[11] Maybe it's time for me to change my position."

"You're doing fine, just improvise."

"Young man, you are starting to get the picture. Anyway, our employees' challenge is to continually make the 'how' work 'now.' This requires that we do everything we can to avoid 'position paralysis.'"

"What is 'position paralysis'?"

"Did you ever hear the story about Rip Van Winkle?"

"Yeah, wasn't that a Frontier America tale by Washington Irving? Actually, I preferred his story of Ichabod Crane, particularly Bing Crosby's narration in that made-in-America Walt

Disney cartoon. Speaking of Walt Disney, did they ever find *Snow White*? I heard that she was lost."

"Very funny, young man! Yes, Disney did find *Snow White* in late 1991. *Beauty and the Beast* was part of the 'quality quest,' but we will talk about that later. Right now we are still on the fickle future and how we had to not only wake up a lot of 'corporate' Rip Van Winkles—who fell asleep because they were paralyzed in their positions—but also keep them awake."

"How did you do that?"

"Through 'the energizer'!"

"What?"

"We 'energized' our Rip Van Winkles and, if you prefer, our Ichabod Cranes, by 'breaking them out of our mold.' You see many of these people had been promoted into dead-end positions and many wanted to do more but could not because there was no process for them to do so. They needed to be 'awakened,' 'renewed,' or 'born-again,' so we gave them a dynamic job description. In other words, we gave them an opportunity to 'early out' their position but to stay in their jobs with us in some other how-now capacity."

"What did you call this program?"

"The 'Brown Cow'! You know I love the ice cream; remember the slogan, 'How now ...'"

"Enough! What did they do to get into this brown cow program?"

"They presented to us a 'position proposal.'"

THE POSITION PROPOSAL

"What is a 'position proposal'?"

"A position proposal is nothing more than a 'turnkey suggestion system.'"

"A 'turnkey suggestion system'?"

"I assume you know about suggestion systems which were used in companies in the days of Welfare America. A problem with the old suggestion systems was that there was often no commitment or follow-through. So many worthwhile ideas were never carried out (i.e., no one was willing to 'turn the key'). Let me give you an illustration of what I mean. Remember the story of the cat and the mouse. All the mice were afraid of this cat who was capable of sneaking up and—without any warning—catching the mice off guard. One of the mice had a suggestion, which was to tie a bell around the cat's neck so that every mouse, when hearing the bell, would know that the cat was coming. It was a great suggestion and guess which lucky mouse got to string the bell around the cat's neck? I believe those mice are responsible for inventing the turnkey suggestion system. Some people also refer to it as 'putting your money—in this case, your talents—where your mouth is.'"

"Sometimes I feel like we are playing a game of 'cat and mouse.' What does a position proposal look like?"

"It normally consists of five parts:

1. **A statement of the problem:** What is 'broken' and needs to be fixed? What opportunities for improvement exist? What new developments are likely to occur and how should Columbus Industries be positioned to capitalize on these developments? Stated simply, where is the cat?

2. **The approach you would take to solve the problem:** What tasks or duties would you be willing to perform? Is there a 'method' to your 'madness'? Are there any unique features to the way you would approach the problem? What will be the benefits to the company? How will Columbus Industries be a better place to be because of your contribution?

3. **Your qualifications to perform the work:** What makes you special? What knowledge, skills, and abilities do you possess and why are they needed in this new position? What is your relevant prior experience and how is it applicable to the problem at hand?

4. **How long it will take:** Is this a one-time project or will it be an on-going program? If it is to be a one-time project, when will it be complete and what time schedule and milestones are needed to monitor your progress? Or if this is to be an on-going program, when can we expect some results and how should these results be measured?

5. **How much it will cost:** What resources will you need? Will this involve any one-time capital expenditures for any new equipment, furniture, or office space? Will it involve an increase in our annual operating costs because of the need for any additional staff to support you in this new 'position'

and to 'back-fill' your present position? What incidental out-of-pocket expenses will there be for any needed travel, communications, and report preparation? Can we expect to save or avoid any costs?

Okay, young man, what do you think about that?"

"Gosh, it sort of reminds me of a management consulting proposal."

"Well, that's where we got the idea. In the midst of Restructured America, we were getting all these proposals on how to downsize our staff. We even got a downsizing proposal from one firm that had a vice president who had just predicted that 'the American phase of downsizing was over.' It was after that statement that we got a little skeptical of using outside consultants as the messenger in any future restructuring. And since some noted management authorities at that time said that restructuring was too important to be left in the hands of outsiders, we figured we better be our own messenger because we felt we would be attacked, one way or the other. So when we started to do the work internally, we asked our managers for 'proposals' and many started putting it in this form."

"And then what happened?"

"At first we were getting all these suggestions but with little commitment or follow-through. Finally our management started getting very impatient and started asking each proposer how they would do it, and would they be willing to do it."

"Did you ever present a position proposal?"

"Sure, how do you think I got where I am today!"

"I should have known. Tell me, what happens when more than one person submits the same proposal and you have difficulty deciding because all the position proposals are pretty good. What do you do then to choose the winner?"

"We don't choose a winner; they are all winners. Then our challenge is to define teamwork."

DEFINING TEAMWORK

"I guess now that we are through talking about management consultants and mice, I am going to hear a sports pitch."

"You are right! Do you have a preference?"

"How about football?"

"Sure. Do you remember the Washington Redskins who won the 1983 and 1988 Superbowls as well as the Superbowls during the 1990s? Do you know why they won in the 80s?"

"Well, they had this really great coach, a couple of great quarterbacks, even though one talked a lot and so he eventually went into broadcasting. And they once had this great fullback who gave some advice to the first lady Supreme Court Justice."

"Please don't remind me. Anyway you don't understand why. The people you are talking about were very good. In fact they were so good they were 'stars,' but they were only a part of the team. And they were not the reason the Redskins won those two superbowls, they were only part of the reason. The 'team' was the reason."

"But why?"

"Because they would only play as a team."

"That sounds like double-talk again."

"No, they refused to play if they could not play as a team. You may be too young to remember, but in the two years the Redskins won the Superbowl there were player strikes that lasted a good part of the season. In the second player strike, the owners decided to really get tough so they brought in these new players and went on with the games without their regular players. Eventually a lot of the players from the other striking teams—particularly the 'stars' who were forfeiting their gigantic paychecks because they had walked out—started to come back 'one by one.' Except for the Redskin players, and even their stars. They would only come back as a 'team'! By practicing the slogan 'all for one and one for all,' they survived through a difficult experience, but made it a mutual bonding experience. Even though it was widely believed that the players lost the strike, the Washington Redskins won their strike. The Superbowl was an easy victory because they played as a team."

"I see, but what does this have to do with defining teamwork?"

"Everything!"

"Pardon me, but I don't understand."

"A team cannot have both winners and losers. If some people win on the team while others lose, the so-called team will eventually fall apart. People will all be out for themselves in order to win. They will 'cut each other's throat' when they get the chance because it will give some of them 'competitive advantage' over the others. People will not cooperate with one another if it is not in 'their interest' to do so. And certainly, there will be no trust. This was the principal tragedy of Restructured America."

"I think I am starting to understand but what do you do about it? You did say it was your challenge."

"Yes, it is our challenge. And this is what we do about it. Let's assume we have five employees who present us with five acceptable position proposals. We simply tell them to go off and do it but not in a way that takes five times the effort and hence five times the cost. We tell them to figure out a way to do the job at about one and one half the cost."

"But why one and one half the cost? Isn't that 50 percent more expensive?"

"It is, but it is a small price to rebuild teamwork and there is always an extra cost to 'regulate redundancy.'"

"Believe me, I'm really trying to understand. What does regulating redundancy mean?"

"You have to recognize that five people came to us with the same position proposal and they all want to be 'stars' or at least 'chiefs.' When this happens there is going to be a certain amount of redundancy for awhile until they are able to organize themselves to get the job done. All we are concerned about is that they get the job done, as we expect they will, so they can all be winners. If they don't, then they all lose. And if one of them tries to get the job done without the others, they all lose. Just like Bob Woodward and Carl Bernstein,[12] who both made 'position proposals' to cover the Watergate break-in, we expect them to organize themselves to get the job done!"

"Hmm ... newspaper reporting. Now you are talking about my line of work and I can remember sharing a few by-lines. I guess you have defined teamwork. But how does this affect the pay rates of these five people? Does it cause problems, particularly if they are not getting 'equal pay for equal or comparable work'?"

"We emphasize pay ranks, not pay rates."

RANKS AND RATES

"Mr. President, when I hear the term *rank,* I think of military service. What do you mean by *pay ranks*?"

"That's a pretty close comparison, young man. While we certainly are not the military, we are a 'service.' We try to instill in all employees that they are here for one reason—to serve the customer. That is our job and if we do that job better than our competitors, everybody at Columbus Industries—including our shareholders—will be rewarded. This is one of the reasons that I formed the Corporate Service Corps for our 'continuing commissions,' which we will talk about later in this tour."

"You still haven't told me about pay ranks."

"I was just getting around to that. Actually our pay rank concept is very much like the military's, except we don't call ourselves 'lieutenants' or 'captains' and we don't wear our ranks on our shoulders. At Columbus Industries a pay rank is the same as a pay grade. And just like a pay grade, your pay rank determines the minimum and maximum salary that you can receive."

"How many pay ranks do you have?"

"We follow 'the rule of ten.'"

"What is 'the rule of ten'?"

"You may have been too young to remember, but to prevent another Great Depression in the 1990s, there was this 'radical movement' to enact some fundamental reforms. One of the reforms was to place a 'cap' on executive salaries so that the maximum salary could be no more than 'ten times' the minimum wage. However, the minimum wage was considered to be too harsh, so "average worker pay" was substituted as the basis. In fact, a formidable group of renowned people, including no less than Peter Drucker, J. P. Morgan, and, would you believe, even Socrates thought that a CEO's salary should be set as some multiple of the average worker. Peter Drucker suggested that a CEO should not earn much more than 20 times as much as the company's lowest-paid employee.[13] Like Drucker, Socrates endorsed a five to one ratio between CEO and an average worker's pay, and Morgan concluded that disproportionately high executive salaries disrupted teamwork.[14]

"So after a lot of town meetings and citizen-initiated propositions, a compromise piece of federal legislation was enacted which effectively said that the maximum executive salary could be 'no more than 10 times' the maximum salary of the lowest-ranking employee in that company. This gave each company the flexibility they needed to set their own pay but still achieved the spirit of the Proutist reform. This became known as 'the Rule of Ten.' Did you know that in Japan they follow 'the rule of six to eight'?"

"Would you mind giving me an example?"

"Sure. If the most the lowest-paid employee in this company can earn is $30,000, then the most I can earn is $300,000. As you can see, I have a real incentive to increase the pay of my employees because I can make up to $10 for every additional dollar our lowest-paid employees earn."

"Okay, but you still have not told me how many pay ranks you have."

"We have as many as we need, but as few as necessary to avoid 'layering.' We believe in having only a small number of wide, overlapping pay ranks."

"How then do you determine the appropriate pay rank for your employees?"

"We use a combination of two methods: (1) the rank of the person, and (2) the rank of the position. Let me explain further:

- **The rank of the person:** While normally a person's rank is the same as the rank of his or her position, the fickle future requires that our employees be flexible, focusing on the 'how now,' and be preparing position proposals under our Brown Cow job enrichment and retraining program. This assures that we avoid position paralysis where people become bureaucratic and hide behind their present, but now obsolete, position description. So we continue to pay our people in the rank they achieved as a person, which is based on the highest-ranked position they achieved. This is why our people are not afraid to take chances by taking on a new position.

- **The rank of the position:** We determine the pay grade of all of our positions, using our job evaluation system. We assign a position to a pay grade based on the total number of evaluation points it is scored under the 'universal criteria'—skill, responsibility, effort, and working conditions. Once we have this score, we net the total based on any negative management points received. So lower-ranked employees can move to the next higher rank if their new position has enough points to be eligible for that new grade and if they have met all of our 'slow-track' promotional criteria.

Are you following me?"

"You are starting to get a little technical. I am dying to find out about all this 'slow track' business."

"Look, young reporter, that doesn't come until later. Relax and 'slow down.' We are almost finished with this part of the tour."

"Okay, but despite all this 'rank in person' and 'rank in position' stuff, you still haven't explained why Carl Bernstein and Bob Woodward are doing equal—or, at least, comparable—work—on the same Brown Cow project, but they might not be receiving equal pay because they are in different pay ranks."

"How do you know they are not getting paid equally? And how can you be certain that the lower-ranked person is not getting paid more than the higher-ranked individual?"

"How can that be? Is this another trick?"

"No, it is just that all of our pay ranges have a lot of overlap. So that a subordinate could be paid higher than his or her boss at any one time. Remembering the military, it was not considered unusual for a bright, but new and inexperienced, young lieutenant to be paid less than a lower-ranked, but older and more experienced sergeant that reported to the lieutenant. You see there is only about a 15 percent difference between the maximums of any two adjacent pay ranges, yet there is about a 60 percent difference between the minimum and maximum of any one of the 10 ranges. So we have an overlap of about 45 percent between Ranks 1 and 2, an overlap of 30 percent between Ranks 1 and 3, and an overlap of 15 percent between Ranks 1 and 4. Does this show how we assure 'equal pay for equal work'? If Woodward and Bernstein are at Ranks 4 and 5, the lower-ranked person can easily make as much or more than the higher-ranked individual. And it is not unusual for some of our employees to be earning substantially more than their bosses."

"I guess it does, but it also appears that it happens at great cost because all your Rank 1 employees can easily make as much as some of your higher-ranked people. How do you control this, so that your people are fairly rewarded for their individual performance while at the same time ensuring that the company does not go broke?"

"That's the next part of our tour."

GETTING REWARDED

MANAGING, NOT MEASURING, PERFORMANCE

"So far we talked about how we bring the right number of people on board and roughly how they fit into the work of Columbus Industries. This is only one side of the equation. The other side is what we do for our employees. Getting rewarded! Moving them through our company through promotions and 'sidemotions'! And preparing them for the eventual time when they will leave! This part of the tour focuses on how we reward our employees for their performance."

"Of course, you do that by evaluating and measuring their performance, do you not?"

"My impetuous young interviewer, you are right, but only half-right. It is true that we do evaluate their performance, but only after we have managed it; we never measure performance."

"Here we go again! How can you evaluate someone if you have not quantified their individual contributions in order to objectively measure it?"

"By managing them! Haven't you ever heard about *The One Minute Manager*?[15] Did you think that it was a book about time management?"

"No, it was about providing 'feedback' to employees. But what does that have to do with performance evaluation?"

"Young man, feedback is performance evaluation!"

"Well, I always thought that performance evaluation was primarily measuring what people are doing; feedback is something you are required to do later, once you got all the facts."

"Young man, unfortunately you are not alone in your thinking. There has always been too much emphasis on performance evaluation 'forms,' appraisal 'techniques,' communication 'programs,' and, of course, objective, quantifiable, and 'measurable' performance criteria. The focus has always been on 'institutionalizing' a performance evaluation system, rather than 'humanizing' it! From all this 'bureaucratic' emphasis, we sometimes forget that 'people,' not paper, evaluate other people."

"But don't people need the forms and the facts before they can provide feedback. What if they are challenged? I have always heard that one of the most difficult jobs of a manager is to sit down and tell an employee about his or her shortcomings. You know people can get pretty defensive once they find out that their performance has been less than satisfactory."

"That's because the manager waited until the last minute to counsel the employee about a problem. It is now probably too late to do anything about it and the employee probably doesn't know what to do because the manager never showed him or her by example. Backed into a corner with no alternative but to fight back, the employee suspects he or she is going to be denied a reward or possibly lose his or her job."

"Well, what would you do differently?"

"First, the manager should not wait until he has all the facts and forms to sit down with the employee. He should stand up to the employee whenever he has reason to counsel the person on some deficiency, and he should praise the employee for his or her good work. And managers do a better job at this when they do it continuously as an integral part of their management responsibility. Can you imagine a football team where the coach did not provide any feedback to his players during the game, but waited until they could all watch the video tapes at a midweek practice session. Next, the manager should base his comments on all aspects of performance, not just those that can be quantified and measured."

"But how can he be objective?"

"You appear to be confusing 'objectivity' with 'ignorance.' Any manager who only looks at numbers will be ignorant of what is really going on because he doesn't have a 'feel' for the business. What if a reporter was only judged on the number and length of his reporting rather than the quality and accuracy of the reporting. Performance evaluation is not a 'numbers game.' In any job there is almost an infinite array of activities and results that can be counted and measured; however, many are not relevant. And when a manager starts to measure employees on irrelevant 'data,' the employees will behave in a way to maximize their 'score' on whatever they think they are being measured on, which can be very counterproductive."

"Can you give me an example?"

"Sure, if you can handle another story."

"It's been awhile, so go ahead."

"In measuring performance the wrong way, some managers focus on activity because it is some indication of the employees' level of effort and how 'busy' they have been. Also there are lot of activities that can be quantified, counted, or measured ..."

"When are you going to tell me the story?"

"Right now, young man. In preparing for my next career in law enforcement, I wanted to ride with police officers in patrol cars to have a better feel for exactly what they do riding around all day besides what we all see on those television programs. Did you know that most patrol officers respond to less than four citizen-initiated calls for police service on an eight-hour shift? For many patrol officers their daily routine involves driving around all day, putting up with hours of boredom that are interspersed with immediate and unanticipated moments of life-threatening terror."

"That is interesting, but what does that have to do with ..."

"Just some background. Anyway, when I rode around with patrol officers in this one department, I noticed something odd. They all drove around at speeds of 30 miles an hour or more, even on some city streets where the speed was only 25 miles per hour. And the other thing I noticed was that whenever they stopped to answer a call, like investigating a burglary or a break-in, they would quickly write up a report and then get back in their car and start driving at 30 miles per hour again. At the end of the day, I happened to ask this other outside observer if he had noticed anything out of the ordinary. He said no, except that he had difficulty learning anything because the patrol cars all went so fast. What we later found out was that the police chief had recently instituted an objective performance evaluation system with quantifiable and measurable criteria. One of the criteria was 'patrol miles driven.' The chief mistakenly believed he could evaluate patrol activity by measuring the miles put on each patrol car. So officers felt they would be penalized if they did not show enough miles on their speedometers. This is just one more case of 'management-by-the-numbers'."

"Why does a CEO want to become a cop?"

"I can't play the violin, I don't like the beach, and there are no openings at McDonald's."

"I think we had better get back to 'managing' performance. Well, if you don't have 'forms and facts,' how do you deal with your, shall we say, 'losers'?"

"By trying to make everybody winners!"

WIN–WIN PERFORMANCE APPRAISING

"Mr. CEO, I am having a hard time understanding all of this 'I'm okay, You're okay,' 'feel good' philosophy. Everyone knows that life is a competitive struggle; there can only be winners if there are losers. Don't you realize that it's a 'zero-sum' game? I'm sure your shareholders don't like all this soft talk. What do they say?"

"My shareholders are the employees. We are a 'born-again' corporation."

"But I read something about Frontier America which said that 'many saw another's fortune as their own loss—the world being a rat race with no rewards for the losers.'"

"Remember this is Competitive America. Frontier America was 200 years ago. And we no longer even have Frontier America's employment laws."

"Okay, just tell me what you mean by 'win-win' performance appraising."

"I think I can better tell you what it is by telling you what it is not."

"Just tell me!"

"There was a time when the so-called management experts—the same people who developed forms and facts for measuring performance—believed that once performance was quantified it could be rated on one of several levels. Typically, they would come up with at least five levels—Outstanding, Superior, Satisfactory, Minimally Satisfactory, and Unsatisfactory. Sometimes they did not even use labels but just rated people as 5's, 4's 3's, 2's, and 1's. And sometimes they would even go further by rating people as pluses or minuses."

"Is that where they got the term *high five?*"

"No, young man. Thank God, there are some expressions in our American heritage that remain pure. Anyway, this all happened before the 'information implosion' when employees were often referred to as 'mushrooms' and they lived in the 'dark.' Because of their 'fear for their heads,' a lot of employees were afraid to ask what their ratings meant and how their rating compared with other employees' ratings. The only time they would find out anything was when it was too late to do anything about it. 'Losers' were informed they were 'losers' well after the fact, typically on their way out the door. There seemed to be this 'we–they' attitude between the evaluator and the evaluatee. There was very little trust and openness. In fact, there was a kind of 'schizophrenic' behavior by a lot of corporations."

"What do you mean?"

"Well, there were even situations where somebody who followed the employee handbook received favorable evaluations, but still got fired in a subsequent downsizing."

"What did they do wrong?"

"They forgot to read the fine print."

"Oh, well, did things start to get better?"

"Not before things got a lot worse! Corporate managers were so impressed with their ability to quantify and categorize performance that they decided to 'weight' it as well. No longer content with only knowing whether an employee was a 'B' or a 'C', they wanted to also know whether he was an '85' or an '84.' And they could do this once they had weighted the performance criteria where one criterion was worth 20 percent, another 30 percent, and so on until the total equaled 100 percent."

"But that seems crazy. How can I determine whether my reporting of this interview is worth 40 percent or 50 percent? Who really can say?"

"No one, even though I believe your report about my company should be worth at least 90 percent, no one can predict that in advance, and this was still true even before the future became so fickle. The problem was that corporate senior management loved the certainty and precision offered by this level of quantification. It was like receiving the 'body counts' from Vietnam. And they knew when they rewarded their employees they were making the right decision. It could not be questioned because the data supported it. And it would not be questioned because no one else had the data."

"Well, how did everything change?"

"It happened after the 'information implosion' when a number of 'sunshine laws' affecting corporations were enacted. All of a sudden employees were able to ask hard questions about their ratings and some did not believe that they should be considered 'losers' relative to some others, if they were rated a 79 and a 'C', compared to someone else rated an 80 and a 'B'."

"What did you do about this?"

"We almost followed Deming's advice and got rid of the entire annual rating system which he felt was counterproductive to improving quality.[16] However, instead, we threw out all the performance categories and all the points and started over, going back to the basics. We believe that, in any organization, you should only group people into three categories. The small group of people who are truly outstanding and would normally be at the top of anybody's list. Next the very large group of employees who do a good job but have not 'distinguished' themselves from the pack. And last the unfortunate, but typically very small, group of employees who seem to have problems and need extra management attention."

"Well, who are the winners?"

"Most importantly, the middle group, which is typically at least 85 percent of our employees. We do not distinguish among them so they feel that their individual contributions have been recognized. They are not concerned about the outstanding few whose distinguished performance reenforces rather than threatens everybody. And we try to make the third group potential winners by showing them the way, either here or helping them into new careers."

"It sounds great but who gets the rewards—the money? Who gains and who loses?"

"We all do!"

GAIN AND LOSS SHARING

"Mr. CEO, what do you mean when you say that 'everybody' gains and loses? How do you attract people to work for you and motivate them to perform well if they can expect to lose money in the deal?"

"You have it backwards, young man. We do not attract them; they are attracted to us because they can expect to 'share' in the gains and the losses. We do not motivate them to perform well; they motivate themselves to perform well so that they can expect to gain—not lose—money in the deal."

"But I don't understand!"

"I can see that. And it is my fault for not making the most fundamental point of this 'employment relations' tour more explicit. And since we are at the very middle of the tour, I will stop to explain."

"What is so fundamental to employment relations?"

"Respect for the individual—the human being at work!"

"But I always thought that employers respected their employees."

"That is my point. The terms *employer* and *employee*—like master and serf—suggest 'elitism.' And by the way, in a large organization 'who' is the employer and 'who' are the employees?"

"Well, you are all employees, and the employer, I guess, would be the shareholders—which, in a born-again corporation, are the employees. But I would think the employer would be 'management,' the people who are charged with looking out for the shareholders' interests."

"You are right. In any large corporation—whoever the shareholders are—'management' has always been considered the employer. And as documented in one of my favorite books, *A Great Place to Work,* much of the management thinking seemed aimed at recognizing an elitist 'managerial class' which runs the organization. According to the author Robert Levering, the 'managerial class sets itself apart as the embodiment of the will of the organization.'[17] This created a 'we–they' attitude among employees and often led to worker alienation. Even 'paternalistic' Welfare America was based on this elitism; and Restructured America's arm's-length climate just hammered the point home."

"What are you doing that's different?"

"We are all 'partners' in Columbus Industries; we have no 'second-class citizens' and we have no elitist group. While some of us are managers, we see that our main job is to coach and guide the other employees; and it is a major challenge not to let our egos, roles, and actions get in their way. Anyone who is part of our 'continuing commission' program has a shared interest in this company which is forged by sharing in our gains and our losses. This partnership is founded on our basic respect for the individual. And as Tom Peters discovered in 1988, this 'alliance' of all our workers—whether unionized or not—has led to many of our quality and productivity gains[18] based on our how-now philosophy. And because of this partnership, all employees are able to share in our gains."

"Gainsharing! What is so revolutionary about 'gainsharing'? That is an old idea that has been around since the 1980s when a lot of companies instituted productivity programs that allowed their employees to share in the gains. What does that have to do with respect for the individual?"

"Nothing, young man. And you are right. Gainsharing is an old idea[19]—nearly 60 years old. It dates back to the days of Frederick Taylor, the father of 'scientific management.' Only the term *gainsharing* was introduced in the 1980s to replace Taylor's 'piece-rate wage standards' where workers could be paid substantially higher wages because of increases in efficiency. But this was not a partnership among equals. There was no trust. Scientific management was rooted in the elitist belief that employees were inherently lazy and needed to be controlled and manipulated. And while I concede that the new gainsharing programs introduced in the 1980s were well-meaning attempts, they were still a long way off from treating the employees as real partners."

"Why?"

"Because real partners share losses as well as gains and they all have some say in how the gains and losses should be distributed. In Restructured America, employees did not share the losses, or the pain of a cost-cutting drive. The laid-off employees bore all of the loss, while many corporate senior executives walked away with most of the gains."

"Well, what do you do differently?"

"First, all of our partners realize that we will have good years and bad years. Second, the likelihood that we will have a good year is in large part dependent on how well everyone of us performs. Yet even if we all give it our best effort, there will be times when business conditions may not be in our favor. These are the years that we must prepare for."

"How do you do this?"

"By placing a part of everybody's pay at risk. Some other companies follow the riskier 50/50 policy; still others follow the less risky 90/10 strategy; we follow the 75/25 program."

"What in the world are you referring to?"

"Under our 75/25 program, our employees are assured of receiving 75 percent of their normal pay in any year; the other 25 percent is at risk. This means that they could lose up to that amount if we have a bad year, or they could double or even triple the 25 percent if we have a good year. If we do have a bad year we can cut 25 percent of our payroll without laying off 25 percent of our employees. As I said earlier, everybody wins and everybody loses—because we spread our losses around. This is the essence of gain and loss sharing."

"Well I think I understand the loss-sharing side, please tell me a little bit more about how you share the gains with your employees."

"No, they share the gains with me. I am only responsible for the more thankless job of sharing the losses."

"How do they do that?"

"Through 'bottom-up' bonuses."

THE "BOTTOM-UP" BONUS

"What is a 'bottom-up' bonus?"

"It is any number of rewards, but what matters is how they are distributed. And in Columbus Industries the rewards are distributed from the bottom up. That's what's important."

"What kinds of rewards are you talking about?"

"Well, at least three come to mind. There may be more, but these are the most important."

"What are the three?"

"The 'bell' awards, the 'intellectual dividends,' and our annual giving program."

"What are the 'bell' awards?"

"The bell awards are named in honor of a group of mice that came up with the 'turnkey suggestion program.' Each year, a committee of the partners reviews the results of our Brown Cow program. In effect, they review the progress made by all our 'position proposers' against their proposals. They check to see if the promised productivity improvements or anticipated cost savings were actually realized because of the how-now suggestions. Then they prepare a list of people to receive the award and the amount of the award, which ranges from $500 to $10,000, which is typically an insignificant payback in relation to their contribution. And in many cases these are team awards. What is really important here is the recognition from their peers. Suffice it to say, it is just a 'ringing' tribute to their initiative and follow-through."

"Very amusing. What may I ask is an 'intellectual dividend'?"

"An intellectual dividend is an annual payout to our 'intellectual shareholders' for the 'intellectual capital' they contributed to Columbus Industries. Again it is not a lot of money, it is more of an honorarium, but it is constant reminder during the life of the patent or the copyright of their important role. And for groups of employees whose contribution cannot be singled out we have the 'Disney animation dividend' for helping us to find our own *Snow White*."

"Oh brother, let's get to the annual giving awards. What is that?"

"That, my young man, is most of our gainsharing—since you seem to be quite interested in how the 'money' gets spread around. We often refer to it as 'carving up the turkey.'"

"Yes, I've heard of that. Typically, management does all the carving and feasting, leaving the rank and file employee with the table scraps."

"You must be referring to the 'trickle-down' theory of economics where the elite siphon off most of the gains, leaving the rest of the populace with whatever is left."

"Yes, but I am not doing a story about politics, I would rather focus on your bonus program. What is different about it?"

"First, it is not my bonus program; the employees run the program. This is not to say that the executives of Columbus Industries do not share in the gains and we can normally expect that our share will be much larger because our duties and responsibilities are much greater. But this is a bottom-up program."

"Please explain. How is the 'turkey' carved up?"

"No, what is more important is who eats first. Did you know that in the military service officers only eat after their men and women are finished. The same is true here. All 25 percent bonuses are distributed to our employees first, then we get our 25 percent of whatever is left. And if there are gains left over, we share equally on a proportionate share basis but they get their proportionate share first. Our managers make a lot more money, but that money is more at risk. This is called taking care of your troops first. As clearly demonstrated in the Persian Gulf, the military always knew this; many corporations are just waking up to it."

"What brought all this on?"

"The 'information implosion,' of course. But I am sure that the 'sprouting spiritualism' and the 'quality quest' also contributed to it."

"Well, I guess that all rewards that you give out are from the bottom up?"

"No, only the monetary rewards. We give out all our nonmonetary rewards from the top down."

THE "TRICKLE-DOWN" THANK YOU

"What is a nonmonetary reward, Mr. President?"

"A 'thank you'!"

"But why make such a big deal over showing your gratitude to employees when they are just doing what you expect of them."

"Because many employees never really know what is expected of them. In many cases they know more about what is wrong with their work than what is right about it."

"Why is that?"

"Because they are told when they are wrong; they are not told when they are right."

"Well, how else will they find out if they are not doing what is expected of them?"

"By not receiving an occasional 'thank you.' If people come to expect that they will be regularly praised for their work, they will try to please, and they will be disappointed when they don't get positive feedback. And it is likely that the employee will do his or her own self-assessment, and come to the manager to find out what they are doing wrong and how they can improve. A thank you—besides being a common social courtesy—is a fundamental communication of 'positive reinforcement.'"

"Thank you, Mr. President. I guess this is what you mean when you say that gratitude should flow from the top down."

"You are right, and by the way, you are also welcome. See how easy it is."

"But if you thank people for only doing what is expected, what do you do when they exceed your expectations?"

"We give them a 'trickle-down' thank you."

"We all know what 'trickle-down economics' is, but what is a 'trickle-down thank you'? It sounds like all the praise is siphoned off by your top management, therefore leaving the poor 'exceptional' employee with only the 'scraps.' And you are telling me that you are not elitist. Come on, what is the real story?"

"Young man, you are right that some of the praise is siphoned off by the employee's superiors because they are responsible for the employee's performance—whether it is exceptionally good or exceptionally bad. How else can they get recognized and receive their thank you's from me."

"See, I knew this tour was too good to be true. The truth, Mr. CEO, is that life is a 'zero-sum' game, yet you act like you have this blank check."

"I do have a blank check when it comes to praising my people, and I give my managers a blank check in giving out nonmonetary rewards. While economics is based on the scarcity of monetary resources, there is no limit to the amount of nonmonetary resources we can give away. It just takes imagination and a willingness to show your gratitude. And every manager who shares in the praise of this exceptional employee will add his own words of gratitude as all the thank you's trickle down. Getting rewarded for your accomplishments is more than getting paid. It is being recognized as well."

MOVING THROUGH

THE CORPORATION CORPS

"Mr. CEO, I just realized that you did not talk about promotions during the last part of the tour. I have always thought that a promotion is the ultimate form of monetary reward and nonmonetary recognition."

"Unfortunately that was true. So everybody believed that they needed to climb the corporate ladder just as fast as they could. Because of this, many employees were more concerned with building their own résumé rather than building the business. This led to a lot of 'grade inflation' as managers tried to be obliging to their employees because everyone else was doing it. And it also led to 'The Peter Principle' and the 'midriff bulge' in a lot of corporations. As a result, many 'fast-track' employees found themselves promoted onto one of the 'shaky staff limbs and branches' and then had to decide how to best 'package' their professional skills before the 'bough' broke."

"What happened then?"

"Well, a lot of people started to parachute off the tree. At one point during the height of Restructured America's turmoil, I saw all these 'stonecutters' jumping out of Cathedral Builders Unlimited in parachutes of almost every color of the rainbow."

"Is that when they started building redwood-and-glass cathedrals?"

"Right. However, some stonecutters, instead of jumping, decided to climb back down the corporate ladder to the 'occupational core' and they were allowed to become carpenters with Cathedral Builders Unlimited."

"Is that because they liked to build cathedrals?"

"You guessed it again! Even more than cutting stones. So they were willing to take a pay cut to get retrained as a carpenter so they could join the Corporation Corps. In fact about one out of every five financial executives takes a lateral or downward move to get operating experience."[20]

"Finally, we get to the point of this chapter."

"Yes, but you are the one who asked about promotions."

"I did, because I wanted to know how people 'move up' within your corporation, which normally happens when they get promoted. Isn't 'moving up' what this part of the tour is about?"

"No, it is about 'moving through,' which means moving left or right as well as up—or occasionally, down. And the only way you can move at all is if you belong to the Corporation Corps."

"How do you join?"

"Well, first, you have to ask yourself whether you have 'the call.'"

"The call?"

"Yes, do you believe in, and enjoy, selling toothpaste or building cathedrals? Or would you prefer law enforcement? Are your interests, abilities, and temperament suited for the job? We have only so much time on this earth, so it is important that we are working at something we like doing. Otherwise you will be unhappy and will not delight in making those subtle extra touches that make all the difference in the 'quality' of what you do for a living. The call is more than making money."

"How do you get the call?"

"The call is different for different people. First, unlike St. Paul, it is not necessary that you get knocked off your horse by a bolt of lightening to realize that you have the call. However, sometimes people need some tragic event, like getting fired, to put them in better touch with themselves in order to understand what their call is, or at least, what it is not. And a lot of people may respond to any number of callings which may even change over their career. What is most important is that they are happy at what they are doing and are not alienated from their work. Otherwise product quality and customer service will suffer."

"Well, once you have the call, what do you have to do next to join the corps?"

"You have to make the pledge."

"What! You have to take some form of oath of allegiance to the company? That sounds so silly. I don't believe it."

"A lot of people didn't believe it, but that is exactly what a lot of company men and women did every day during the Welfare America period of employment relations and they got very little in return. We don't ask them to make any pledge of allegiance to the company, we only ask that they pledge to provide service to their customers. That is what the Corporate Service Corps is all about, and in return we grant them a 'continuing commission' with the company."

"What does a 'continuing commission' do for the employee?"

"It assures them that they will not get fired except for good cause, and if we ever have to lay employees off we will provide them with ample warning and adequate severance benefits commensurate with their length of service with the company."

"Well, how do people move through your corps?"

"By moving through the occupational core of our company."

"How do you do that?"

"By grooming generalists."

GROOMING OF GENERALISTS

"Generalists?" The reporter looked bewildered. "I have grown up to believe that we are in the age of the specialist. Don't you recall all that has been written about the 'professionalizing of industry'. In fact, you are aware of the 'professionalization push,' the movement to 'certify' a person's occupational fitness. Why do you need generalists?"

"To protect the company from the 'tyranny' of the specialist."

"Tyranny? Excuse me for laughing. Here I am interviewing the president of this powerful transnational corporation about how they treat their employees and he needs to be protected from some specialist. I think you've got it backwards. How can some poor specialist 'tyrannize' you?"

"By misusing their power and influence in a way that puts the narrow interests of their profession above the broader interests of this corporation. 'Tyranny' may seem too strong a statement because they may think their actions are for the good of the company when they press their power and influence."

"But what real 'power and influence' does the specialist have?"

"The 'power of knowledge work' and the 'influence of the expert.' As a reporter, you should be able to appreciate what I am saying, both as a generalist and as a specialist. You are a 'generalist' when it comes to the subject of 'employment relations.' Since you are not an employment relations expert, you need to interview 'the experts' and skeptically weigh, cross check, and simplify what they may tell you in technical 'throw-weight' terminology. Then you must report a story that touches and influences your readers to make choices regarding their own survival. However, once you start reporting, that is when you become the 'specialist' because you are relying on the tools of your chosen profession. You then have power in how you report the knowledge you have gained and can influence your readers with your 'spin' to the story."

"I am starting to understand. I sure hope we have some generalists working on nuclear disarmament. Okay, how do you 'groom' a generalist? Does the Educational Testing Service offer a certification exam? Do you have to become a member of some professional society?"

The president smiled, "Not yet, thank God, but anything can happen. However, if we ever needed to 'certify generalists,' I would 'examine' people for the following:

- **Is their calling broader than the call of their profession?** For example, our stonecutter has to see his job as building cathedrals.
- **Does their vision permit them to see 'the situation as a whole'?** Do you remember Sir Alec Guinness as the general who as a prisoner of war of the Japanese built the bridge on the River Kwai? It was only at the end, when his last words were, 'What have I done?' that he was finally able to see 'the situation as a whole.'
- **Do they have a 'catholic curiosity'?** I am not suggesting that they be of a particular religion but that their curiosity be 'universal.' This requires 'holistic thinking' which can never be limited by the boundaries of their profession. It also requires starting out with a 'blank sheet of paper' so that they do not limit their thinking to the status quo.
- **Are they nosey?** It is not good enough to be curious if you are not willing to: (1) ask 'hard questions' and (2) only accept 'straight answers.' While you don't have to be like Ronald Reagan's favorite TV reporter, Sam Donaldson, there are times when it is necessary to say 'Hold on, Mr. Specialist!'
- **Can they 'put things together'?** This often requires being able to 'synthesize information.' Other times it requires being able to 'integrate the activities of other professional people.' All the previous qualities of a generalist do not matter if there is no added value. This is where the generalist really makes a difference.

Young man, do you believe your interviewing me on this 'employment relations' story 'certifies' you as a generalist?"

"I have yet to put it all together. Let's just say that I am still being 'groomed.' But 'hold on Mr. President!' You just told me what you look for in a generalist, but so far you haven't told me how they are 'groomed.'"

"Very slowly!"

THE "SLOW-TRACK" CAREER

The reporter, looking impatient: "Well it's about time! I have been waiting to hear about this 'slow-track' business for several pages now. What is so great about a slow track and what does it have to do with grooming generalists?"

"Bright young people who are in a hurry with their careers tend to miss out on a lot of things. Even *Business Week* found that 'the era of rapid promotions created a cadre of executives whose experience was often shallow.'[21] MBAs who are skilled at reading financial statements and developing strategic plans, probably know very little about actually running a business. When I was going to business school I remember this myth that was going around, in fact it was promoted by some of my business school professors and readily swallowed by everyone."

"What was the myth?"

"That a graduate business school education—an MBA— prepares a person as a generalist. This is the educational fast track. A 'quantified generalist' after two years. Many corporations had their own version of this with their management training programs. For two years the new recruit was rotated around the company, so that every six months they were in a new assignment— never staying very long to really get a feel for what was really going on. Instead of a true generalist, we were 'mass producing' a new breed of manager who could conceptualize our business but could not run it. However, because many were quantitatively trained, their concept of the business was primarily a financial one. We had 'the best and the brightest.' However the Vietnam war was over now. They had moved up on a fast track into the executive offices of the Fortune 500. So when all the competitive pressures of the 1980s caught many of these executives off guard, they reacted like financial specialists, rather than generalists."

"What did they do?"

"They became overly concerned with short-term profitability, so they cut costs. And they did this by laying off long-service employees because their employment was at-will. It was easy to do because this new breed of manager did not have a feel for these people any more than many in leadership positions really had a feel for what was going on in the Vietnam war outside of the daily 'body count.' Only this time we had turned the guns inward and the bodies we were counting were our own people. And I guess what made this palatable was that this new breed of manager did not know and therefore did not have any personal loyalty to these people or their families. They had no time to meet these employees, to care about their families, and to understand their value to the company. After all, the best and the brightest were on a fast track to the top. Because of this, they could only count profits and losses because the traumatic experiences of employees did not show up on balance sheets![22] In fact, back in 1989, *Fortune* observed that a lot of them think that 'everybody who doesn't have an MBA from Stanford, or possibly Harvard, is some lower form of life.'"[23]

"Hmm, you have told me earlier what qualities you look for in a generalist. What don't you like to find?"

"Superficiality!"

"Would you explain that."

"I think I told you earlier that some people think that if you don't know anything about a subject, then you are totally objective. I call that 'total ignorance'! The same people also think that if you know a lot about a subject then you are a specialist, which means you cannot be a generalist at the same time. They doubt if you can get the same characteristics in one person.[24] So the only people who qualify to be generalists are the ones who know very little about a lot of subjects and are intent on remaining that way because they are constantly on the move or, shall we say, the fast track. For a while the management literature saw these people in a more positive light, and equated this lack of interest—or not having a penchant for detail—with the notion that these hard-chargers were easily bored—a sign of a real executive."

"What happened then?"

"That's when we entered the age of the specialist, because people started to realize that these fast-track generalists had nothing to say or worth saying at all. Their knowledge was superficial."

"Well, finally, how do you 'slowly' groom generalists?"

"We season them. We let them age. We make sure that they have a lot of 'batting practice' and a 'lot of trips around the track.' This is what 'grooming' is all about. Do you remember the 1988

Republican Convention when they nominated this 41-year-old vice presidential candidate and all that controversy developed. It was not really about the National Guard: it was just that he had not been 'groomed.' We believe in the saying in that old commercial, 'As I got older, I got better!' But most importantly, we believe all our specialists are potential generalists and that's why we formed the Corporation Corps."

"How do you make a specialist into a generalist?"

"They do that for themselves. We just offer them 'sidemotion' opportunities."

PROMOTION AND "SIDEMOTION"

The reporter had heard it before. "Sidemotion, huh. I guess that is the next 'cute' term you are going to use to describe 'horizontal' movement of your professional employees into other positions outside their specialty. And you move people around the organization in order to keep them enthusiastic and 'awake' so they don't become Corporate Rip Van Winkles. And by broadening their career paths you are able to slowly groom all your generalists. Am I right so far?"

"You are right, young man."

"This is only 'Theory Z' management that has been around since 1981."

"You are right again."

"Well, what is new and different about your sidemotion concept?"

"Nothing."

The reporter interrupted, "So why do my readers have to listen to you rehash the same ideas that William Ouchi advanced in 1981 when *Theory Z* was published?"[25]

"Because a lot of American corporations failed to follow Ouchi's advice during the 1980s. You can't have sidemotion if you don't have stability of employment and a climate of trust. People will be afraid to go into a new area for fear that they may not succeed and then they will not have their old position to return to."

"Well, how do you make sidemotion work? It would seem to me that you have a number of hurdles to overcome. Wouldn't employees be worried that once they gave up their position to start learning in a new position, they may get 'downgraded'?"

"That's a valid concern; however, you must have forgot that we have a 'rank-in-person' pay system. Sidemotion will only be attractive to our people if they are able to maintain their salary level and their stature in the organization. If you recall, a military officer is always thought of as a generalist first and a specialist second. This is why the military services are able to easily rotate an army captain from commanding a hundred-person field unit to a staff position where he supervises no one. The rank once earned stays with the person."

"Okay, Mr. CEO, but how can you transfer a specialist—for example, an accountant—and expect the person to perform in a totally new position?"

"You can't. The accountant can only be transferred to a related area but there are a lot of those areas—data processing, purchasing, human resources, and even line management. In data processing, the accountant could assist in designing an accounting system. He would be learning about computer systems while contributing his knowledge of accounting. The important result of sidemotion is the 'ripple effect,' which is the key ingredient of grooming a generalist."

"What is the 'ripple effect'?"

"The ripple effect is how people develop when they are literally thrown into a new situation and are expected to 'swim for themselves.' Just think of their skills as a pebble that hits the water. At first the splash is small, but then it starts to ripple outward as more and more water is displaced. The specialist becomes rounded out with each new ripple which is caused by the preceding one. Our organization must provide the same 'fluidity' and position displacement if our employees are going to have an opportunity to broaden their careers."

"This is starting to sound a little 'fishy' to me. Why would department managers want someone who was not qualified for the position since it would only make their work harder?"

"My foolish young man, I thought we covered that at the start of this tour. You are getting 'qualified' confused with 'quantified' again. Once a specialist is 'sidemoted' he is no longer Mr. Right, he becomes a Mr. Roug . . ."

"Don't say it! But how do your department heads manage a Mr. Rough?"

"By teaching and coaching him. All our managers have to become teachers and coaches, that is part of their development. Don't forget learning is a two-way street. The employee has to be willing and open to learning a new field, but that is not enough. There has to be someone to teach him."

"Where do your managers get the time to teach?"

"They don't have the time."

"Well, how do they do it?"

"By example!"

The reporter looked tired, "I think I have heard enough about sidemotion and I am starting to get seasick. So far you have not said anything about promotion. How do you handle that?"

"Through our 'intracker' program."

OUTPLACERS AS "INTRACKERS"

The reporter seemed furious. "Mr. CEO, I am beginning to think that you are the chief 'editing' officer and your challenge is to come up with all these neat little labels. 'Sidemotion,' 'Mr. Rough,' and now 'intracker.' Who is this 'intracker'?"

"The 'outplacer.'"

"Another label!"

"Yes, young man, but I didn't come up with that term. That was invented before my time somewhere in the middle of Welfare America. 'Outplacers' were kind of like a 'halfway house' that processed 'terminated' employees who were 'released' from their jobs so that they could undertake their 'campaign.'"

"Were these employees running for political office?"

"No, they were at-will employees who had just been fired and they were launching a 'campaign' to find another job."

"Wait a minute! 'Terminated,' 'released from their jobs,' and 'campaign'; this is all double-talk. Did these 'outplacers' actually 'place' these people in a new job?"

"No, the fired employees did that for themselves or they were placed through an executive recruiter."

"But why would the fired employees pay this 'outplacer' who doesn't do the placing?"

"The fired employees didn't pay the outplacer. The fired employees' ex-employer paid the outplacer."

"Why would the ex-employer want to do that?"

"Because after firing an employee, the ex-employer wanted to befriend the fired employee by providing some free career management advice."

"Why didn't the ex-employer hire the outplacer to give the fired employee some 'free career management advice' before the ex-employer became an ex-employer by firing the employee?"

"Young man, you've got me on that one!"

"Well, I guess I am starting to catch on, Mr. President. Maybe your ripple effect is starting to work on me. But anyway, while I am on a roll, how did these 'outplacers' become 'intrackers'?"

The CEO looked tired. He was being forced to recall the really turbulent period of Restructured America when he and many people he knew were going through outplacement. It reminded him of when he was really young. The days when kids said "How Now, Brown Cow." The days when kids got polio.

"Mr. President, what's wrong?"

"Oh, I was just thinking about 'job loss' and what it does to a person. How it paralyzes people—and even worse, their families—because it strikes people in 'unpredictable, mysterious, and catastrophic' ways. Young man, after living through Restructured America, I vowed this would never happen again. Did you know that with all the firings going on, the outplacement market really grew at an astronomical pace and the industry was having a hard time keeping up with the growth."

"What did the outplacement industry do?"

"They started growing like crazy. They could not keep up with the demand so some outplacers started to offer fired employees outplacement jobs. I guess they were following our sidemotion strategy, because they figured that one fired employee could at least relate to another fired employee while they picked up their other outplacement skills. Did you know that I was even offered a job as an outplacer?"

"I didn't know you were fired."

"Everybody was then."

"Well, what happened then? How did outplacers become intrackers?"

"After awhile everybody was joining the outplacement industry. There were less jobs in investment banking after 'The Crash of 1987.' All these baby boomers were playing 'musical chairs.' But all of a sudden there was no one left to fire. The Fortune 500 had lost 400 of its members. And they apparently discovered a new 'salk vaccine.' Once this happened we had an oversupply of outplacers who were now trained in how to manage other peoples' careers. And they had this gift."

"What gift?"

"They cared about people! And they could do something about it because they were now trained in career management. There were so many of these outplacers. So corporations started getting them involved in our employees' careers, the moment the new employee came on board."

"Well, what did they do?"

"They started to manage the careers of Messrs. Right and Rough once they started 'moving through' Columbus Industries. One innovative outplacement firm started the concept of "lifework," which abandons thinking of a career in the old vertical pattern of graduating from college, climbing an organization's career ladder, and retiring with the same company. They believe instead that a multiple career may happen over a lifetime in related and unrelated businesses—a career continuum. One outplacement firm, Janotta, Bray, suggested that career management issues should be dealt with before termination or before a career hits a rut, suggesting that a lifework evaluation should take place every three to five years.[26] So every few years all our employees had to go through a 'self-assessment' of their career. Because they cared, a lot of our employees started to become very attached to these intrackers. They wanted them as an employee benefit."

"Why?"

"Because they realized that the intracker had a conflict of interest, since they were paid by the corporation, yet they were supposed to be working for the employee. The employees felt that it was not fair to the intracker to have two bosses. So the employees reasoned that the only solution was to have the intracker work for the employee and be paid for by the employee out of his or her benefits."

"Did this happen?"

"Well, it took a lot of time to make it work. Unfortunately, some employers saw these outplacers as their agents and did not want to give them up. But they finally acquiesced."

"So the outplacers became intrackers?"

"Yes, and many became 'player's reps.'"

PREPARING TO LEAVE

HUMANE "UP AND OUT" SYSTEMS

The reporter, realizing that he was near the end of the tour, started to look concerned. "Mr. CEO, I can't believe that we have been through 'getting rewarded' and 'moving through' and you still have not said anything about 'promotion.' Why not?"

"There is very little to say."

"Why?"

"Promotion has been overemphasized for too long because people always had too much to say about it. So we try to say very little about promotion, so our employees will not expect too much."

"You keep your employees in the dark?"

"No, but we keep anybody we promote out of the spotlight."

The reporter was once again puzzled, "But why? I always thought that getting promoted was the ultimate form of recognition for the 'rising stars' of the company."

"Young man, that is the problem. Every time we announce that some employee has been promoted, we also are sending out a message to the other fully qualified candidates who were not promoted. Although we can only promote the best-qualified candidate among all the candidates competing for the position, we want all our fully qualified employees to believe that they are stars. So we want to share the spotlight with them."

"I certainly can understand that, Mr. President. If you didn't do something like that, then all the candidates passed over for the promotion would believe that you are sending them a signal that they should be preparing to leave."

The President hesitated, "No, we hope that they would be preparing to leave."

The reporter was really taken aback by this statement. He jumped to his feet, "Mr. Chief Ethics Officer, I can't believe I heard what you just said, after you have been trying to convince me about how much this company cares about all of its 'partners.' Why would you want your fully qualified employees to be preparing to leave?"

"My young reporter, it is because we care about our employees that we want all of them to be prepared to leave."

"I don't understand."

"Then you had better go back and read the first four parts of this book again, because it is about leaving your employer in a way other than retirement. In fact, it is about building a career around yourself, not someone else. And that means that you have to be prepared to leave not one, but several employers, over your career."

"But why would anyone want to leave here? This is a good place to work!"

"We don't want our employees to leave. We need them. We just want them to be in control of their own destiny. Because if business conditions ever get out of control again, we don't want these employees to be expecting clear sailing and to fall asleep or become complacent on their 'watch.'"

"Their watch?"

"Yes, and we give all of our new employees a gold watch when they join Columbus Industries."

"A gold watch? But I thought you only gave gold watches to someone who retires after spending 30 or 40 years with your company. Why give a gold watch to a new employee?"

"Because the days when a retiring manager could expect a gold watch for 35 years of service are over. Furthermore we want them to watch their time! Young man, everybody used to think that gold was so valuable. Did you know why?"

"Well, gold is a scarce commodity. But wait a minute. So is time!"

"There is never enough time, so we want our employees to start watching it from day one. And by giving them their gold watch when they join, they don't have to wait around to get one 30 or 40 years later. In essence we give them the organization's blessing to leave at the beginning, so that when they do leave they are doing it with honor. And we make sure our employee benefits programs are flexible enough to allow our employees to leave."

FLEXIBLE BENEFITS

The reporter began to wonder, "Gold watches to new employees! Employee benefit programs which allow employees to leave your company! You have got it all backwards. I always thought that these benefit programs were designed to be a form of 'golden handcuffs' to tie people to your company. What happened to change all that?"

"Welfare America."

"Welfare America? *You* better go back and read the first part of this book. Remember Welfare America's personnel systems were not 'flexible' enough to meet the challenge of Restructured America's business conditions. Employees were tied to their corporations' benefit programs. Don't you recall it was Restructured America's turmoil that caused many employees to become second-class citizens because they were no longer tied to these generous benefit programs. How can you say 'Welfare America'?"

"Because an increasing segment of the U.S. electorate started to lose their corporate-sponsored benefits, a comprehensive set of reforms were enacted to make health, accident, long-term disability, and life insurance benefits more 'universal' and more 'portable.' In other words, this reform movement culminated in ensuring the welfare of all Americans."

"What was reformed?"

"The tax laws."

"Why the tax laws, Mr. President?"

"Because up through the 1980s, American tax policy was subsidizing the cost of providing employer-paid fringe benefits. These benefits were the same as giving the employee more tax-free income, yet the employer could use the benefit costs as a deduction from their corporate income taxes. The employer and the employees came out as winners; the only losers were (1) the taxpaying public at large who had to make up for this by paying higher taxes, and

(2) the growing number of ex-employees who no longer were eligible for this tax-free benefit."

"I suppose they tried to make employer-paid benefits taxable to the employee."

"They did try to make these benefits taxable, but to overcome organized opposition, they settled for a compromise."

"Well, what tax policies were reformed?"

"The 'Flexible Spending Account Program'—also known as FSAP—was modified so that any taxpayer could establish a FSAP, rather than restricting its use to employees of participating corporations. Under the former FSAP, the luckier employees were able to pay their share of their medical bills with pre-tax earnings. Now this program was open to all taxpayers, regardless of whom they worked for, and whether they were 'employees' or worked for themselves. However, under the new program all taxpayers were entitled to a maximum credit of $3,000 per year. Corporations which paid more than $3,000 per year for each employee in health premiums were required to report the extra amount to the IRS as income to the employee."

"Did this plan help to reduce the federal deficit?"

"Well, it did help to slow the runaway costs of health care."

"So I guess these changes do allow employees some additional flexibility when it is time for them to be preparing to leave. But you have not mentioned the most important reason that stops them from leaving. What about the need to wait 20 or 30 years to build up enough service credit in their retirement program?"

"We put them on a 'fast track.'"

"FAST-TRACK" RETIREMENT PLANS

"Hold on, Mr. President, you just told me that all of your people are on 'slow-track' career advancement. How can you now say that they are on a 'fast track' to retirement? Isn't that inconsistent?"

"Yes, it seems that way. We have employees who really understand all facets of our business because of their slow-track development through our 'occupational core.' Because they have been groomed to be generalists they are now capable of really contributing to Columbus Industries. However, because they were on a retirement fast track, they are now prepared to leave."

"Well, if you admit that it is inconsistent, why do you allow it?"

"Wait a minute young man, I said it only seems inconsistent. And for that matter, it is no more inconsistent then what happened when the reverse was true. In the past, American employees advanced on a fast track within their occupational specialty and quickly climbed onto a shaky branch in their narrowly defined career path. However, once there, they had no place to go. And many were forced to stay there for 15 or 20 years because the retirement plan was on a slow track. Unfortunately these people were not groomed to contribute beyond their specialized area and they were not prepared to leave. Young man, the older I get, the more I find that life is paradoxical, often filled with inconsistencies. However, some paradoxes are 'win–win' situations while others are 'lose–lose.' I believe we now have a 'win–win' paradox."

"But aren't you worried that you will lose these good people who now know your company the best?"

"No, just because they are prepared to leave, that does not mean that they will leave. After all they are probably more valuable here than somewhere else. And I would rather have employees giving me some painfully straight advice because they are not afraid to leave. A long time ago Peter Drucker warned that 'the greatest obstacle to organizational mobility' was the 'golden fetters,' such as pension plans, which tie people to a particular employer."[27]

"Well, how do you make this work? What is a fast-track retirement plan?"

"There are two basic types: the defined-benefit plan and the defined-contribution plan. A 'defined benefit' is where you know that you will be entitled to something like 60 percent of your pay at your normal retirement date, provided you have, for example, 20 years of service. The benefit you will receive is defined; the contribution is not, because it depends on employee turnover, the rate of inflation, and other actuarial assumptions. On the other hand, a 'defined contribution' is where you know how much tax-deferred income you can put into the plan. The amount you will get out depends on the number of years you contribute, the amount of those contributions, and rate at which your contributions appreciate."

"Gosh, the defined benefit plan seems so complicated and technical that I guess you would need several actuaries to figure it out. Why do people like it?"

"Because it was so simple!"

"What I can understand is the simplicity of a defined contribution plan. It is just like a savings account; the more you save and the longer you save, the more you will get back. But what is simple about a defined-benefit retirement plan?"

"The vision! The 'seductive' promise of how much you will receive if you are able to stay until your normal retirement date. The promise worked fine during Welfare America, but it was broken for many people in Restructured America because of another vision. The selfish vision of corporate raiders who realized that they could lay off at-will employees with long service and siphon off the excess funds that this had generated in the pension plan."

"That must have been terrible. Why didn't they just get rid of all these defined-benefit plans and let employees save money the old-fashioned way in a defined-contribution plan?"

"Well, they tried. Most employees started to realize that they needed a retirement program that was more than a seductive promise, so defined-contribution plans became widely popular. However, there were two forces working against this. On one hand, the federal government was looking for new revenue sources to trim the deficit, so they all but destroyed a very popular program at the time, called the 401k plan. On the other hand, all the actuaries were afraid that they would be put out of work if there were no more defined-benefit plans. So they came up with several fast-track changes to these plans."

"What kind of fast-track changes?"

"Changes that would allow employees to reach normal retirement in 10 years."

THE 10-YEAR CAREER

The reporter had now heard it all. "Normal retirement in 10 years! You have got to be kidding. That certainly is quite extreme."

"Well, actually it is. Most of our employees normally retire after 12 to 15 years, but our retirement plan allows for normal retirement as early as 10 years."

"What? You vary normal retirement eligibility of your employees. Don't you think that unfairly discriminates against your 15-year employee?"

"Young reporter, we don't vary our employees' retirement eligibility; they do it for themselves."

"How can they do that?"

"By choosing their retirement option. I am sure you are aware that some health insurance plans offer their members a variety of optional coverages. For example, plan members who elect the 'high option' will receive greater health coverage but will pay a higher premium. All we have done is apply this same principle to retirement protection coverage. Any person who elects a 10-year normal retirement will at the end of 10 years be eligible for a lifetime annuity."

"But isn't that very costly?"

"No, the cost will depend on the employee's age, the amount of their annual contribution, and the size of the defined benefit they will be entitled to receive at the end of 10 years."

"But if you call this a 'defined-benefit' plan, how can the size of the benefit be altered? Are you sure this is not a defined-contribution plan in disguise?"

"No, it is a defined-benefit plan; our employees know the size of the benefit when they enroll in the plan. But, as I was saying before, the size of the benefit they elect depends on whether they choose a high-option or low-option plan. Typically, our younger employees who are on their first career can only afford the low-option plan. And after they leave to go onto their next career they may also choose to defer their retirement benefits until later when they really need the money. Our older employees when they start working here typically choose the high option. They can afford it, because many are 'double and triple dippers.'"

"What is 'triple dipper'?"

"A triple dipper is an older worker who has several successive 10-year careers. In each career they have managed to accumulate retirement benefits and they are now 'dipping' into at least two other retirement incomes; our paycheck is the third 'dip.'"

"This all seems quite complicated. You have all these high-and low-option plans, different normal retirement dates, and all these multiple dippers. How do you keep track of, and administer, all of these figures? Your actuaries must hate it."

"No, our actuaries really love it. Remember they came up with the idea as part of our Brown Cow program. It has created a lot of work for them and something even more important."

"What is that?"

"Job security!"

"I guess I am starting to understand. But what happens when you have groomed a generalist on your slow track who is eligible for normal retirement after 10 years. What happens at the end of 10 years if you don't want that person to leave because they are now groomed to take on even more responsibility? What happens after they pass their normal retirement date?"

"They receive negative retirement credit."

"Negative retirement credit? Do you mean you actually penalize them for staying on with you?"

"No, we reward them with negative retirement credit. It is sort of like a reverse mortgage, where instead of paying interest on the mortgage, an older person can actually start drawing down on their home equity. What we do is let them receive in cash the amount we would be paying into their retirement if they were staying here another 10 years, or we let them start another defined-benefit program, only this time we make their normal retirement 5 years out instead of 10. Our actuaries just love it."

"I am sure they do, Mr. CEO. By the way, this tour is almost over. Yet at the very beginning you said that you were going to explain to me about your plans to go into a law enforcement career. When do you plan to do that?"

"As soon as I become an 'emeritus employee'!"

THE EMERITUS EMPLOYEE

The reporter knew he was at the end of the tour of Columbus Industries. He was now getting anxious to file his story with his editor and hoped it would be published quickly. He had two concerns. First, as a reporter, he wanted to get the story out to the public to make them aware of this revolutionary change in American employment relations. Second, as a person, he wanted to be the first to report these developments because it would only be a matter of time before the word would leak out. Yet, before he left this interview with this CEO, he had one more question, "What is an 'emeritus employee'?"

"Young man, an emeritus employee is what every 'loyal' working man and woman strives to become when they are working for somebody else. They know that someday they will leave the organization; they hope that their leaving will be seen as 'normal', and many hope that this will occur at 'normal' retirement. In today's fast-moving world, it is not normal or good business sense to hold out the seductive promise of lifetime employment. It is better to expect that it is normal for employees to work for several different employers—including themselves—over their lifetime. And it is normal to expect that American employment law and corporate personnel systems—most importantly, defined-benefit retirement plans—adapt to this business reality. And lastly, if these expectations normally become a reality, it should become a normal occurrence to see a lot of emeritus employees of corporations working: at law enforcement, at McDonald's, or in a satellite business, having found their orbital niche to the mothership they just 'retired' from . . ."

"Mr. President, I have a deadline! What is an emeritus employee?"

"A person who retires from active service and leaves with the organization's blessing!"[28]

CHAPTER 6

FOLLOWING THE RIGHTSIZING REMEDY—AN INTEGRATED HUMAN RESOURCE MANAGEMENT APPROACH

All progress depends on the unreasonable man[ager].

George Bernard Shaw[1]   (*brackets added*)

The downsizing dilemma is the outgrowth of reasonable men and women managers following outdated scripts—extrapolating Welfare America's human resources practices into an uncharted Restructured America future. The CEO of Columbus Industries (or the person responsible for his script) may be too downright unreasonable or just too unrealistic. In terms of what? The past? The present? What about the future? Has anyone been there yet? Christopher Lloyd summed it all up at the end of the original *Back to the Future* movie when he says to Michael J. Fox as they are about to time travel to the 21st century, "Where we are going there are no roads."

Also there are no roadmaps for those "behemoth corporations" that just can't seem to get their "restructuring drill" right. So where does this leave management in responding to this downsizing dilemma? Perhaps one downsizing consultant unwittingly touched on the problem when he related the process of corporate restructuring to trying to navigate an aircraft carrier, or for that matter, a jumbo jet on a runway. For the managers of a "jumbo corporation," this may well be the problem, because they approach restructuring in a linear lockstep fashion. All the managers—especially those responsible for human resources—are compelled to move in one direction. But is this still the right direction? There are no roadmaps, because there are no roads!

The rightsizing remedy is about blazing trails just like our forefathers and foremothers did in Frontier America. It is also about getting beyond blazing a trail through (or eroding) the "soiled" doctrine of employment-at-will and, instead, finding new paths for human beings to pass through employment systems. Remember, it is better to pursue employment relations opportunities than to try to solve insoluble employment relations problems.

To do this, corporate CEOs are going to need to rely increasingly on their human resource experts, in addition to their accountants. When the plant or the factory is in somebody's head, the traditional bottom line cost-accounting conventions of "material" and "labor" no longer apply. Senior management will need to reframe its view of human resources as an investment rather than an expense. Human resource practitioners will need to gear up to literally lead the way by blazing their own trail and providing their employer and employees a navigational direction if there are no roads.

And when there are no roads, there are also no boundaries. The dimensions of choice are unlimited. There is no reason why an unreasonable manager cannot maneuver several paths simultaneously. The trick is to understand and balance many interrelated dimensions into one integrated human resource management approach. The Rightsizing Remedy does not view restructuring as a one-time change in the size and form of the organization, but as an ongoing balancing of many interrelated dimensions:[2]

- The **external environment** of the enterprise and the need for management to be continually alert and agile enough to react to a wide variety of "fickle" external forces and to invent the future.
- The **culture** of the organization—particularly the degree of openness, trust, teamwork and, of course, loyalty—which bonds management and employees into an oath of allegiance focusing on quality and service to the customer.
- The **autonomous employees** who make up the company, with particular emphasis on their "roughness," their nonautonomous "families," and the need to upgrade their knowledge and skills and their ability to move from one job to another, as markets, customer needs and preferences, and competitive conditions change.

- The **processes** of the corporation (e.g., job evaluation and performance measurement systems) and the extent to which these processes empower or impede individual employees in responding to unforeseen events.
- As well as the organizational **structure**, with special emphasis on the degree of autonomy that managers have to reorganize and redeploy their staffs to meet changing conditions.

For managers to follow the rightsizing remedy, they will need to pave their own roadway which balances all of these dimensions. Simply moving or eliminating boxes on an organization chart will not change behavior unless: (1) human beings at work have the right skills, (2) management demonstrates the right values, (3) the right processes are in place to recognize and reward these behaviors, skills, and values, and (4) all of these changes respond to the competitive environment.

This concluding chapter offers some suggestions on how to achieve this balance.

STEP 1: INTERNALIZE YOUR ENVIRONMENT

START WITH A BLANK PIECE OF PAPER

Jean Valjean is nothing now.
Another story must begin!

Les Misérables[3]

With these words, the hero of this magnificent musical tears up his yellow "ticket-of-leave"—the reminder to the world that he was a convict, a paroled thief—who stole a loaf of bread to save his sister's dying child. He would no longer be "prisoner 24601"—a number—but would become part of "some higher plan." Jean Valjean was reborn with a calling and started his life again on a blank piece of paper.

"Rebirth" ... "renewal" ... "calling" ... "blank piece of paper" are merely words on another piece of paper for most of us most of the time. Until we experience a crisis—a death, divorce, job loss—which disrupts the linear, more or less predictable, patterns of our personal lives. This is also true for all forms of organizations—corporations, cities, and nations. Germany and Japan, nations in crisis at the end of World War II, had no choice but to start with a blank piece of paper. Many of our cities and states are experiencing financial crises today but still hang onto old patterns of behavior; they will soon have no choice but to start with a blank piece of paper in questioning their ever increasing linear expenditure patterns as taxpayers continue their revolt. Corporations increasingly caught in a downsizing dilemma will have no choice but to start with a blank sheet of paper in questioning their linear patterns of thinking and behaving. Another story must begin!

The first step is always the hardest one to take. It is one of awakening to the fact that we are now in Restructured America and the restructuring will go on and on and on. The reason it is hard is that we are still managing and being managed by Welfare America's rules. We are a nation of employees! Our substance of life (our jobs, our salaries, our health and retirement protection, and our careers) are in another man or woman's hands. Throughout all the past restructuring, when we fire someone, or are fired, the reaction is to outplace the ex-employee, or be outplaced. To what? For the most part, the outplaced seek to get inplaced, so the substance of their life ends up in another man or woman's hands. Another musical chair. Until the next restructuring.

This observation is not meant in any way to be critical of human resource practitioners, or most outplacement firms and employees. Most are attempting to do the right thing, but they are doing things within the context of Welfare America's employment systems. It is time to do the right things differently within the context of a new era.

Consider what Charles Handy has to say about employment in this new era: "Where our fathers thought it normal to spend 100,000 hours, or nearly 50 years, in their organization, our children will spend only half of that, whether they cram it into 25 years or spread it out more thinly."[4] Handy's "upside-down thinking" about work has tremendous human resource implications, particularly if employees chose to spread their 50,000 hours of life work over 50 years. Imagine developing human resource policies and systems for people who take half the year off! But this is the direction that corporations are moving in when they rely increasingly on the contingency work force.

The contingency work force. Up till now we have been viewing contingency workers as losers. But again, only in the context of Welfare America's entitlements. Contingency workers are really in the vanguard of this new era. They probably don't know it but they are pioneers because they have to blaze their own trails in search of work. They have to accept different life-styles from those of many employees who are still "pampered" by their organizations. Yes, they are pampered with a steady salary, generous benefits, a role, and, of course, the prospect of a better salary and benefits and a bigger role. In fairness, these employees are only pampered within the context of the new Restructured America era. In Welfare America this was the "organizational glue." Now these entitlements are considered costs. Which is why downsizing goes on and on and on. And more and more pampered employees are downsized out of a job and become contingency workers unless they get another musical chair.

There are more contingency workers today because there are less musical chairs. So the frontier of this new era is being filled with a lot more immigrants from the old era. Again they come seeking a better life for themselves and their children. The good news is that America is still the land of opportunity, regardless of the era. However, unlike 200 years ago, the opportunities are not external (cultivating the endless land) but internal (cultivating the endless reaches of our intelligence). The contingency workers of today and tomorrow, if they are to succeed in this new frontier, will need to recognize that they carry the means of production in their head, and there will be an increasing market for what they have to sell. The human resource buyers of their services in companies will need to harness this opportunity.

To harness the contingency work force as well as many other realities of Restructured America, we need to wipe the slate clean of our lifelong beliefs about employment. Handy describes this as upside-down thinking—"considering the unlikely if not the absurd."[5] Peter Schwartz considers this as "reperceiving" the world—that is, making the best possible use of information by opening one's mind to the fanciful, the intuitive, even the unthinkable.[6] But what is unthinkable? What is unlikely? What is absurd? The fall of the Berlin Wall? The invasion of Kuwait? Arabs fighting Arabs? The end of the Soviet Union? The fact that in the same time frame, fewer Americans were killed in the Operation Desert Storm theater of operations than in the District of Columbia? Lee Iaccoca in an ad in *Fortune* telling us—in his same old Japan-bashing way—how to respond to the new American Century?[7] Take your pick.

Whether it is rethinking the phenomena of the contingency work force or the phenomena of a Lee Iaccoca, this chapter is about viewing the reality that surrounds us with a blank piece of paper. To accomplish this, we need to internalize our environment. To smell its roses as well as tolerating some of the stench. Most importantly, we need to recognize the environment for what it is now and will likely be in the future, not for what it was from our past.

THINK HOLISTICALLY

How do we internalize our environment? Consider for a moment the following front page story, entitled "A generation's vast wealth is a baby boomer windfall," which appeared in *The Philadelphia Inquirer* on May 26, 1991:

> "There is no doubt that we will soon be seeing the largest transfer of income in the history of the world," according to economist Robert Avery of Cornell University. The passing of the extraordinary wealth, estimated at $8 trillion, created in America in the past five decades will speed up in the 1990s, as those alive and working during those years reach their 70s and 80s.[8]

What relevance has this to human resource management? There is no direct relevance perhaps. For certain, this story will not appear in a corporate annual report unless the firm is made up of probate attorneys or investment advisers. But that is the point—this social phenomena is occurring outside of the bounds of the organization but will indeed impact in varying degrees on the material substance of life of people who work inside the organization. According to Edward N. Wolff, a New York University economist, "If it weren't for gifts and inheritances, most baby boomers would never be able to accumulate any real wealth."[9] What happens if a valuable at-will employee who has been privately questioning "what is in it for me to stay here" all of a sudden receives a several hundred thousand dollar inheritance?

This "transfer of income" story is but one example of any number of events—the AIDS epidemic, the high-tech household, the health-care crisis, the plight of the homeless, the threat of global warming, the demise of the Soviet Union, the sprouting spiritualism, etc.—which are converging on us to ensure that our future is not a linear extrapolation of the past. Increasingly, managers will need to integrate these unconnected "blips on their radar screen" into their own holistic vision of the future. How do you it? By simply reading parts of the newspaper that deal with news about events occurring in ordinary lives—as opposed to news of celebrities such as Madonna, Michael Jackson, and Nancy Reagan. John Naisbitt calls this the "content analysis" which formed the factual underpinnings of his predictions in his best-seller *Megatrends*. He argued that "the analysis of the content of newspapers is an effective way of monitoring social change because newspaper space is limited—when something new is introduced something else is deleted."[10]

And while reading these "bottom-up" news accounts is the necessary first task, the next essential task is letting your upper-right brain draw pictures of the implications for the future.

INVENT THE FUTURE

Noted columnist George Will, also an occasional (no quotes) luncheon companion of Nancy Reagan added his two cents to the controversy surrounding Kitty Kelly's unauthorized biography of Mrs. Reagan. Mr. Will, however, did not attack Ms. Kelly, the messenger; he attacked her readers! His argument was that anyone who would read this book was in essence leading an "arid" life.[11] Perhaps he thought that they should be conducting "content analysis" by reading newspaper stories about the "income transfer" phenomena or at least reading his syndicated column. His recommendation was that these "readers" should "get a life." Mr. Will: readers—and writers—already have a life. What we all need is a future!

How do we get the one that we need? Remember, necessity is the mother of invention. How do you invent a future? By first drawing a picture of what we think we need and then envisioning how all these holistic social phenomena we are reading about are going to converge to create it. This sounds crazy? Maybe so, to reasonable men and women who stopped dreaming after their childhood days and who as "adults" consume their time rationalizing life as it exists.

Although this is not *Mary Poppins* and we can't end this story by going out and "flying kites," there are certain universal truths that rational managers sometimes lose sight of because there is no time or "reason" to consider them. History is full of stories of heroes who impacted history—Walt Disney, who discovered *Snow White*, or Christopher Columbus, who discovered America. Disney invented his future because he not only understood his environment but he followed a dream on how to make a difference in this environment. Although America is now trying to rediscover Columbus (was he a hero or villian?), there is no question that Columbus's voyages set off a chain of actions and reactions that continue to influence the course of history in our own day.[12] In different ways, Disney and Columbus shaped America.

At no time in human history do more and more people have so much opportunity to shape their work lives and the organization they work for in so many ways. In addition to all the trends and developments which impact on our environment, we are singularly and collectively impacting our environment. We are not bystanders in our lives, we are already living. Thank you, Mr. Will, we are making a difference.

One question is, what kind of difference do employers want their employees to make? What is the vision? A leaner organization with fewer but better people? Growth in earnings per share? Bottom line improvement? These are financial projections, but what is the holistic vision of how this will occur in a new environment? This kind of "by-the-numbers" thinking may have led to the observation that "many U.S. companies would be better off hiring one good science-fiction writer for a month than buying 1,000 IBM personal computer spreadsheets for a year."[13]

Perhaps this science-fiction writer ought to construct some new bottom lines.

CONSTRUCT NEW BOTTOM LINES

Why do we have bottom lines? To keep score. Business is like a sporting event except for one critical difference. The game never ends. Firms are going concerns. Corporations are immortal. There is no ninth inning. Instead there are accounting periods—months, quarters, fiscal years—in which to keep score. There are also "generally accepted accounting principles" on how to keep score in business. And there certainly are enough scorekeepers.

While not meaning to offend the business scorekeeping profession, it is true that their principles, practices, and conventions are contrived; they are not naturally a part of the business. This is not to say that they are not useful to the owners and management of the business—who collectively need to know the periodic score by taking the corporation's pulse. But remember, an EKG only records the heartbeat, it is not the heart. The health or wellness of a corporation, like its mortal counterpart, often requires many other "tests" as well as a holistic assessment of the "individual's" medical history. There is no one bottom line but a lot of contrived and often conflicting bottom lines that are useful in keeping score.

The human resources profession has a job to do in constructing their own bottom lines to measure corporate health and wellness. What is the bottom line on the "trust gap" in Restructured America? What are the generally accepted human resource principles, practices, and conventions to keep score on this front? Or stated another way, what is the value of knowledge worker loyalty and dedication to a company or its investment community? Where is this accounted for on a corporation profit and loss statement and balance sheet?

But this measure of a company's human resource health is not all that is not accounted for by numbers. *Fortune* reports that "intellectual capital" is becoming corporate America's most valuable asset,[14] but "intellectual assets" appear on no balance sheet.[15] Moreover, the value of employee loyalty and dedication becomes even more important when you consider a new phenomenon called the "competency perspective." According to *The Washington Post,* C. K. Prahalad, a professor at the University of Michigan business school, believes that "the real value of a company is in its organizational portfolio of strategic competencies."[16]

Is "strategic competency" really a new phenomenon? Hardly, when you consider the animators and other crafts people Disney brought into his organization. Their shared values for excellence created an organizational core of competence, coupled with creativity and imagination, which was nurtured and sustained for years. What is new is a reawakening among corporations obsessed with strategic plans, quarterly profits, and organization headcounts that people—their competencies and shared values— are their greatest asset. In fact, some would argue that "the allocation of talent becomes more important than the allocation of capital."[17]

But how can the people asset be measured and reported on the bottom line?

QUANTIFY THE UNQUANTIFIABLE

Fifteen years ago, a major U.S. bank was forced by law to divest itself of all of its nonbanking activities—which meant that it had to get out of the management consulting business. The bank's corporate management had an idea: It would place the management consulting firm on the market to see who would be willing to buy the firm at the highest price. The management consultants had a different idea: The bank would sell the firm to the senior consultants at a mutually agreed price. The consultants did not have as much financial capital as potential buyers from the outside; in fact most of them had hardly any capital at all. But the bank agreed to sell them the firm under a very attractive financial arrangement. Why? Because these consultants controlled all the "intellectual capital" in their collective craniums and could have voted with their collective feet if the bank sold the firm out from under them to a third party. Without this portfolio of competencies, a third party would own only the furniture, the office supplies, and office rental contracts—because these consultants were considered at-will employees. To effect this deal, the bank and the consultants were able to quantify the unquantifiable.

There is a lot more interest today on the part of corporations in general, not just consulting firms or whoever owns their intellectual assets, in quantifying "brainpower." *Time* reports that in an "economy increasingly based on information and technology, ideas and creativity often embody most of a company's wealth."[18] The traditional vehicles—patents, copyrights, trademarks, intangible assets such as "goodwill," advances to authors which place some value on their intellectual talent, and so forth—are coming up short. These are only accounting vehicles which worked in a different era—when intellectual achievement, such as research and development, were "indirect" to production and sales. They were indirect costs in the production process. They are not reflected in the salaries of employees because salaries are based on a "position" evaluation system (a role or an organizational script), not an "intellectual assets" evaluation system. How do you compensate an employee who has invested "intellectually" in the future of the company?

The typical response coming out of Welfare America is that this employee's intellectual capital will be compensated, that is, the person will be recognized as having "potential" and hence a "good (extrapolated) future" with the company. Times have changed! In today's arms-length employment environment, it's hard to extrapolate the future when the employment relationship may not last beyond sundown. How can someone's intellect be capitalized in an at-will employment relationship? What is the legal value of their "intellectual assets" to employees when they can be fired at-will? And what is the asset value to the employer? Employers who fire at-will are going to come up short of intellectual capital. Knowledge workers will be at-will to vote with their feet.

What is needed now is more concerted attention to "quantify the unquantifiable" in the same manner that the bank and the consultants did 15 years ago. By negotiating an agreement as to what those intellectual assets are worth. In the case of employees, these will be employment agreements, continuing commissions, and endable enlistments—which "value" the employment relationship.

But there are no commonly accepted accounting principles to "quantify" this asset. Come on. Do things differently, invent them! Jeffrey Hallett argues:

> It will not suffice to argue that we are trapped by "commonly accepted accounting principles" unless we do not really believe that

people are assets. When the industrial revolution began, people were confounded by the ideas that pieces of metal—inventory—could have value. It took a long time to develop accounting procedures which allowed a company to declare these scraps as assets. Similarly, we may now need to develop accounting procedures that recognize the intellectual and human capital represented by employees are assets. The arguments that assume people are assets must begin now.[19]

Once employment relationships are "valued," the accountants can assume their normal role of working out generally accepted accounting principles for "depreciating" or "amortizing" employment agreements and working out more "LIFO" and "FIFO" techniques for changes in employee "brainpower."

STEP 2: EXTERNALIZE YOUR CULTURE

GET RID OF YOUR "TANKS"

There is a nationally renowned management consultant on the general subject of employee (particularly police officer and firefighter) behavior. He has spent time in public meetings of local governments across this nation telling a story about his neighbor. It seems his neighbor, a graduate of the Army's Armor School, has a love affair with armored tanks—thanks to the doctrine he was exposed to at the U.S. Army's tank school. The doctrine that this neighbor believes in is that "a tank is the best defense against another tank." This "truth" dates back to some time in Welfare America, perhaps when Rommel and Patton faced off in some North African desert (remember the movie *Patton*, where George C. Scott peers down from some mountain overlooking an impending tank battle). The management consultant has articulated clearly to cities across the country that the problem is this doctrine (tank versus tank) is out-of-date. The best defenses against a tank these days are an airplane with armor-piercing bombs, also missiles, and a whole host of high-tech air-to-land, sea-to-land, and land-to-land weapons. We are in a new era where the best defense against a tank is a plane or a missile. Thank God, Saddam Hussein did not realize this.

This management consultant was not talking about tanks in the literal sense. He was really talking about the blinders or blind spots that all professions have when they continue to inwardly focus on the age-old tenets of their faith rather than sense what relevance these beliefs have to the here and now. Companies have been relying on their tanks. What was successful yesterday may not be successful tomorrow.

What are tanks? Some call tanks *paradigms*[20] (i.e., patterns of human behavior) which are counterproductive to organizational goals. No thanks, I prefer *tanks*. Tanks are the embodiment of what drives behavior into "patterns," like the web tracks that appear in the sand where there are no roads. The "tank" is the culture of an organization moving ever forward into the future protected from the outside by its armor. Defending itself against what it knows—other tanks. Unaware that there are now planes with armor-piercing missiles.

Many organizations are moving ever forward today into places where there are no roads. The people in the organization are feeling protected from the outside by the armor of their shared values and their sense of corporate "manifest destiny." The IBM corporation—the mother of all that was good about Welfare America employers—has its own tanks. Fortunately for IBM, its leader—John Akers—wants to destroy IBM's tanks. And if he does, he will owe a lot to Brent Henderson, the IBM branch manager who unwittingly "externalized" IBM's culture by taking Aker's message to heart—and to the media. Akers was quoted by Henderson as saying: "I'm sick and tired of visiting plants to hear nothing but great things about quality and cycle time—and then visit customers who tell me of problems .... (IBM workers) too damn comfortable at a time when the business is in crisis ... standing around the water cooler waiting to be told what to do."[21] Welfare America employees are marching lockstep into the midst of Restructured America's turmoil. Akers and his earnest follower and messenger may deserve medals. Corporate tanks (i.e., patterns of behavior) need to be destroyed by CEOs.

But that is not enough. Cultural change requires not only the employer (Akers—the head IBMer) to decree it; it also requires employees (all the other IBMers) to accept change. Before there were tanks, there were pharaohs and emperors who ruled by decree. For example, the late Yul Brynner, who epitomized the role of kings and of pharaohs, had one standard line in *The Ten Com-*

mandments. As the Egyptian pharaoh, Brynner would rule by saying: "So it is written, so it is done."

Brynner's pharaoh and, later, his king found that it is not always easy to get people to do what you say. And, it is becoming even more of "a puzzlement" for Akers and many other CEOs to get people to do what they say when employees are fed up with how CEOs act. Although they may not have been "standing by the water cooler," many employees believe that it is Akers and his peers who have been "too damn comfortable"! The modern day pharaohs of America's 200 largest industrial and services companies were rewarded with an average of $2.4 million in pay in 1990 at a time when many of their employees lost their jobs.[22] It is also about time that America's self-appointed royalty accept that cultural change is a two-way street. Although the message is clear and it is getting louder, many CEOs still have not heard it. Perhaps we should use Henderson's electronic mail to get out this message.

TELL THE EMPEROR TO DRESS UP HIS ACT!

After hearing Akers message, *Business Week* reported the IBMers worldwide were debating whether the fault lies in them or their bosses. At the same time that IBM was losing marketshare, Akers' pay jumped 138 percent to $4.6 million in 1990.[23] *Time* questions why "at a time when millions of American workers are being asked to share the risks in pay-for-performance schemes, economists and shareholders are beginning to ask why the boss should be immune to reality."[24] *The Washington Post* states that "most studies have shown that executive compensation is generally not correlated to executive performance—improving working conditions, employing more people, and increasing value to shareholders."[25]

There is no dearth of external critics of executive pay practices. Stephen O'Byrne, a compensation expert, is reported as saying that "CEO pay packages are so large that they represent investment decisions on the order of building a plant."[26] Kendall Hutton, director of Special Projects at Electronic Data Systems (EDS) says: "No one is worth more than $300,000 a year in salary

... you should be a really exceptional individual to get more than that in bonuses and options." He adds that "in too many firms (pay for performance) is allocated based on management rank and salary, and there's nothing left for the people who actually do the work. ... We need to turn the pyramid upside down. There is nothing wrong with someone in the front line making more than managers in the back offices."[27] According to Jim Kouzes, president of Tom Peters Group Learning Systems, "To improve their credibility, executives themselves need to take steps, such as enacting a pay cap."[28]

However, there are not enough internal critics. Graef Crystal (according to *The Washington Post*) says the core of the problem is that corporate boards are too cozy with the managers they are supposed to supervise. "Most of these boards are asleep at the switch. They do not represent the shareholders' interest."[29] Because of this (as reported in the same news article), big institutional investors and other large shareholders—such as the California Public Employees' Retirement System (Calpers)—are taking an increasing interest in executive pay. For example, "Calpers has pressured two of the nation's largest companies to adopt corporate by-laws designed to strengthen the independence of the committees of the boards of directors that set the pay for top executives. The companies—W. R. Grace & Co. and ITT Corp.—have had the distinction of providing generous pay packages to their CEOs who have delivered only mediocre performance records. Both companies reluctantly agreed to the rules change rather than risk a potentially embarrassing fight over the issue at the annual meeting."[30] Because corporate directors have been part of the problem rather than the solution, the Securities and Exchange Commission is considering allowing shareholders to vote on how companies set executive pay.[31]

And what about the Emperor's subjects—the employees? We think we know what they feel but what are they saying? And who is saying it for them? The human resource practitioner faces the uncomfortable task of being the internal messenger for the rank-and-file employees to tell the emperor that he stands naked against these critics. The only reason that CEOs have received this kind of pay is because people—directors, consultants, employees, managers, and CEOs themselves—believed that top executives have the power to get away with it. There is no other reason.

This "power dilemma" faced by the human resource profession is painfully outlined in an *HRNews* article entitled, "CEO's Pay and Philosophy Cause Trust Gap." The article posed the following question:

> How can you—or should you—realign compensation systems and executive pay without biting the hand that feeds?[32]

Recognizing that the human resource profession may be increasingly called on to become the "human conscience" of the corporation, the article goes on to predict that "HR policies will invariably come into conflict with broader corporate strategy—perhaps the very strategy middle managers seem to have little faith in."[33] What effect will this have on the HR professional's role as a "strategic partner"? In responding to this question, it is not clear what effect HR's speaking out will have on its prospects for full partnership. However, there is one thing that is very clear. There are no "silent partners." The HR profession—the experts on compensation matters—needs to be heard from on this issue.

PRACTICE MANAGEMENT-BY-NEGLECT

And while speaking out about executive pay, ask yourself and your CEO one more question: Why are employees standing around by the water cooler "waiting to be told what to do?" In response to Aker's criticism, many people—inside and outside of IBM—believe that it has less to do with the employee than the culture of a largely centralized corporation in which "many can nix an idea or project but few have the authority to approve."[34] When autonomy and independence are stifled, people will wait around to be told what to do. Even for one of the most successful corporations in the world, this is institutionalized negative leadership and goes against its corporate credo: respect for the individual.

For sure, IBM is not alone. All behemoth corporations[35] are trying to navigate an aircraft carrier or a jumbo jet when it's time to change course. The problem with these vast institutions is that they are often overmanaged and underled. This is why communism has been failing all over the world. They were able to control every economic decision and so the communist people waited by the water cooler to be told what to do. Although America's system of federal, state, and municipal government is facing serious fiscal problems, in most (not all) communities the garbage gets picked up, the streets are paved and kept clean, and police and firefighters respond to their emergency calls within minutes. Would it be this way if the federal government was involved in the management of every city?

We should be thankful that our Founding Fathers thought most local municipal matters were none of their business. Charles Handy calls this "subsidiarity," which he characterizes as "giving away power." Handy writes that the principle of subsidiarity is based on a traditional doctrine of the Roman Catholic Church which states that "it is an injustice, a grave evil and a disturbance of the right order for a large and higher organization to arrogate to itself functions which can be performed efficiently by smaller and lower bodies."[36] How else could the Catholic Church's behemoth transnational organization manage itself for the last 2,000 years? Because this goes against the "hands on" philosophy of too many modern managers, it is probably more appropriately called "management-by-neglect."

Managers in the future need to practice management-by-neglect by learning to let go of not only how employees' jobs are performed but also what they are doing. This goes one step beyond the overly bantered phrase—"it is more important to do the right things than to do things right." A manager in Armonk, New York, may know what "the right things are for his or her employees today. But unless the manager is clairvoyant and omnipresent, only the scattered employees will know "what different things" need to be done tomorrow all over the world. All that matters are the results that employees achieve.

But even here there are pitfalls. Employees not knowing what to do will do what they know. They will follow an old pattern of behavior. Instead of formulating "how now" strategies and "position proposals" they will look for a cookbook solution. Future managers will have to burn a lot of these cookbooks, and be coaches and counselors to their employees. In much the same way, Alec Guinness's Ben Obi-Wan Kenobi was to Mark Hamill's Luke

Skywalker when he was teaching him to be a Jedi in the original *Star Wars* movie. His simple advice: "Act on instinct!" Today's employees often have better information available to them than their management. They need to react to unforeseen events by using their instinct, not by trying to be Mr. Right who looks for the "quantified" solution that will make it appear that he or she did the right thing according to the book.

One of the two best things managers and human resources staff can do is to train and motivate employees to know how to act on instinct, using the information available to them (not their managers). The other thing that a manager can do is to be forgiving when their subordinates act on their instinct but, alas, "the force was not with them." Employees should possess the ingrained notion that it is "better to seek forgiveness for having done the wrong thing than to seek permission to do the right thing." However, they should also be ingrained with another credo: It is *best* not to seek either permission or forgiveness! To do this they will need to empower themselves with "the force." Follow Obi-Wan's advice: "Let go of your conscious self." Become the audience.

BECOME THE PERFECT AUDIENCE

Stephen Spielberg, when asked about why he was such a successful moviemaker, replied: "Because I am the perfect audience." There are two ways to interpret Spielberg's comment. On one hand, he enjoyed watching movies and hence he would only make movies he enjoyed watching. On the other hand, he would "let go of his conscious self" and take on the consciousness of the audience. Either way is fine and both taken together are even better. By wanting to make movies only he would want to see, it is clear that Spielberg was "following his call" and "delighting in the results when adding subtle extra touches." Spielberg builds cathedrals. And by taking on the consciousness of his audience, Spielberg knows when to switch from redwood and glass (for example, *ET* and *Raiders of the Lost Ark*) genre to more stately cathedrals of marble (for example, *The Color Purple* and *Empire of the Sun*).

The only way Spielberg can become the perfect audience is to get rid of the armor of his profession—the importance of deals, the concern about "egos," the obsession with special-effects technology, and the "consensus" thinking—follow-the-latest blockbuster mentality—of Hollywood. Hollywood only makes movies; the audience pays to watch them. And what they pay to watch over and over again are good stories executed well on the screen; the stars are only an expensive insurance policy. All of what Hollywood does exists to satisfy audiences.

It is no different for others who earn their livelihood by satisfying someone else's need for a good or a service. Employees don't really work for companies, they work for customers. Even autonomous employees who carry the means of production around in their cranium are not autonomous of the customers they serve, whether they are internal or external to their organization of the moment. Why does this simple truth need so much exposition? Because employees in large companies—particularly companies that have a long record of success—sooner or later begin to believe that only they know what is good for the audience.

Although IBM's Akers can be attacked by his employees and other critics, his message cannot be attacked! IBM has dominated the computer market for decades to a degree that the only threat to the company was from antitrust action. The computer market has been changing dramatically. Small is beautiful and IBM's competitors know exactly what the customer wants—an IBM-compatible PC but not at IBM prices. These customers are not concerned with whether the people who "clone" this commodity wear stuffy white shirts, move around a lot, have a good Welfare America culture, or that they work for IBM—one of the best and most successful companies in the world for the past three decades. The only people who care about this are IBM employees.

Success inevitably breeds arrogance and complacency. This is true of IBM, moviemakers, authors, baseball players, and every other human being on the face of this earth. Complacent/arrogant organizations inevitably forget about the customer and operate for the benefit of the employees. Can you imagine a restaurant that has managers, maître-d's, waiters, and cooks who prefer to work a typical weekday 9–5 shift because it fits better with their personal needs. The only waiters and cooks who work evenings and weekends to handle the dinner and weekend traffic are the people with little or no seniority or organizational clout. What about a hotel, a hospital, or a police department where the more senior employees adjust their schedule to have normal working hours. How many times have you had a problem in a nationally ranked hotel at an inconvenient hour of the evening to find that there is no one in charge or with authority to do anything about it. Contrast this with a "mom and pop" operation—who don't have all the fancy systems and advertising—but have real people who care about each customer because their personal livelihoods depend on the customer. They have no armor. The only water coolers that exist there are for the guests.

Managers face an ongoing challenge of inspiring their employees to not only take on the consciousness of their customers but also to pattern their behavior in a way that satisfies the customers' needs first. The challenge is to break down the walls around the company and "go public" with the culture, that is, the shared values of employees should be valued in the marketplace. If these values (e.g., white shirts and three-piece suits) are not valued, it is time to let go of your conscious self and view the movie from where the audience sits.

"CUSTOMERIZE" YOUR CODE OF ETHICS

Over the past several pages, there has been a lot of reference to IBM's "dirty laundry." This was not planned when this writer started this book. In fact, up till now, IBM has been pictured in only a good light because of its culture of caring about its employees. There is no question that it still does care about their welfare, but business conditions are playing havoc with IBM's employer/ employee relationship. Not even the best corporate cultures are immune from Restructured America. IBM's human resource system—its culture, people, systems, and structure—will need to change to meet its new competitive environment. IBM, like many other companies, will need to rethink their corporate values. However, there are certain absolutes which will work in any environment. The most important are to "honor thy fellow human being (whether it be a customer, a co-worker, or anyone else) and to honor thyself." This is, after all, the only pattern of behavior that really matters. It is also good business.

Tom Lewis, a senior vice president of Oxford Realty Services Corporation, articulated what amounts to a "code of ethics" for treating customers (in this case, elderly residents) of one of Oxford's subsidiaries—Oxford Retirement Services, Inc. (ORSI) —that he once managed.[37] These service principles which are shown in the following exhibit are based, for the most part, on fundamental truths—they will work in any environment, including IBM's.

ORSI Principles to Deliver Oxford "At Your Service"™

1. The resident is the most important person in our business. Honor them. Treat them with dignity and respect. They are #1—there are no #2's.
2. Be honest at all times. There is no excuse for dishonesty. Remember, well-intended failure is okay.
3. Emphasize the positive. Try to catch people doing things right.
4. Be professional. There is no substitute for courtesy and good manners.
5. Create a satisfying work environment and develop a high morale of company loyalty and team spirit.
6. Communicate problems early. Develop solutions quickly. Remember an unresolved problem grows geometrically with time.
7. Trust your employees. Give them independence. Provide them the training and tools to get the job done and then get out of the way.
8. You are expected to work the necessary hours to get the job done.
9. No surprises. They are not appreciated.
10. Inspect what you expect. Document and tell your employees exactly what you expect. Follow up and follow through.
11. Lead by example. Be a solid and visible role model. Have a positive attitude and enthusiasm for your work. Take time to teach. Never tell a person to do something without first showing them how.
12. Perfection is the ideal. Our lobbies, dining rooms, offices, restrooms, common areas, parking lots and grounds are to be neat and orderly at all times. We are constantly marketing our communities.
13. No star gets to outshine the team. Don't worry about who gets the credit. If management didn't think you were good, you would not be in your position. We want to build a team and we want the <u>team</u> to win.
14. Success has to be earned each day. Remind yourself of this each morning. Remember, it's doing a thousand little things each day that counts.
15. Be proactive instead of reactive. Make things happen rather than waiting around for it to happen.
16. Strive for results. Look sharp, feel sharp and be sharp. Be the healthiest, most productive and best-looking professional team in the industry.
17. Create a warm community environment that supports and enriches the productive life span of our residents. Care about what you do and for whom you are doing it.
18. Have fun. Create a healthy balance between work and the rest of your life.

STEP 3: UPSIZE YOUR PEOPLE

GO FOR THE "A" WORD

A long time ago in a galaxy far, far away (translation: several chapters back and a few years ago in the dusk of Welfare America), a corporate executive recruiter (translation: headhunter) said that companies were getting rid of "B" and "C" players and hiring "A's." Perhaps this executive recruiter was fed-up with management-by-the-numbers and decided it was time for management-by-the-letters. But, did he have the right letters? Perhaps. Many companies are starting to become full of A's, the C's are disappearing, but there are no B's. In Welfare America, most companies were full of C's; most A's eventually became C's, but there were still no B's! What B's was that headhunter referring to? And what did he mean when he referred to A's? Perhaps we need one more translation.

Putting aside for a moment what this headhunter was talking about (we will, of course, come back to his comments later), the "A" stands for at least two things: "autonomous" employee and "adult." What does the "C" stand for? Career employee, company employee, committed employee, and, of course, "child." There has been a silent, bottom-up graduation occurring among American workers. It is happening subtly and unevenly across the nation. There are no diplomas and degrees being awarded. There are no "pomp and circumstance" ceremonies. People with knowledge and skills are graduating to a new age—an age of no roads and no boundaries.

Hallett envisions the "changing social contract" and says that we need a new model. He argues that "the new model we must use to define rights, responsibilities, and expectations is obvious, but it is extremely difficult to implement because it represents a dramatic change in the perceived power, status, and responsibilities for those who have grown and worked under the old model." He goes on to state:

> The key to the understanding of the new model—and why it differs so greatly from the prior model—is the emergence of a reality where the business's core enterprise activities occur at what has been traditionally the "bottom" of the organizational structure.[38]

Perhaps, this is why IBM's Akers wants to get his employees away from the water coolers. He has likely realized that this is where IBM's core enterprise activities occur—these employees are IBM to the customer. IBM's employees, employees of all of Restructured America's other behemoth companies, employees of "would-be" behemoth companies, and "would-be employees" of any company are likely realizing the same reality. They are the company because they have the company's "means of production" crackling away in their craniums. With this realization, employees become autonomous of their corporation of the moment. Employees become adults! Hallett reasons that "if the old (employment relationship) model was Adult/Child, the new model is Adult/Adult. This new model is reflective of a totally new set of relationships, expectations, responsibilities, and roles."[39]

The challenge for management is to "upsize" their regard for people. These new adults with power-packed craniums. Wait a minute! Perhaps the executive recruitment profession was on to something when they coined the term *headhunter*. What a way for one of Welfare America's professions to stay relevant in the new age of Restructured America. These stonecutters know how to build cathedrals. But what did that one executive recruiter mean when he said that companies were hiring A's, and B's? What is a B?

One more translation. Perhaps his "A" is Mr. Right. In that case, a "B" would have to be . . . Mr. Rough? Let's continue, for the moment, to manage-by-the-letters.

HIRE B's AND MAKE THEM A's

A long time ago, there was a "would-be" management consultant. He aspired to be part of a major management consulting firm which was considered to be one of the best and most established, albeit small management consulting firms in the nation. When he applied to the firm in 1974, he was flatly rejected. He tried the next year and was almost turned down again. One of the reasons was that he lacked "sparkle." What is sparkle? Perhaps it is some form of "star quality." Whatever it is, if you got it (or more importantly if other people perceive that you have got it) then you are Mr. Right. If you lack sparkle, or a "quantified résumé," then you are, in other people's eyes, Mr. Rough. Despite his apparent handicap, this Mr. Rough made it the second time. In 1990 he became the head of this firm, the same organization which initially rejected him because of misgivings about his prospects for success.

This person was one lucky Mr. Rough. He got his opportunity to sparkle. We hope he will help others to do the same because there are many Mr. Roughs who don't make it. A lot of organizations are only looking for Mr. Right. Because of this, there are factories producing Mr. Rights and increasingly Ms. Rights. They are called business schools. Their product is the MBA graduate. MBAs are an ever growing legacy of Welfare America. Business schools stepped up there production of Mr. and Ms. Right to meet Corporate America's penchant for bigness. According to Samuelson:

> The MBA boom was originally driven by the needs of large firms, which were growing bigger and more diversified in the 1960s and the 1970s. The new MBAs helped assure top executives that these empires could be controlled. The MBAs were smart and adept with numbers. They were quick studies: they could talk confidently about subjects they understood only superficially. These were skills perfected in the classroom. By the thousands, MBAs flooded management consulting firms and executive suites. They abetted corporate America's delusion that conglomerates could be run efficiently. The result was too much bureaucracy and too little attention to making high-quality products at low costs.[40]

Mr. Rights out of control? The A's of the past have become the "scarlet letters" of the present? Hardly! Let's be reasonable. They were only becoming *C*'s! These *c*hildren of Welfare America are only following extrapolated futures. In the process, many gave up their "A" status to become *c*reatures of the *c*ompany; the brightest men and women were *c*o-opted to find *c*omfort in the *c*ollective effort of their *c*ompany. They, after all, had *c*areers!

But many middle-age MBAs are finding out that being Mr. Right is a momentary accomplishment. Many have been fired, as their company decided to do things differently without them. Even Mike Doonesbury, a Mr. Right of advertising who sold his soul to the tobacco companies, was laid off by his agency. Listen to him:[41]

Zonker: Whatcha doin' Bro?
Doonesbury: Trying to make my life look good on paper
               . . . I never had to do this before. There were a

zillion jobs last time I was looking. Now so much depends on my getting it right . . . But when I look at this résumé, it looks so puny! What have I done with my life? Zip! The only thing that I did that really **mattered** was to start a family I now can't support!

This famous *Doonesbury* comic strip character belatedly realizes that he has become Mr. Rough when he laments that the only "accomplishment" he can add to his résumé is that he has become the head of a family and because of this he has taken on a lot of material obligations. Michael has suddenly realized the perils of putting the material substance of his life (and that of his wife and little girl) in the hands of someone else. People trained to do the right thing—the *c*orrect thing—are finding life to be rough.

Company human resource managers are also finding it rough to find the right people for jobs at all levels of the organization because of a growing skills gap. America's public schools are systematically not turning out enough A's, B's, or even C's; they are turning out F's. This is a growing national problem and a greater threat to the future security and well-being of this country than any number of Iraqs. Alas, it is a problem beyond the scope of any company, or of this book, to solve. What is immediately solvable is how to salvage Mike Doonesbury and the other Mr. and Ms. Roughs who have fallen off their musical chairs and are now trying to reinvent their futures.

What to do? Get rid of your tanks (your preconceived notions) that these people are "damaged merchandise," that they will not fit into a younger work force, and, of course, that they lack sparkle. Consider this tank-buster: A Commonwealth Fund study concluded that long-held beliefs that older workers (55 years and older) are harder to train, cost more, are inflexible, and don't work as efficiently are wrong.[42]

Consider this scenario: What if the U.S. Army after the Vietnam war went through a downsizing and a military officer by the name of Schwarzkopf was "outplaced" to the private sector. What is your guess as to whether he would have been hired by General Motors, for example. Consider the evaluation feedback on Schwarzkopf's candidacy: earnest individual but no relevant experience, too intense, questionable interpersonal skills in dealing with peers and subordinates—possible temper, overweight, name too difficult to spell; stronger candidate by the name of Roger Smith: right background, American automotive industry experience, a real team player, fits in, easy name to remember and spell. What would have been the "right thing" for General Motors to do at that time? David Gergen asks: "If Schwarzkopf had been running General Motors for the past 20 years, would the company be any better off than under Roger Smith?"[43] Who knows? But General Motors, it is never too late; Retired General Schwarzkopf may be interested.

There are any number of Mr. Roughs trying to get into or stay in your organization. Take time to get to know them and their families.

REMEMBER WHAT "F" STANDS FOR

"F" has gotten a bad wrap by society. It is used to denote "failure," and other unspeakable terms. However, it also could stand for "friendship." It also happens to stand for "father." Most importantly, it stands for "family." In Welfare America, there was a lot of talk about the "corporate family." And some *Brave New World* theorists predicted that corporations or institutions would replace the family. Because, by 1991, "all people would be the same" or, at least, they would be "alphas, betas, and gammas."

Well, guess what! Families are still "in," fathers are still coaching Little League and doing a lot more to bond with their children, and corporations are trying to become "family-friendly." Families are alive and well. Well, some are not that well. They are fragile human structures which need to be nurtured in order to keep from breaking apart. And if families do break up, there needs to be understanding and comfort for the family members.

Divorce! It is also like polio—"every case, however rare, was unpredictable, mysterious, and catastrophic." It happens to the best couples—they tried to do everything right but it did not work. And worse, it happens to their children.

There is a story of a 90-year-old man and his wife who had been married for 65 years who decided to get a divorce. The judge who was hearing their case looked at both of them and asked: "Why are you getting a divorce now, your marriage has worked for 65 years! The elderly couple, in unison, shot back: "No, it didn't work, neither of us could stand each other for the past 60 years." The judge simply asked: "Well, why did you wait this long to break up?" The couple, again in unison, responded: "We were concerned about the children so we waited until after they were dead!"

What about the children? Divorce, like downsizing, is a relatively new phenomena of any magnitude. There is a lot to learn about its implications. There are victims—children. Beware, this is a sensitive area. There are "single" parents who want to do right by their children; they don't need a lecture or any expository prose. They need understanding from their employer and equitable (not special) treatment given to their circumstance. Most employers continue to apply a Welfare America model, which is sexist! The "man in the gray flannel suit" is the breadwinner. Single women heads-of-the-household are Ms. Rough when it comes to promotion or pay equity. But, this is not a women's issue; it is a parents' issue. Working fathers are not finding it any easier, according to James Levine, director of the Fatherhood Project of the Families and Work Institute,

> Men are caught between today's different set of expectations about what it means to be a father and yesterday's old set of rules for the workplace. . . I talked to one expectant father at a progressive company who told me that when he made plans to use the company's new parental leave policy—widely praised in the business press—his manager said, "Bob, let me speak to you as a friend, not a boss. I know you are entitled to parental leave, but take vacation days instead. If you take a leave, you'll be branded around here forever as uncommitted.[44]

It is even harder for divorced fathers. In *Kramer vs. Kramer,* Dustin Hoffman ends up losing his job because he is trying to be a good parent. And what about "working women"—the double "w"—how are they doing? "Super-moms" have a come a long way, but many don't want to be "super"; they just want to be a good parent, which unfortunately takes many out of the work force. According to Ellen Galinsky, co-president of the Families and Work Institute: The numbers are small, but we are seeing more and more women saying it's not worth trying to be both mothers and hold down full-time jobs."[45] There is a debate going on about whether women are choosing a life at home with their children over another day at the office.

But why have a debate? Why do women need to spend another day at the office? The technology exists today for all fathers and mothers to give their time and attention to their jobs and their children at the same time. But their managements will need to grow up to concepts like flextime and flexi-place. Unfortunately, we are ingrained with the notion that it is socially and psychologically important to show up for work, as if each day there is a boss waiting to tell us what to do that day. This is a factory mentality! But most managers and co-workers reinforce this stereotype, so the would-be "homeworker" feels the social and psychological pressure to get back to the factory. Perhaps this is because of the old saying, "half of the job *is showing up*." High-touch, but who is being stroked? Managers standing around the water cooler or in the conference room. Another "meeting," but for what purpose? High-touch only matters when the *customer* is being stroked.

"Family and Work" is a growing issue in business today. Company attitudes about mothers and fathers at work—whether married or divorced—better keep one thing in mind: all, or at least most of us, are working for our children. This is true whether we are, in Hallet's words, "singles, mingles, mixed marriages, single-parent households, dual-career marriages, etc." Hallett argues that the "real issue needing to be confronted here in the workplace is the growing insistence by people in the workplace that they be treated as whole individuals who have important needs that cannot be ignored... This holistic view of the individual is alien to traditional concepts of life, of caste, of position, of organization, and of work which was rigidly structured into a series of tightly defined boxes."[46]

Welfare America's lockstep industrial methods dehumanized the individual. Employees were molded into the image of the organization. Even their families needed to fit into that image; spouses (wives in those days) went through their own charm schools to please the boss and, of course, his wife. However, the reverse is now occurring. Employees are doing more of the molding these days to meet their family responsibilities for child care and, increasingly, elder care—a baby boomer's responsibility that is only starting to emerge in importance. Handy says, "Shaping work to suit our lives means, first of all, taking more jobs outside of the organization, so that the job is more in our control." He goes on to argue that "jobs do not necessarily belong in organizations any more."[47]

If jobs don't belong in organizations, then how do you get people to feel that they belong in organizations? By perfecting "the three R's!"

PERFECT "THE THREE R's"

No, we are not talking about "reading, (w)riting, and (a)rithmetic." It is clear, however, that someone else should be doing more than talking if we are going to produce high school graduates who will be employable by the year 2000. It is estimated that 2.5 million illiterate Americans enter the work force each year; about one half of all job applicants lack certain basic skills, such as writing, verbal communications, English language capability, basic reading, and math.

Speaking of the next millennium, it may come as a surprise that 85 percent of the people who will be employees in the year 2000 are already in today's work force. Perhaps this is the reason that Anthony Carnevale, chief economist at the American Society for Training and Development has said that, "There is too much focus by CEOs on fixing schools and not enough time on fixing their own organization to better utilize people." Carnevale was quoted in a *Fortune* article on "The Workers of the Future." The stated conclusion is that "To prosper in the Nineties and beyond, companies must concentrate on the three R's: recruiting is important but so is retraining, as is retaining high-quality people."[48] The three R's all focus on how do you get and keep the best people, and get the best out of people. Consider the following:

- Fifty percent of the jobs performed in the late 80s did not exist in the late 60s. At this rate, by the early 21st century all work will be new.
- Nearly three quarters of the information available to workers by the year 2000 will have been created during this decade.
- Employees will need to be retrained in increasingly large numbers, as many as three to four times during a normal employment period.

How can managers, particularly human resource practitioners, better utilize people—these new autonomous "adults," the "diamonds in the rough" whose "sparkle" needs to be found, these Michael Doonesbury's of the world, whose latest accomplishment is the taking on of family responsibilities? How do behemoth corporations, such as IBM, get the best out of all of its people? By simply making them better (that is, high quality) people by investing in their future.

You are probably scratching your cranium at this point and asking: What is new about that? Corporations have been doing this for years. They have, but in lockstep fashion; more or less like the public school systems have been "educating" high school students. This is not an indictment of corporate training programs; it is more of an indictment of the employees of these programs. All too often, they go through these programs because they are offered to them; they come to be trained about being a good supervisor, how to use computer language, how to use a new piece of equipment; how to improve their interpersonal skills, how to "time manage," how to be a better public speaker, how to write reports, how to cope with stress; the fundamentals of a new corporate strategy; et cetera, et cetera.

The training is fine. What is often missing, however, is the context of the training—how does this fit within the individual's life work. What is his or her calling(s)? What are the person's attributes, ambitions, skills, limitations, and shortcomings? What future do they want to invent for themselves? Why is it that these kinds of questions normally only get asked of someone before they are hired and after they are fired? This is not how you "perfect" the three R's.

What is needed is periodic "lifework" exams to focus the training to make better people. Outplacers spend a lot of time and employer dollars getting people in tune with their individual "lifework" but only after they have been fired. Is this a good corporate investment? What if this attention was given to employees during their employment? Would they become better employees? Would the company be better able to focus its retraining and retaining investment in high quality people? Would not all parties be better off? Even the outplacers—who would now be "inplaced" within the company as an integral part of a company's human re-source management function. Tom Cody, a partner with the outplacement firm of Janotta Bray & Associates, has been ad-vancing the concept of *lifework*. Cody believes that career manage-ment issues should be dealt with before termination or before reaching a career rut, suggesting that a lifework evaluation (psycho-logical testing and other forms of assessment) should take place every three to five years.[49] Janatta Bray has a separate division, called Lifework Partners, which works with executives and their spouses, in attempting to integrate life goals (e.g., family and spirit-ual well-being, and service to others) with work goals (e.g., continu-ing self-development and self-worth).[50]

But what good is all of this added outplacer/inplacer expense? Won't we still have to pay a new "inplacer" when we want to outplace employees we chose not to retain and retrain? They may sue us. And why should our company pay inplacer/outplacers to give "lifework" exams to our best people? What if those ex-amined find they are in the wrong profession, or company? Why do we want to invest in their future if they can leave the company at-will?

One answer: Make them an offer that they cannot refuse. Give that person a contract!

GIVE YOUR EMPLOYEES A "C"

Any Orioles baseball fan knows what fame is. It is to catch, or oth-erwise secure, a baseball hit into the stands. Aside from their catch, they can be assured that Rex Barney, the Orioles' announcer, will send out a proclamation to the stands: "Give that fan a contract." Baseball and contracts are as American as apple pie. Baseball is our national pastime. Contracts are how free men and women struc-ture their affairs—whether it is getting married or unmarried, buy-ing a house, or buying a car.

So why is it that two thirds of the American work force work "without fences" to define the boundaries of their rights and re-sponsibilities? Raymond Hilgert observes: "As we move into the 1990s, human resource managers should rethink the whole employment-at-will question." He goes on to say that it is possible that, eventually, employers will be required by law to follow a "just" or "reasonable cause" standard."[51] But how is this going to be possible? Should employers, employees, and their human resources managers look to the federal government, state legislatures, and the courts for leadership and action?

There is an old saying: "If you ask for assistance you don't need, you are liable to get assistance you don't want." Quite frankly, it is better for individual employers and their employees to decide on what they want to do—and then agree to it. For the past 200 years, employers have benefitted from the at-will doctrine at the expense of their employees who have not had any contractual rights. As Hilgert suggests, this may be changing.

James Heller and Douglas Huron of a Washington, D.C., law firm, Kator, Scott & Heller, are not convinced that employers will move en masse to draw up specific contracts with their middle managers and professionals; such employment contracts will continue to be limited to attracting senior executives. Heller and Huron believe that a more practical alternative would be to use employee handbooks for this purpose by simply removing the disclaimers which state that the handbook is not to be considered a legal contract. *With* these disclaimers the handbooks are telling employees what their obligations are to their employer but are denying the employee any rights.[52]

However, there is a growing trend on the part of many companies to use contingency workers and other temporary workers. In fact, *HRMagazine* reports that the growth of contingent personnel in the American work force is easily outpacing total work force growth. This is because every human resources manager is using some form of contingent personnel to achieve benefits of a more variable work force. It also reports that "the most innovative approach to establishing a contingent work force may be the increased use of the oldest and most long-standing device—independent contractors."[53] So we will undoubtedly be hearing Rex Barney's proclamation more and more—Give that fan (of the company) a contract! To this end, Heller and Huron offer the following points to consider in drafting employment contracts.

Points to Consider in Drafting Employment Contracts

1. Identify the parties to the agreement (the Company and the employee) and its binding effect on any successor to the Company (e.g., through merger or acquisition).
2. Specify the term of the contract and what will happen when the contract expires. If the contract is ordinarily automatically renewable, specify the terms and conditions under which the contract will not be renewed. In particular, specify how much notice will be given if the contract will not be renewed.
3. Outline the duties and responsibilities of the employee, any specific performance requirements, the supervisor the employee is to report to, and whether the employee is expected to devote all of his or her time, energy and ability to the business.
4. Document the cash compensation to be paid to the employee (salary, bonus, commission, etc.), how any variable incentives will be computed, the method for any salary adjustment during the contract, and any fringe benefits (e.g., life, medical, disability, and accident insurance and retirement protection) and perquisites (e.g., travel and entertainment reimbursement; automobile allowance; club memberships).
5. State whether the employee agrees not to enter into future competition against the company, defining in sufficiently narrow terms the period of time, the geographic area, the lists of clients and customers for such noncompetition.
6. Outline the conditions for termination of the agreement, e.g., failure to perform duties; "no fault" termination upon specified notice, provisions for severance protection and outplacement assistance, how disputes will be handled (e.g., arbitration, litigation) and what State or jurisdiction's laws will govern in case of any dispute.
7. Specify that the contract constitutes the entire agreement between the parties and can only be waived or amended by written consent of both parties.
8. Strive for clarity.

Source: James H. Heller and Douglas B. Huron.

STEP 4: DOWNSIZE YOUR SYSTEMS

UNCOUPLE THE TRAIN

"I think I can, I think I can..." The "little engine that could" could! Many bigger engines are having a more difficult time getting over the mountain these days because they are carrying too much baggage. Not passengers necessarily—even though it appears that people are the first ones thrown off the train—but baggage! Baggage comes in all forms—outdated tanks and also outdated and overly cumbersome "systems." What is a system? Like organizational culture and shared values, a system provides "glue" to an organization by interrelating the components. Managers have had a love affair with systems all during the era of Welfare America—analyzing, designing and installing, marketing, manufacturing, distribution, accounting, information, human resources, job evaluation, performance appraisal, compensation, and retirement . . . systems.

One of the first systems many managers were exposed to were model electric train sets. It is no doubt a coincidence that manufacturers, such as Lionel and American Flyer, started turning out these train sets back in the 1930s and 40s—Welfare America's early years. These systems could be elaborately constructed with switches, painted landscapes and molded mountains, villages, and several engines coupled with a variety of rail cars all synchronized to travel in the same or different patterns. Or, the train could be simply set up to circle a Christmas tree. In Welfare America the system designer had all the tracks and cars necessary; the task was to "couple" these components together so as to synchronize human activity as organizations became ever bigger.

NAPALM! No, not napalm, NAPALM (*N*ational *A*DP *P*lan for *A*MC *L*ogistics *M*anagement). Although NAPALM and napalm do not mean the same, both terms came onto the public consciousness in the late 60s; however, only a relatively small public was conscious of NAPALM.

AMC was the U.S. Army Materiel Command, a behemoth organization which was the culmination of the merger of seven U.S. Army "commodity commands" (Aviation, Electronics, Weapons, Missile, Tank, Ordinance, and Transportation). NAPALM was a plan to integrate the logistical information systems of all these separate "commodity" organizations into one megasystem; no different that integrating seven model train sets into synchronous activity. NAPALM was a massive undertaking, involving the work of scores of contractors, civilian and military employees, and the attention of four-star generals, including the army chief of staff. It required unprecedented standardization; data elements, formats, and programs needed to be the same or the separate commodity systems could not be linked together. One overly bantered phrase to the skeptics was: though we may all wear different-sized shoes there is no reason the color can't be the same. The only reason to have shoes of the same color was to have a more cost-effective logistic system. In simple terms, this meant (or should have meant) that if the troops in the field (Vietnam at that time) were better fed and equipped, they would be a better fighting force and win the war. What else should have mattered then?

NAPALM—and its infamous cousin—did not win the war. Bigger logistical systems did not matter in Vietnam when the human element was missing. There was no willpower to win at that time. The moral of this story is this: corporate systems are the tracks, the switching devices, and the rail cars: they are not the engines. Today, there are a lot of "little engines that could" locked onto the wrong tracks, carrying the wrong freight, and being switched by top/down command and control systems. Behemoth organizations seeking to synchronize activity in nonsynchronous times. It is time to downsize any number of corporate systems by uncoupling their parts to allow individual employees to make it over the mountain. It is a time to allow people to wear different color shoes (and if you are with IBM, shirts).

COUPLE PERFORMANCE

It is also a time to tolerate "sameness." There is a certain irony in the behavior of organizations. Many organizations expect people to behave in the same way—whether it's wearing white shirts, wingtips, three-piece suits, or suspenders, showing up at the office to work, not moonlight, and be team players. At the same time that organizations preach conformity, they attempt to force employee performance ratings into a statistical distribution: "outstanding" (no more than 10 percent of the employees), "excellent" or "superior" (about 20 percent), "fully satisfactory" (around 60 percent), and "unsatisfactory" or "minimally satisfactory" (about 10 percent). The human resource profession and a lot of management consultants have a tank that is running loose and unchecked: the belief that the performance of employees follows some statistical curve—whether it be a normal or skewed curve. This "tank" presupposes that performance can be measured (appraised) along a continuum.

Performance appraising "by the numbers"! Normally, it does not end there. Of course, there are some who are "plus" and "minus" each of these categories: O+, O, O−, S+, S, S−, FS+, FS, FS−, MS, and U. There is no doubt that employees could fit all of these distinctions if their performance were measured by strict numerical performance, for example, number of units sold, dollar sales produced, revenues generated, percentage above or below one or more numerical goals. But surprisingly, there are many jobs where quantified targets have only limited relevance because of the importance of other nonquantifiable goals: quality, customer service, teamwork, staff development, and so forth. Even where there are jobs that can be measured by meeting sales and revenue targets, it is important that managers "qualify" the numbers (Was this a hard or an easy sale to make? Is this a new account or "over the transom" business from an old account? Was the sale the result of teamwork? Is this business that will enhance, or possibly hurt, the firm's reputation?). Given all of these factors, managers should have the flexibility to grade their subordinates' performance accordingly. The problem is that many do not have this flexibility; they are motivated to discern "differences" rather than "sameness" in their staff.

How and why does this happen? The typical knee-jerk response is that if there is no forced distribution of ratings, managers would choose the easy route by tending to rate all their employees the same, and many would give out too many "outstanding" and/or "excellent" ratings. So "their" solution is to "couple" the manager's own rating on the way he rates his employees. Managers are not only expected to grade performance along this type of continuum but their own performance is graded on the *extent* to which they grade performance. So they rank their employees against each other and fit them into categories that they may or may not believe in. You may ask how this writer knows what these managers believe in. Another writer who purports to be able to get in the minds of his subjects? Yes, but only to this extent: How many managers would be willing to post their appraisal ratings (−O+, O, O−, S+, S, S−, FS+, FS, FS−, MS, and U) on a bulletin board for all their employees to see and be able to compare their performance with their peers and teammates? How many managers are prepared to defend their ratings to their employees? All of a sudden, there are many mind readers!

The human resource profession's "tank" of a forced-rating appraisal system works as long as employees are treated like mushrooms—kept in the dark about how they stand relative to others. Is this any way to run a railroad, or at least a performance appraisal system? No, because it is conceptually wrong in the first place. People don't perform "by the numbers" or even "by the letters"; they normally perform in one of three ways: they do what is expected of them, they don't do what is expected of them, or they perform extraordinarily—positively or negatively. Most people do what is expected; trying to grade their performance is unexplainable, which is why it is hardly ever explained! And employees are kept in the dark. The other categories are noticeable to the whole organization and don't need explanation. When "outstanding" performance is not measured under a forced rating system it will emerge naturally, rather than artificially, as when it is forced. Only when employees are forced to be different for grading purposes do they demand to be graded "outstanding." Who wouldn't try to be the best in this system? Can you imagine for a moment what would have happened if we had had a forced rating system for the "employees" who worked in "Desert Storm"? Do you think this would have produced a better outcome? Should the welcome-home parades in New York and Washington have distinguished between O+, O, O−, S+, S, S−, FS+, FS, FS−, MS, and U performance?

Jackson C. Tuttle, the city manager of Williamsburg, Virginia—a delightful place that thrives on the memory of pre-Frontier America—may have the answer. Mr. Tuttle, like this writer, grew up believing in the doctrine of forced-appraisal ratings but found they did not work, so in the end he stopped practicing what was preached to him. Why would any manager want to make the vast majority of his employees feel that they are only "average" or "below average"? Consider that, first, no one really knows, or can honestly define, in advance, what "outstanding performance" is for most jobs. Second, because it can't be defined, it can be left up to anyone's interpretation. Many employees therefore naturally interpret their own performance as outstanding when what they really are saying is that they don't want their performance to be interpreted as "below average." Remember, the best defense is a good offense. So Tuttle decided the best way to eliminate all this fuss and make the vast majority of his employees feel like winners was to devise the following rating scheme:

Full Merit Increase	_____	(for fully satisfactory performance)
Partial Merit Increase	_____	(for minimally satisfactory performance)
No Merit Increase	_____	(for unsatisfactory performance)

What Tuttle did was "uncouple" any *higher* rating from the system. There was no place to mark "outstanding" or "excellent" performance on the form. This did not mean that there was no reward system for outstanding performance; it just was not (*form*) *alized*. Managers had to make an exception to the form and explain why someone's performance was above his or her peers. As a result, the system took care of, and motivated, most of the employees to feel like winners—after all, they received the highest rating on the form; the managers took care of the few exceptional workers.[54]

This revisionist concept clearly goes against the grain of most "modern management" thinking. But for a good reason: How many organizations can honestly say that they are "outstanding," "exceptional," or (as Reagan once said) "any better off today" because they have a forced-ranking performance-appraisal system which rates people as outstanding performers? These "outstanding" systems also make it more difficult to level with employees about their performance. Most employees are complaining about why they are not rated "outstanding" when they are in fact only performing as good as their peers (what is "outstanding" about that?). Some employees who are rated as only "fully satisfactory" (below these "outstanding" workers) are not fully satisfactory at all. They are marginal performers buoyed up by an inflated ratings system. They are only told they are marginal (a "B" or a "C") when they are fired; so they sue for wrongful discharge and win because the documented evidence is on their side. James Buttimer, an organizational and operations expert with Arthur Andersen & Co., states the following:

More rigorous evaluations are needed to keep top employees on their toes in an environment of tough competitiveness. Managers must deal with problem employees sooner and with directness. They must prepare candid evaluations and encourage feedback. If the company resumes its old habit of evaluating without taking serious action, fat will start to build up again.[55]

Perhaps, we don't have more outstanding performance because we don't have outstanding positions. It's because we don't have outstanding position evaluation systems.

REEVALUATE POSITION EVALUATION PLANS

The late John J. Corson was one of the early deans of management consulting—head of McKinsey's Washington office during the 1950s and early 1960s, chairman of the board of Fry Consultants in the early 1970s, author of numerous books, and counselor (or friendly co-pilot) to numerous CEOs, university presidents, and government leaders. Dr. (or as he preferred it, Mr.) Corson was a man who lived through the Welfare America era, helping to put together what we know today as the Social Security Administration, and writing one book (around 1970-71) entitled *Business in the Humane Society.* Mr. Corson once had some words for something else that came out of Welfare America: position (often inaccurately referred to as job) evaluation plans. In 1972, being exposed to a position evaluation plan that was being used to evaluate the top 80 jobs of a company of which he was a board member, Mr. Corson referred to the plan as nothing more than "a lot of organized mumbo-jumbo."

Despite Mr. Corson's concerns, a position evaluation plan was developed to grade the jobs of the these 80 executives—in the belief that at least the mumbo-jumbo was organized and hence more explainable than the mumbo-jumbo it was trying to fix. Organization! Position evaluation plans "institutionalize" organizations by attaching a point score, a salary grade, and a dollar sign to each organizational box. The plans "value" the "pecking order"—the higher the organizational layer, the higher the value of the job. These plans provided ground rules for not only how to pay people in their current position but also how to pay people if they advance (get promoted or transferred) to another position. If there was one system that provided "organizational glue" it was the position-evaluation plan. The importance of position/job evaluation was strikingly evident throughout the 1980s when it became the battleground for *comparable worth*. Comparable worth advocates quickly realized the importance of job evaluation in deciding the worth of jobs, so they fought to ensure that these plans did not undervalue the work performed largely by women (teaching, nursing, library services, secretarial/clerical, etc.) versus the work largely performed by men (trades and crafts, police and firefighting, etc.). However, they were doing this within the framework of Welfare America's assumptions about organizations and its attendant systems. It is now Restructured America, and people who used to worry about relative positioning now worry (or should worry) about absolute positioning, that is, whether they keep their job.

Job evaluation plans are increasingly getting in the way of restructuring efforts, not only hurting employees but also negating the progress of companies that have downsized. Robert Tomasko, as noted earlier, argues how job evaluation plans have encouraged employees to advance up the ladder of supervision (become middle managers when the middle is being cut out of the organization) or up their profession (become advanced stonecutters when there is no longer a market for cathedrals made of stone). Many of these middle managers and "senior" stonecutters have been downsized out of the evaluation plan and their job. However, while the employees are forced to leave (because "knee-jerk" managers can see immediate savings by firing people) what often stays is the evaluation plan that caused the problem in the first place.

A case in point was that of the so-called baby bells after Judge Harold Greene ordered the breakup of AT&T. An audit of the human resources system of one of these behemoth "babies" ordered by a state public service commission revealed the following: This "baby bell" had been going through an organizational downsizing brought on not only by the breakup but, more importantly, by technological advance in switching. AT&T, and these "seven sisters," had *initially* built the number of organizational levels over the number, and type, of "long-distance" operators it needed to switch calls; it also built its management structure on top of this. There were 10 pyramidal levels of district manager to manage all of these operators. Technology changed all of this; the switching became automatically controlled by computers. There has been noticeably much less operator intervention in phone calls. AT&T, and its children, did what they believed was necessary; they downsized their people—fewer operators and fewer managers. But they had not downsized their position evaluation plan—which was built on the assumption of a 10-manager pyramid. So here was a "leaner" organization alright, but one that had gone on a fad diet. And so the underlying system which institutionalized and valued the "fatter" organization remained.

Fad diets and fad downsizings don't work over the long term. It is important to change the systems which put on the weight. However, the answer is not to get rid of job evaluation plans. Remember, organized mumbo-jumbo is better than disorganized and unexplainable mumbo-jumbo. Just make the mumbo-jumbo relevant to today's conditions. Make the compensable factors really factors that you want to compensate people for in their work. Reward "utility players" (that is, reward cathedral builders rather than stonecutters); reduce levels in the plan (you will see that this will reduce levels in your organization), and institute a "sunset" provision to make the plan disappear after five years unless its continued usefulness can be positively justified.

Will this eliminate "position paralysis"? It will at least eliminate many of the rungs, so there will be less to cling to. However, people will continue to cling to their jobs, even without job evaluation. Why? Because of the benefits. They need to be "refringed."

REFRINGE THE BENEFITS

Back in the mid-1980s, one consulting vice president based in Washington, D.C., submitted a proposal to study the compensation of employees of a Colorado city. In doing so, the unsuspecting consultant incurred the wrath of another of his firm's vice presidents who was based in Colorado. Because the study was to be performed in his geographical area of responsibility, the Colorado vice president expressed concern that he and his staff were not afforded sufficient opportunity to provide "input" to the proposal. His argument: the proposal was technically deficient because it lacked this input. When asked what the specific deficiencies were, the Colorado vice president, who also was a benefit specialist, said something to the effect: "You (meaning the D.C. vice president) obviously are not abreast of the latest developments in the benefits area; in the proposal you kept referring to "fringe benefits"; we now refer to them as "employee benefits"!

Well, what do you think about that? Welfare America may be coming to an end but its legacy endures. One can easily sympathize with the benefits consultant from Colorado. After all, who would want to be in a business or a profession that has the prefix "fringe?" Human resource managers, who used to be referred to as "personnel administrators," can appreciate what is in a name. And the Coloradan was right. When an employer shells out around one third of an employee's salary in benefits, they are hardly a fringe. Ask any employee who has been asked to make a greater contribution to the cost of the employee health plan, whether the benefit is a "fringe." Better yet, ask a 15-, 20-, or 25-year employee, whether he or she considers the company's retirement plan a fringe. Best yet, ask a contingency worker who no longer has these benefits whether this loss is merely the absence of a fringe. They truly are "employee benefits" as long as you remain an employee.

In Restructured America, an increasing number of employees are losing their "employee benefits" along with their job. Handy, in an interview with *Business Week,* states "This is the end of the age of big corporations as employers and providers of health and pension benefits for millions of people."[56] Some who end up going to work for smaller companies are not getting the same generous benefits they enjoyed as part of a big firm. Why? Because the smaller firm cannot afford to pay someone 130 percent or more of their salary. You may wonder why large firms can afford to do so. Increasingly, they cannot! This is why they are downsizing in the first place. It is also why any number of "large" companies are increasingly relying on independent contractors, contingency workers, temporary service firms, and various other staffing arrangements. These receive no benefits—fringe benefits, employee benefits, or any other kind. Even outplaced workers who manage to get back on a musical chair with full benefits in some other large firm have lost years of "retirement credit" in the process.

There is an old saying: "Where you stand depends on where you sit." There are a lot of us who are sitting quite comfortably with our employer-paid benefits who will not agree with this stand. *All benefits given by the employer should be taxed to the employee as ordinary income.* For those who don't agree with this stand, what is your argument? Why should the federal government (i.e., the American taxpayer) be subsidizing the cost of employer/employee health care and other insurance benefits? What public purpose or social good is served by the federal government subsidizing the cost of health insurance to an ever decreasing number of workers (already subsidized by their employer) while many contingency workers and people employed by small business cannot afford health insurance. Not only is this federal "employee benefit" subsidy serving to increase the federal deficit, it is also driving up the cost of health care—which has skyrocketed in recent years. Consider this:

- Health-care costs are now about 11 percent of the gross national product and increasing by about 11 percent a year.
- Because of the medical insurance crisis, increases of 20 to 40 percent are expected each year in insurance premiums.
- The present value of retiree health benefits is estimated at as high as $2 trillion.

Employees who pay little or nothing for health insurance have little incentive to control their health care costs, to foster "wellness" habits, or to take individual responsibility for their health, health care, and health-care costs. They have an "entitlement mentality," so they continue to stand where they sit.

But alas, there is a growing shortage of "employee seats" these days. Baby boomers and musical chairs! "Human resource managers" and "employee benefit professionals" (whatever you choose to be called these days) have another challenge ahead: To rethink the role of employee benefits in your human resource strategy. What kind of a person are you trying to attract and develop? Someone who wants their compensation to be subsidized by others? Someone who will eventually feel locked into your health or retirement plan because they fear it is too late to get into another one? Will this kind of person be flexible to new ideas? Be innovative? Be willing to take risks?

It is time to "refringe the benefits." This does not mean "refringing" the benefits profession. Quite the contrary. By making individuals more directly accountable for their cost, there is much more that needs to be done in the areas of managed health care, individual retirement protection, and insurance plans. Employers and employees need systems (individual health-care scorecards, retirement bank accounts, etc.) that make employee benefits an earned and valued "right" that is protected throughout the "life-work" of an employee rather than a lot of "entitlement fluff" that can disappear when one walks out the door of an organization.

Tax the fringe benefits? Hmm. This book has taken on a lot of sacred "tanks"—Lee Iaccoca, CEOs, IBM, MBAs, accountants, employee benefit specialists, and employment-at-will—to say the least. Let's be fair and reasonable. Why haven't you picked on lawyers! Stay tuned. They are about to get their day in court.

KILL ALL THE LAWYERS?

Christopher Lloyd, at the end of the original *Back to the Future* movie, not only said, "Where we are going there are no roads," he also said that there were no lawyers. Did Shakespeare finally get his wish? Who knows? After all, it was only a movie. What about real life?

Lawyers are everywhere. In TV ads, at the scene of the Bhopal and Valdez tragedies, in emergency rooms, in board rooms, and leaving their mark on human resource systems and personnel policy manuals. There are a disproportionate number of lawyers in the United States as compared to Japan; most reside in Washington, D.C., Chevy Chase, or Bethesda, Maryland, or the state of New Jersey. The only thing greater in number than lawyers are lawyer jokes. But there is one leveling factor, as stated by one Washington law-firm partner: "Everyone ridicules or criticizes lawyers until they need one!"

In Restructured America, a lot more people need lawyers. Employees who are suing their ex-employers for wrongful discharge or some other exception to employment-at-will; employers who are defending themselves from these suits, both reactively and proactively, before a suit is ever filed. Lawyers have had to put down boundaries or fences around personnel policies and in employee handbooks—because there are no roads! *The Washington Post* reports that the growth in litigation is because of an uncertainty about the law:

> Where people of honest intention are suing each other in large numbers, it is because they are baffled in their efforts to learn any other way what the law expects of them. "No profound social theory is needed to explain why people are more litigious today than ever before," as Richard Epstein of the University of Chicago puts it. Legal uncertainty "breeds litigation. . . . It's that simple."[57]

The article goes on to say that "vagueness creeps into the law on the padded feet of words and phrases like fairness, equitableness, good cause, good faith—pillowy expressions that tend to soften the blow of what is in fact a grant of wide judicial discretion over some area."

Come to think of it, exceptions to at-will employment include a lot of phrases such as "fairness," "good faith," and "good cause." Given this vagueness of the law—a virtual frontier without roads—it is no wonder that there are so many lawyers trying to construct fences and boundaries where they heretofore did not exist. What is missing are fences and boundaries for the lawyers themselves.

Let's start constructing a few for the human resource profession.

1. **Use an attorney to guide your decisions, not to control them.** Remember, if you ask for advice you don't need, you will likely get advice you don't want! As in the tobacco industry, there are some businesses where attorneys dictate what managers can do and not do. In tobacco companies, all corporate executives must pass a legal review before they make a public statement. The reason is simple. No company executive can ever say that smoking is beneficial. If they do, the warning on the pack goes out the window and the litigation for product liability will drive a wedge into the heretofore successful record against civil prosecution. This is an industry under siege and their lawyers are their last defense.

   This is not true in employment relations, which makes one wonder why many companies adopt "siege mentalities" with respect to their employees. Perhaps it was on the advice of counsel; after all, a good offense is the best defense. Of course, you may want to appear defensive. Lawyers are great but they cannot run your business; you have to do this. In hiring good lawyers, you should have the humility to listen to what they have to say but also possess the wisdom to decide what to do on your own.

2. **Hire good people and don't fire them unless you have a good reason.** One way to be sure that you can do this is to hire the best people; not just the quantified ones. The quantified employees will be more interested in staying quantified, which means they are likely to retain their own lawyer to protect their "quantified" reputation. Just hire good people; you will need no fences. Good neighbors make for good neighbors. Systems, fences, and even lawyers can't do that. Remember that people, not corporations, hire people. And people, not corporations, fire people. However, good people don't fire good people. In this regard, this writer is reminded of the lament of one corporate human resources vice president who said: "I don't mind managers being entrepreneurial except when it comes to employment decisions." His point was that managers left on their own would likely get the company in trouble (wrongful-discharge suits). You wonder what decisions this executive would entrust his middle managers to do if they are not empowered to manage their employees. Let good people deal with good people; reserve the law, the lawyers, and this vice president for the rest.

3. **Be explicit and clear about the employment relationship.** Most litigation comes about because conditions of employment are vague and uncertain. Fired employees sue their ex-employer when they perceive that an expressed or implied agreement has been broken. Ex-employers defend their actions because they feel it has not been broken. If the employment relationship was contractual there would be less vagueness and uncertainty about what was agreed to. Just look at the contract.

4. **If you can't write personnel policies that you are willing to stand behind in court, don't write any.** Legal caveats in personnel manuals may appear to be a good defense if attempts are made to use the manual against an employer in court, but it only contributes to more vagueness about what your policy really is—which breeds more uncertainty on the part of managers and employees as to what they can or cannot do. To alleviate this uncertainty and resulting distrust on the part of their subordinates, managers will inevitably make reassuring comments to employees, which will be used in court against the company as an implied oral agreement in the absence of a clearly stated corporate policy.

5. **Provide your employees with a legitimate alternative to litigation to resolve their disputes.** Undoubtedly, there will still be misunderstandings between employees and management. One of the biggest mistakes employers often make is to rally around their management to show support and solidarity. Although this is often well-intended, what may be missing is the element of "due process" for the employee. Jonathan A. Segal, who comments on legal trends for *HRMagazine*, writes: "At a minimum, due process requires that: (1) The employee know the employer's expectations. (2) The employee receive notice of any failure to meet these expectations and the consequences of this failure. (3) The employer's rules and regulations must be administered consistently. (4) There be an internal appeals procedure by which employees can challenge managerial decisions affecting job security."[58] With respect to point (4), the internal appeals procedure or some other nonjudicial, dispute resolution mechanism provides employees "their day in court" but in a much less expensive way for all concerned.

6. **Remember employees are human beings too.** Employment disputes are often not about violations of the law; they are always about violations of human trust and ethical behavior. And if an employee's livelihood is significantly damaged by these perceived violations, it is inevitable that vagueness will creep "into the law on the padded feet of

words and phrases like fairness, equitableness, good cause, good faith." However, once employment disputes in particular, and employment relations in general, move out of the hands of managers and human resource practitioners to those of attorneys, there is a breakdown of the human dimension. The attorney's role is to protect the interests of one party at the expense of the other. The "other party" ceases to be a human being but someone to be dealt with at arm's length and in a "take no prisoners" manner. Managers need to control these disputes, like marriage counselors, so if a divorce is inevitable it will occur as amicably as possible where everybody is a winner, not just the divorce lawyers.

The preceding sections of this chapter have focused on steps to take to bring your environment, culture, people, and systems into balance with the era of Restructured America. It is now time to bring your *structure* into balance with these other dimensions by making it virtually disappear.

STEP 5: FLEXSIZE YOUR STRUCTURE

FIND THE INVISIBLE ORGANIZATION

Charlie Brown, the comic strip character, was the manager of a baseball team made up of all the other *Peanuts* characters. Charlie Brown had a problem; his team had a perfect record—they had lost all their games. Like most managers, Charlie Brown knew he couldn't just stand by, he had to do something. He reasoned that his team had lost every game because they were not organized properly. So he held a press conference to tell all of his readers how he had solved the problem. His answer: "I just wrote down everybody's name and the base they played on a piece of paper. Now we have organization."

As the decade of the 1980s came to a close, a large number of CEOs were losing ball games in the eyes of their investment community. Like most managers, these CEOs knew they couldn't just stand by; they had to do something. They reasoned that they were losing out to the competition because they were not organized properly. So they individually held press conferences to tell all their investors how they had individually solved the problem. Their answer: We have had our staffs write down on a piece of paper everybody's name and the "musical chair" he or she would hereafter occupy. Now that we have downsized, we are organized!

It is not a coincidence that terms such as *restructure* and *downsize* dominate management thinking. Tables of organization and staffing are tangible—you can see them, you can count boxes, lines, and people, and, most importantly, you can write them down on a piece of paper. And if you are in one of the top boxes, you can "start with a blank sheet of paper" and redraw the lines, add, and (of course) eliminate boxes and numbers of people below you, because you are in control, thanks, in part, to employment-at-will. So CEOs, when they appear to be losing ball games, restructure and downsize and then show the investment community another piece of paper to demonstrate that they are in control—they are organized. "So it is written, so it is done!"

What is harder to show on the piece of paper is what they have done to (1) influence their competitive environment, (2) change their organizational culture, (3) upgrade the skills, abilities, and dedication of their people, and (4) overhaul their systems. These changes are not always tangible. And, they are not easily controlled by the person who sits at the top of the pyramid of boxes. It is the invisible organization.

The challenge to management is to find this invisible organization and influence its dimensions. To become less preoccupied with formal structure and body counts. But it is not going to be easy. Robert J. Samuelson, a critic of MBAs and the "emptiness of what passes for modern management" writes:

> In the 1980s, corporate America made much of how it was cutting bureaucratic fat and eliminating layers of unnecessary middle managers. A lot of this actually happened. But the defects of American management go beyond the number of boxes on an organizational table. They also involve patterns of thinking and habits of self-deception. These, unfortunately, endure.[59]

"Patterns of thinking" and "habits of self-deception"! Sound like "Tanks" to you? Please Mr. Samuelson, tell us more.

GET RID OF THE "NUMSKULL FACTOR"

Samuelson was making these comments in an article entitled "The Numskull Factor," where he argues that what produces a lot of bad corporate decisions is "executive insularity." He also writes:

> Our corporate elites are awash in empty jargon that masquerades as serious thought. . . . Surely the dreary performance of so many huge companies in so many industries is an indictment of something about American management practices and style. One problem is an infatuation with making big plans based on sweeping generalizations about the future. Our top executives are forever "devising strategies," or "reinventing their companies," or proclaiming "new visions" for their industries.[60]

Samuelson was commenting on the "silliness" of a questionnaire sent to him and other opinion leaders in 12 countries. The study was being conducted by one of the largest consulting firms in the world—ironically, for IBM—to define the "worldwide human resource strategies that will enable companies to be effective in the highly competitive 21st century." The unlucky firm which sent Mr. Samuelson the questionnaire was a management consulting firm with scores of offices around the world and literally thousands of people. It is one of the premier "mega' firms in the consulting industry. It became big because the number and size of its offices has grown, and through acquiring other consulting firms.

But does "big" equate to "better"? There are undoubtable strengths to being a large firm—buying power, strong specialized staffs, and the ability to synergize a network of skills, information, and business leads, as well as an omnipotence of presence (after all, being there, or just showing up, is half the battle). However, bigness alone doesn't make us any smarter than our smaller competitors. It all too often only breeds arrogance and insularity on the part of senior executives. They think they can produce a "landmark study" aimed at defining the "worldwide human resource strategies that will enable companies to be effective in the highly competitive 21st century." Apparently, this "landmark" survey questionnaire did not demonstrate any "landmark" thinking. According to Samuelson:

What IBM will get is synthetic information—meaningless statistics that, if analyzed, will produce meaningless conclusions. They will be meaningless no matter how many tables the final report includes or how glossy its cover. It offends common sense to think that people will strain to squeeze significance from the survey's data.[61]

Only time and the actual survey results will determine whether this firm deserves this harsh an indictment. What is indictable now are the "top-down, command and control" numskulls who devise grand strategies, visions, and organization charts on pieces of paper while forgetting to focus on "the people factor." Landmark studies are not conducted by large corporations; they are conducted by people. People who don't have to spend a lot of time and energy catering to the arrogance and insularity of the people in the boxes above them—whose skulls have gone numb because of the protective armor of their big corporation.

THROW OUT ALL THE SCRIPTS

People, particularly in large companies, are not having that many good days anymore. According to IBM's Akers, "We have a very low level of separations for poor performance. That level will go up—must go up."[62] Akers has a people problem—his people are not selling enough computers; they are not having very good days. One of the biggest problems that large corporations, such as IBM and General Motors, have today is that they are increasingly organized around people rather than ideas and ideals. These behemoth organizations have lost their way as they march their legions of people into an uncertain future where there are no roads and roadmaps. Many major corporations have become like large occupying forces, but the terrain of their industry keeps changing so the force keeps finding its competitors elusive. It is not the deserts of Iraq but the jungles of Vietnam.

People march in "bureaucratic lockstep" because they are boxed into organizational positions. Whenever, two (or more) people join in any endeavor, whether it's a marriage, a rock concert, a presidential campaign, Operation Desert Shield or Desert Storm, or working for IBM, there has got to be a division of labor; everyone has to know their role. Just look at our national pastime—every baseball player has to have a position. So it starts early in life; kids on Little League teams want to know what their position is on the team and then compete with each other to hold onto their position or seek out a more coveted one.

People want to change, but they don't want to lose the position they have worked hard to achieve in the organization; this is their only stakeholding from Welfare America—a musical chair that provides them with the material substance of life. Even when one person is willing to change—to make a position proposal—there is someone else (probably many someone elses) who must weigh in on the decision because of their position(s). An organization that was formed with a mission—an idea or ideal—has lost sight of this calling. We are no longer in the business of building cathedrals but of protecting stonecutter jobs and their relative internal positioning. Even management consulting firms—the masters of strategic planning, restructuring, and downsizing for someone else—are not immune from occasionally focusing away from their calling. Partners in one firm that was devising its own grand strategy in the late 1980s, when asked whether they would buy into it, were quick to ask who will be in what boxes. Human beings at work!

Alas, what to do? Change human nature? It would be easier to wait for the next millennium when organizations may be staffed by robotrons without feelings, insecurities, jealousies, and original sin. But, even there, one would have to worry about Hal, the 2001 computer. What will we do?

Nothing! This is an insoluble problem. It's better for corporations and the people they employ to pursue opportunities in their organization of the moment or elsewhere. IBM will get rid of its bureaucracy by focusing its bureaucracy on opportunities; so that people boxed into positions will want to break out with new position proposals. People will invent their own futures out of necessity—to survive—for material sustenance. People within IBM will do this, not IBM; they will do this with or without IBM. Remember, IBM is not a real person. Like other corporations, it is only a person in the eyes of the law, not in fact. Corporations are immortal in the eyes of the law; they only remain relevant as long as they serve an idea or an ideal. There is no more telling example than the U.S.S.R. Remember Khrushchev warning the United States, "We will bury you"? The only thing that has been buried these days is the Soviet Union, by the Russian people no less! The Russian people, the other "soviet states," and their balking Baltic satellites lived before this "organization," and will live beyond it. The Soviet "Union" was just a more global version of Charlie Brown's infamous organizational plan.

So, managers, throw out your script. Your role is changing. Get out of the way of your people. Lead for once by following *their* advice, facilitating *their* movement, and franchising *their* futures. There is much talk about the "manager of the future" being like the conductor of a symphony orchestra, coordinating the efforts of a wide variety of players. This is true but it's only a snapshot of a manager in action, and it is misleading because it demeans the players, as if they need to wait to perform on cue. Future managers will be much more than that—future managers will play any combination of roles. They will be screenwriters, casting directors, and producers of an endless array of "motion pictures." The one role that managers will not play will be that of director—because increasingly, work will be played out in a theater of "improvisation." How now, Brown Cow!

Brian Dumaine in a *Fortune* article, entitled "The Bureaucracy Busters," talks about the "adaptive organization" which "incorporates the informal organization and draws its power from the same energy." This is people power. He goes on to say that:

> Instead of looking to the boss for direction and oversight, tomorrow's employee will be trained to look closely at the work process and to devise ways to improve it, even if this means temporarily leaving his regular job to join an ad hoc team attacking the problem. . . . When people move from one team to another, they and their companies will have to think about careers and pay in new ways.[63]

In essence, they will be following the "Rightsizing Remedy." They will have taken steps to bring their environment, culture, people, and systems into balance; this fluidity will make the organizational *structure* balance with these other dimensions. It will virtually disappear as we have known it. What will emerge in its place will be a new form of structure: information/service channels. Success in this new environment is getting into the right channels.

GET INTO THE RIGHT CHANNELS

What do the Atlanta International Airport, the Mall of America, and Suite 400 have in common? They are "organizations of the future." Alvin Toffler describes the significance of the Atlanta airport in *Powershift*:

> It is a giant mosaic consisting of scores of separate organizations—everything from airlines, caterers, cargo handlers, and car rental firms to government agencies like the Federal Aviation Administration, the Post Office, and the Customs Service. Employees belong to many different unions, from the Air Line Pilots Association to the Machinists and Teamsters. . . . The wealth flowing from this meta-mosaic is precisely a function of *relationships*—the interdependence and coordination of all of them. Like advanced computerized data bases, the Atlanta airport is relational.[64]

Toffler probably did not mention the Mall of America (Bloomington, Minnesota) in his 1990 book because it had not been built yet. When it is completed sometime in 1992, this 4.2 million-square-foot, $625 million complex will be the largest shopping center ever built in the United States. According to *The Washington Post*, it will consist of "four department stores, about 400 specialty shops, a seven-acre, enclosed theme park, a 1.2 million-gallon walk-through aquarium, a two-story, 18-hole miniature golf course, the largest Lego structure ever built, multi-multiplex cinemas, restaurants, bars and 13,000 parking spaces."[65]

There are many malls and airports dotted across America which are the hubs of relational networks for creation of wealth. Toffler describes these hubs as "hyper-flexible" organizations. They can be quickly brought into balance with changing industries and market conditions. He argues that "an economy of small, interactive firms forming themselves into temporary mosaics is more adaptive and ultimately more productive than one built around a few rigid monoliths."[66]

And what about Suite 400? Walk into the lobby of the south-west corner of International Square in Washington, D.C., and read the office directory. You will quickly discover that over 125 businesses, associations, professional firms, and Washington offices of major companies are in Suite 400! Take the elevator to the fourth floor and there is a sign above the door: "Suite 400." But the names of the organizations listed in the lobby are not shown. This is an Atlanta airport or Mall of America in miniature. HQ, the organization that manages this "mall" provides office space, services, and "corporate identity" for its clients listed on the directory downstairs. Some clients are working there and some are working out of a home office. These "home office" satellites are networked to this "mothership" by a sophisticated phone system. Thus, unlike malls and airports, HQ's capacity for stimulating wealth creation goes well beyond its physical size; the only limitations are the "craniums" and resourcefulness of its clients. HQ has similar Suite 400s (though they may be called something different) in other cities in the United States and around the world. Unlike malls and airports, HQ is largely invisible—a well-kept secret—because it exists to promote its clients' corporate identity, not its own.

In an age of the "electronic cottage," services such as HQ are critical for homeworkers to be tuned into the right information channel. Is there a lesson here for behemoth companies? Yes, if you want to go on creating wealth. Don't be monolithic. Bust the pyramid. Become invisible like HQ. Don't expect that you can control employee behavior as in an adult-child relationship. The world is growing up around you. Your survival is in adding value; creating a wealth-creation network that your employees can't create for themselves. Become a hub, a mothership, an information/service channel!

Corporate "HQ" staff should become the "nerve center," channeling information/services among and/or between their employees and/or their clients/customers. Perhaps the most exciting vision of the future relates to what any corporate "headquarters" can be. They can become value-added "switchboard centers"—the center of an hourglass—channeling information/services back and forth among their autonomous employees and other service/goods providers in their network. The organization of tomorrow will not be labor intensive, but information/service intensive. Its competitive advantage will be determined by its ability to channel information and services. It will become a mothership networked to any number of satellites not constrained by the dimensions of space and time because of "flexispace" and "flextime" arrangements worked out with its partner "employees." It will become an "atomistic" organization. All the organization of the future has to do is nurture a network of "atoms" or, more precisely, "Adams" and "Eves."

NURTURE A NETWORK OF ADAMS AND EVES

Organizations have long had a nurturing role. It has changed with the end of Welfare America. Employees are on their own more today and that's good. They will adjust to the challenge; just like children do when they grow up. They adjust but they still need to be nurtured. They still need structure. However, the structure will no longer be a top-down pyramid but a "constellation" of orbiting "satellites" of Adams and Eves pulled together by the force of harmonious relationships. The core of this constellation will be a corps of people (e.g., the Disney animators; the inhabiters of Suite 400) which differentiates this "organization" from others in the galaxy. Whether they are unified by a core competence (animation), a vision (build cathedrals), or a place to work (the Mall of America), it will not matter. What will matter is that there will be a "clearer measure of loyalty-up, loyalty-down" which will fit business conditions.

Employees will have a contractual stake in their job—a franchise—whether it is a continuous commission, an endable enlistment, or just an employee handbook without legal disclaimers. This franchise will give employees the autonomy they need to improvise and build their ownership stake in this new enterprise. This is now starting to happen. According to one observer, "the common thread running through the diverse operations as they scale back management is employee "ownership"—of ideas, of working conditions, and in some cases, of the company itself."[67]

And when employees become autonomous "corporate citizens," employers will be able to get out of the "welfare" business; they can stop acting like parents who must nurture children. They can concentrate on working with adults both inside and outside the organization, expanding and contracting to meet changing business conditions. This is, according to *Fortune,* "just another hallmark of the adaptive organization—its openness to outsiders—greater use of alliances, joint ventures and other relationships with parties from the outside."[68]

The organizations of tomorrow will provide their new autonomous employees with a home away from home even if they are still working in their home; it will give them a sense of belonging to something bigger than they could be on their own; it will channel information and services to them that would be unobtainable anywhere else; and it will build on their relationships and their skills. Lastly, it will give them a new franchise on life. At last, the "material substance of life" will be in each employee's own hands.

EPILOGUE

A TRIBUTE TO PRESENT EMPLOYEES

HONORING THE DIGNITY OF WORKERS

> At the end of the day you're another day older
> And that's all you can say for the life of the poor.
> It's a struggle, it's a war,
> And there is nothing that anyone's giving.
> One more day standing about
> What is it for?
> One day less to be living![1]

It is the end of the day. The musical *Les Misérables* has a "work" scene entitled, coincidentally, "At the End of the Day." This day ends with a worker being "fired at-will" for bad cause! Fantine is told by the foreman, "Right, my girl. On your way!" because she wouldn't give him "his way" with her. An 18th-century Ms. Comerford.

We have come a long way from the days of Jean Valjean, Fantine, and the people who were "standing in their graves." Or have we? Technology has advanced, but has human nature? We are in many ways no different from Adam and Eve or Cain and Abel. We are still human beings.

We are human beings at work. Restructured America with its unending downsizing has stripped away the dignity of a lot of at-will workers. It has been a "struggle" for many people. All you have to do is look behind the mask.

LOOKING BEHIND THE MASK

>. . . save me from my solitude . . .[2]

This is one of the climactic lines from another very successful musical. It is called *The Phantom of the Opera*. It is an old story. The Lloyd Webber version is a romantic love story, but it is also something more. It is about a very talented person who was terribly scarred. This person hides his scars by wearing a mask. A mask of solitude.

There are a lot of talented people in America today who are also scarred. They were at-will employees who were fired for no cause or bad cause. They were victimized by their ex-employers' "broken promise." Unfortunately, victims have always had to bear the guilt and the shame associated with their predicament. As Dr. Cohen noted, they are being forced to leave an organization "without its blessing" and people will assume that they are "totally to blame." These fired employees cope with their misfortune by wearing a mask before the public. After all, who wants to be stigmatized as "damaged merchandise" or as what one executive recruiter callously labeled them—"B's and C's." But there is a tremendous sense of betrayal and injustice that hurts just the same. And it is made all the more painful because it has to be experienced in solitude.

Peter Drucker once said that "job loss was like polio." He was right when he said that job loss and polio are catastrophic. He was also wrong. Polio victims and their families were not forced to wear masks; they could share their grief with their neighbors. We all knew when a neighbor had gotten polio; we normally don't know when a neighbor loses a job. They try to hide it behind a mask, for fear that we would assume it was their fault. So while we hear numbers about people being laid off and underemployed, it is difficult to understand the real human cost until it happens to us or someone we know and care about. If this book can accomplish one major purpose it would be to unmask and demystify this national epidemic which has scarred, and continues to scar, a lot of talented people.

Fortunately, there is one other striking difference from polio. People are much more able to recover from job loss.

MAKING THE INDIVIDUAL TRIUMPHANT

> Do you hear the people sing
>   lost in the valley of the night?
> It is the music of a people
>   who are climbing to the light.
> For the wretched of the earth
>   there is a flame that never dies.
> Even the darkest night will end
>   and the sun will rise.[3]

Songs! Musicals! They lift the human spirit. This is part of the finale of *Les Misérables*. It is a story about the triumph of the human spirit despite remarkable odds. It is a story about redemption. One way or another the victims of Restructured America will ultimately become victors. They will be forced to reach inside themselves to tap some inner strength that they never knew existed. They will build back from the ashes and turn their "failure" into success. In an article, "The New Executive Unemployed," David Kirkpatrick says:

> Being laid off is never going to be an easy experience, no matter how common it becomes. The secret is remembering that, done right, it can represent an opportunity for greater self-knowledge, heightened self-fulfillment, and ultimately a better career. And if awareness of the possibility of being laid off makes each of us a little more self-reliant, we'll all be better off.[4]

After all, we all have time on our side—we now have the rest of our lives. We have *Les Misérables'* "One day more" and Annie's "Tomorrow." Many will go on to becoming the CEO of a "mothership," the founder of a "satellite" business, or the head of a "hightech household." Many go to do something else they have always wanted to do but never had the compulsion or time to do it. These "noble individuals" are the real heroes of our day, whose stories have yet to be told.

At the end of the day, what is it for? One day *more* to be living!

NOTES

Prologue

1. Mindy Fetterman and Julia Lawlor, "Workforce Redefined by Tough Times," *USA Today*, December 20, 1991, p. 1B.
2. Carol Hymowitz, "The Agonizing Decision to Cut Corporate Staff," *The Wall Street Journal*, July 26, 1982, p. 1.
3. Timothy D. Schellhardt and Amanda Bennett, "White-Collar Layoffs Open 1990, and May Close It, Too," *The Wall Street Journal*, January 15, 1990, p. B7.
4. L. Z. Lorber et al., *Fear of Firing—A Legal and Personnel Analysis of Employment-at-Will* (Alexandria, Va: The ASPA Foundation, 1984), p. 1.
5. Bob Baker, "Downsizing: An Annual Edgy Rite," *The Washington Post*, April 22, 1990, p. H3.
6. Paul Hirsch, *Pack Your Own Parachute—How to Survive Mergers, Takeovers, and Other Corporate Disasters* (Reading, Mass: Addison-Wesley Publishing, 1987), pp. 7–18.
7. Schellhardt and Bennett, "White-Collar Layoffs Open 1990," p. B1.
8. Editorial, "When the Bonds of Loyalty Are Broken," *Business Week*, October 7, 1991, p. 158.
9. Evelyn Roberts, "When the Company Leaves the Employees," *The Washington Post*, August 12, 1990, p. H3.
10. Steve Painter, "Middle-Management Spread Hits Corporate America," *The Washington Post*, May 26, 1991, p. H2.
11. Donald Regan's remarks on "The Phil Donahue Show," May 11, 1988.
12. David Gergen, "Bringing Home the 'Storm'," *The Washington Post*, April 28, 1991, p. C2.
13. Anne B. Fisher, "The Downside of Downsizing," *Fortune*, May 23, 1988, p. 42.
14. Frank Swoboda, "Pink Slips and the White-Collar Blues," *The Washington Post*, August 14, 1988, p. H5.
15. Alvin Toffler, *Powershift* (New York: Bantam Books, 1990), pp. 215–16.
16. David Halberstam, *The Next Century* (New York: William Morrow & Co., 1991), p. 15.
17. Otto Friedrich, "Freed from Greed?" *Time*, January 1, 1990, p. 76.
18. "The Pacific Century," *Newsweek*, February 22, 1988, pp. 43–51.
19. Carla Rapoport, "The Big Split," *Fortune*, May 6, 1991, p. 39.

20. Margaret Shapiro and Fred Heath, "Confident Japanese See United States in Serious Decline," *The Washington Post,* July 3, 1988, p. 1.
21. Peter Schmeisser, "Taking Stock—Is America in Decline?" *The New York Times Magazine,* April 17, 1988, p. 24.
22. Paul Kennedy, *The Rise and Fall of the Great Powers: Economic Change and Military Conflict from 1500 to 2000* (New York: Random House, 1987).
23. Baker, "Downsizing: An Annual Edgy Rite," p. H3.
24. Thomas R. Horton and Peter C. Reid, *Beyond the Trust Gap* (Homewood, Ill.: Business One Irwin, 1991), p. 221.
25. David Kirkpatrick, "The New Executive Unemployed," *Fortune,* April 8, 1991, p. 36.
26. Michael Schrage, "Rather than Spreadsheets, Companies Need Scenario Software," *The Washington Post,* April 12, 1991, p. C3.
27. Hirsch, *Pack Your Own Parachute,* p. 110.
28. Shoshona Zuboff, *In the Age of the Smart Machine: The Nature of Work and Power* (New York: Basic Books, 1988).
29. Robert M. Tomasko, *Downsizing—Shaping the Corporation for the Future* (New York: AMACOM, 1987), p. 17.
30. Charles Handy, *The Age Of Unreason* (Boston, Mass.: Harvard Business School Press, 1989), p. xi.

Chapter 1

1. Thomas R. Horton and Peter C. Reid, *Beyond the Trust Gap* (Homewood, Ill.: Business One Irwin, 1991), p. 221.
2. L. Z. Lorber et al., *Fear of Firing—A Legal and Personnel Analysis of Employment-at-Will* (Alexandria, Va.: The ASPA Foundation, 1984), p. 3.
3. Charles A. Reich, *The Greening of America* (New York: Random House, 1970), p. 27.
4. Ibid., p. 24.
5. Lorber, *Fear of Firing,* p. 3.
6. Robert B. Reich, *Tales of a New America—The American Liberal's Guide to the Future* (New York: Vintage Books, a division of Random House, 1987), p. 9.
7. Lorber, *Fear of Firing,* p. 4.
8. Charles A. Reich, *The Greening of America,* p. 47.
9. Alvin Toffler, *The Third Wave* (New York: William Morrow & Co., 1980), pp. 23–24.
10. James Fraze and Martha I. Finey, "Employee Rights between Our Shores," *Personnel Administrator,* March 1988, p. 50.
11. William H. Whyte, *The Organization Man* (New York: Simon & Schuster, 1956) p. 3.
12. Charles A. Reich, *The Greening of America,* pp. 67–68.
13. Michael Maccoby, *The Gamesman—The New Corporate Leaders* (New York: Simon & Schuster, 1976), p. 81.

14. Allan Bloom, *The Closing of the American Mind* (New York: Simon & Schuster, 1987), p. 203.
15. Maccoby, *The Gamesman,* p. 80.
16. Louis Uchitelle, "The Uncertain Legacy of the Crash," *The New York Times,* April 3, 1988, Sec. 3, p. 1.
17. Peter Schmiesser "Taking Stock—Is America in Decline?" *New York Times Magazine,* April 17, 1988, p. 67.
18. John S. McClenahen and Perry Pascarella, "America's New Economy," *Industry Week,* January 26, 1987, pp. 27–28.
19. Thomas J. Peters, *Thriving on Chaos—Handbook for a Management Revolution* (New York: Alfred A. Knopf, 1987), p. 13.
20. Ibid., p. 14.
21. Tom Forrester, *High Tech Society* (Cambridge, Mass.: The MIT Press, 1987), pp. 245–46.
22. Alvin Toffler, *Powershift* (New York: Bantam Books, 1990), pp. 75–76.
23. David Halberstam, *The Next Century* (New York: William Morrow & Co., 1991), p. 123.
24. Warren Brown, "Chrysler to Shift K-Car Production to Mexico, Angering UAW Officials," *The Washington Post,* April 23, 1988, p. B1.
25. Forrester, *High Tech Society,* p. 254.
26. Paul Blustein, "Japan Inc. Stretches Its Global Foothold—Strategic Shifts Bring New Heights of Success," *The Washington Post,* March 24, 1991, p. H7.
27. Judith H. Dobzynski, "Merger Mania—Why It Just Won't Stop," *Business Week,* March 21, 1988, p. 122.
28. Brian Bremmer, Kathy Rebello, and Joseph Webber, "The Age of Consolidation," *Business Week,* October 14, 1991, p. 86.
29. Dobzynski, "Merger Mania," p. 126.
30. Brian Bemmer et al., "The Age of Consolidation," *Business Week,* October 14, 1991, p. 89.
31. Dobzynski, "Merger Mania," p. 126.
32. Claudia H. Deutsch, "Keeping the Talented People," *The New York Times,* August 12, 1990, p. F25.
33. Joseph Weber, Lisa Driscoll, and Richard Brandt, "Farewell, Fast Track," *Business Week,* December 10, 1990, p. 192.
34. "The Economy of the 1990s," *Fortune,* 1987.
35. "Helping Middle Managers Survive the Job Squeeze," *Resource,* ASPA, March 1988, p. 5.
36. Janice Castro, "Where Did the Gung-Ho Go?" *Time,* September 11, 1989, p. 52.
37. "Helping Middle Managers Survive," p. 5.
38. Hirsch, *Pack Your Own Parachute,* p. 163.
39. Michael Korda, *Power! How to Get It and How to Use It* (New York: Random House, 1975), p. 150.
40. Claudia H. Deutsch, "U.S. Industry's Unfinished Struggle," *The New York Times,* February 21, 1988, Sec. 3, p. 1.
41. Frank Swoboda, "Firms Dump Labor to Lighten Debt Load," *The Washington Post,* January 6, 1991, p. H3.

42. Robert M. Tomasko, *Downsizing: Shaping the Corporation for the Future* (New York: AMACOM, 1987), pp. 41–42.
43. Andrew C. Siglar, "U.S. Industry's Unfinished Struggle," *The New York Times*, Sec. 3, p. 1.
44. Sally Lehrman, "Middle Managers Face Squeeze As Firms Try New Structures," *The Washington Post*, September 4, 1988, p. H2.
45. Dr. Stephen Cohen, *When the Going Gets Rough—Best Strategies for a Job Gone Sour* (New York: Bantam Books, 1987), p. 180.
46. Korda, *Power!*, p. 150.
47. Claudia H. Deutsch, "Why Being Fired Is Losing Its Taint," *The New York Times*, January 24, 1988, Sec. 3, p. 1.
48. Janice Castro, "CEOs: No Pain, Just Gain," *Time*, April 15, 1991, p. 40.
49. Joani Nelson-Horcher, "What's Your Boss Worth?—35 Times Your Salary? 1,000 Times? The Workforce Gets Angry," *The Washington Post*, August 5, 1990, p. D3.
50. John A. Byrne et al., "Who Made the Most—And Why," *Business Week*, May 2, 1988, p. 53.
51. John Hillkirk, "High Salaries Draw Fire in Austere Times," *USA Today*, April 26, 1991, p. 1B.
52. Byrne, "Who Made the Most," p. 53.
53. Graef S. Crystal, "At the Top: An Explosion of Pay Packages," *New York Times Magazine*, December 3, 1989, p. 25.
54. Ibid., p. 50.
55. John Holusia: "Chrysler and the UAW—A Union Pact to Restrict Executive Privilege," *The New York Times*, May 15, 1988, p. E4.
56. Alan Farnham, "The Trust Gap," *Fortune*, December 4, 1989, p. 57.
57. Frank Swoboda, "Suggestions for Solving Part-Time Employees' Problems," *The Washington Post*, March 31, 1991, p. H2.
58. Andrea Knox, "Many Laid-Off Managers Aren't Managing Too Well," *The Philadelphia Inquirer*, August 21, 1988, p. 1-E.
59. Robert J. Samuelson, "Temps: the New Work Force," *The Washington Post*, July 12, 1989, p. A23.
60. Dale Russakoff and Cindy Skrzycki, "Growing Pains in the Contingent Work Force," *The Washington Post*, February 11, 1988, p. A18.
61. Peter F. Drucker, *Management—Tasks—Responsibilities—Practices* (New York: Harper & Row, 1974), p. 290.
62. Louis Uchitelle, "As Jobs Increase, So Does Insecurity," *The New York Times*, May 1, 1988, p. F25.
63. Frank Swoboda quoting Richard Beleous, "The Contingency Question," *The Washington Post*, January 8, 1989, p. H2.
64. Tamar Lewin, "High Medical Costs Affect Broad Areas of Daily Life," *The New York Times*, April 28, 1991, p. 1.
65. Tomasko, *Downsizing*, pp. 45–46.
66. Claudia H. Deutsch, "U.S. Industries Unfinished Struggle," *The New York Times*, February 21, 1988, Sec. 3, p. 1.
67. Bruce Nussbaum, "I'm Worried About My Job!" *Business Week*, October 7, 1991, p. 94.

68. Castro, "Where Did the Gung-Ho Go?" p. 52.

69. Ibid., p. 52.

Chapter 2

1. Cindy Skrzycki quoting Robert Fitzpatrick, "Just Who's in Charge Here, Anyway?" *The Washington Post,* January 29, 1989, p. H1.

2. Kenneth Labich, "The Innovators," *Fortune,* June 6, 1988, pp. 50–64.

3. Paul Blustein, "Japan Inc. Stretches Its Global Foothold—Strategic Shifts Bring New Heights of Success," *The Washington Post,* March 24, 1991, p. H1.

4. Robert B. Reich, *Tales of a New America—The Anxious Liberal's Guide to the Future* (New York: Vintage Books, a division of Random House, 1987), p. 90.

5. Paul Blustein and Warren Brown, "Iacocca Faces the Paradox of a Japan Basher," *The Washington Post,* April 14, 1991, p. H1.

6. Paul Hirsch, *Pack Your Own Parachute* (Reading, Mass.: Addison-Wesley, 1987), p. 26.

7. Sally Lehrman, "Middle Managers Face Squeeze As Firms Try New Structures," *The Washington Post,* September 4, 1988, p. H2.

8. Michael VerMuelen, "Who's Afraid of Carl Icahn? Who Isn't?" *TWA Ambassador,* September 1984.

9. John A. Byrne questioning Windle B. Priem, "Business Is Bountiful for Elite Head Hunters," *Business Week,* April 18, 1988, p. 28.

10. Thomas J. Peters, *Thriving on Chaos—Handbook for a Management Revolution* (New York: Alfred A. Knopf, 1987), p. 364.

11. Anne B. Fisher, "The Downside of Downsizing," *Fortune,* May 23, 1988, p. 50.

12. Ibid., p. 42.

13. Lorber et al., *Fear of Firing—A Legal and Personnel Analysis of Employment-at-Will* (Alexandria, Va.: The ASPA Foundation, 1984), p. 1.

14. "Employment-at-Will Erodes, Union Membership Shrinks," *Resource,* December 1989.

15. Paul M. Barrett, "Wrongful-Dismissal Laws May Feel Effect of Dispute before Montana's High Court," *The Wall Street Journal,* November 8, 1988, p. B1.

16. Lorber et al., *Fear of Firing,* pp. 7–14.

17. Frank Swoboda," A Growing Challenge to the Right to Fire Workers," *The Washington Post,* January 31, 1988, p. K4.

18. Ibid.

19. Claudia H. Deutsch, "Making the Anger Pay Off in Cash," *The New York Times,* January 24, 1988, Sec. F, p. 11.

20. Milo Geyelin, "Fired Managers Winning More Lawsuits," *The Wall Street Journal,* September 7, 1989, p. B1.

21. Elizabeth Spayd, "Companies Fighting Fire with Fire," *The Washington Post,* November 5, 1989, p. H3.

22. Daniel Moskowitz, "Toughening Employee Handbooks," Washington Business, *The Washington Post,* January 9, 1989, p. 20.

23. Thomas R. Horton, "If Right to Fire Is Abused, Uncle Sam May Step In," *The Wall Street Journal*, June 11, 1984, p. 1.
24. Patricia Bellew Gray, "Smoking Foes Cite New Evidence Emerging in Tobacco Liability Suit," *The Wall Street Journal*, April 4, 1988, p. 19.
25. Jeremy Main, "Look Who Needs Outplacement," *Fortune*, October 9, 1989, p. 85.
26. Hirsch, *Pack Your Own Parachute*, p. 153.
27. Main, "Look Who Needs Outplacement," p. 85.
28. Ibid.
29. Dr. Stephen Cohen, *When the Going Gets Rough—Best Strategies for a Job Gone Sour* (New York: Bantam Books, 1987), pp. 204–5.
30. Main, "Look Who Needs Outplacement," p. 85.
31. Bob Baker, "Downsizing: An Annual Edgy Rite," *The Washington Post*, April 22, 1990, p. H3.
32. Keith Bradshes, "Signing Away the Right to Sue," *The Washington Post*, July 31, 1988, p. H2.
33. Raymond L. Hilgert, "Employers Protected by At-Will Statements," *HRMagazine*, March 1991, p. 60.
34. Bonar Menninger, "Cresap Remodels the World Bank, Cuts $50 Million in Role of Heavy," *Washington Business Journal*, December 21, 1987, p. 1.
35. James B. Treece with Robert Ingersole, "GM Faces Reality," *Business Week*, May 9, 1988, p. 114.
36. Sally Lehrman, "Middle Managers Face Squeeze," *The Washington Post*, September 4, 1988, p. H2.
37. Cindy Skrzycki, "The Drive to Downsize," *The Washington Post*, August 20, 1989, p. H1.
38. Kenneth R. Blanchard and Norman Vincent Peale, *The Power of Ethical Management* (New York: William Morrow & Co., 1988), p. 6.
39. Hirsch, *Pack Your Own Parachute*, p. 163.
40. Carl R. Boll, *Executive Jobs Unlimited* (New York: Macmillan, 1979).
41. Richard Nelson Bolles, *The 1987 What Color Is Your Parachute?* (Berkeley, Calif.: Ten Speed Press, 1987), p. 12.
42. Robert Ringer, *Looking Out for #1* (Beverly Hills, Calif.: Los Angeles Book Corp., 1977).
43. William Barry Furlong, "Namath's Best Deal Was His Counselor," *The Washington Post*, August 3, 1975, p. D1.
44. Hobart Rowen, "A Look at Jacksonomics," *The Washington Post*, April 1, 1988, p. H1.
45. "Will Mergers Help or Hurt in the Long Run?" *The Wall Street Journal*, May 2, 1988, p. 1.
46. Fisher, "The Downside of Downsizing," p. 42.
47. Richard Reeves, "In America's Perestroika, the Rich Get Richer," *The Philadelphia Inquirer*, July 10, 1988, p. 7-C.
48. Eliot Janeway, "What's Behind Those Funny Numbers? A Depression?" *The Washington Post*, May 5, 1991, p. K1.
49. Dr. Ravi Batra, *The Great Depression of 1990* (New York: Simon & Schuster, 1987), p. 183.

50. John Holushia, "Chrysler and the U.A.W.—A Union Pact to Restrict Executive Privilege," *The New York Times,* May 15, 1988, p. E4.

Chapter 3

1. George Gilder quoting Peter Drucker in response to a question by Ken Adelman, "Chip on His Shoulder," *Washingtonian,* April 1991, p. 28.
2. Otto Friedrich, "Freed from Greed?" *Time,* January 1, 1990, p. 76.
3. Janice Castro, "The Simple Life," *Time,* April 8, 1991, p. 58.
4. Allan Bloom, *The Closing of the American Mind* (New York: Simon & Schuster, 1987), p. 57.
5. Ibid., p. 56.
6. Don Oldenburg, "Kids and Morals in a Me-First World," *The Washington Post,* March 25, 1988, p. D5.
7. Georgi Arbatov, "America Could Use Some Perestroika," *The Washington Post,* May 15, 1988, p. B2.
8. Ronald Henkoff, "Is Greed Dead?" *Fortune,* August 14, 1989, p. 40.
9. Castro, "The Simple Life," p. 58.
10. John Naisbitt and Patricia Aburdene, *Megatrends 2000* (New York: William Morrow & Co., 1990), p. 271.
11. Antony Jay, *Corporation Man* (New York: Random House, 1971), p. 300.
12. Robert L. Dilenschneider, "Where Competiveness Starts: Values Are the Means to the End," *The New York Times,* December 3, 1989, p. F3.
13. Cindy Skrzycki, "More Firms Trying to Instill Ethical Values," *The Washington Post,* May 21, 1989, p. H3.
14. Laura Sessions Stepp, "In Search of Ethics—Alcoa Pursues a Corporate Conscience through Emphasis on 'Core Values'." *The Washington Post,* March 31, 1991, p. H1.
15. Rod Willis, "What's Happened to America's Middle Managers?" *Management Review,* January 1987, p. 28.
16. Marilyn Gardner, "Companies Seeing Need for a Family-Friendly Workplace," *The Philadelphia Inquirer,* July 31, 1988, p. 1–D.
17. Michelle Neely Martinez, "Making Room for Work/Family Positions," *HRMagazine,* August 1990, p. 45.
18. Robert D. Hershey, Jr., "Employee Stock Ownership Plans: Including Labor in the Division of Capital," *The New York Times,* April 24, 1988, p. E5.
19. Peter F. Drucker, *Management—Tasks—Responsibilities—Practices* (New York: Harper & Row, 1974), p. 735.
20. Ibid., pp. 738–41.
21. James Fraze, "Meeting the Challenge of Understanding," *Resource,* American Society of Personnel Administration, April 1988, p. 6.
22. Kenneth J. Albert, *Handbook of Business Problem Solving* (New York: McGraw-Hill, 1980), pp. 2–68.
23. Claudia H. Deutsch, "Losing Innocence Abroad," *The New York Times,* July 10, 1988, Sec. 3, p. 1.

24. Martin E. Payson and Philip B. Rosen, "Playing by Fair Rules," *HRMagazine,* April 1991, p. 42.
25. Howard A. Simon and Frederick Brown, "International Enforcement of Title VII: A Small World After All?" *Employee Relations Law Journal,* Winter 1990/91, pp. 299–301.
26. Daniel Kendall, "Rights Across the Waters," *The Personnel Administrator,* March 1988, pp. 60–61.
27. L. Z. Lorber, *Fear of Firing—A Legal and Personnel Analysis of Employment-at-Will* (Alexandria, Va.: The ASPA Foundation, 1984), pp. 15–16.
28. Daniel Heneghan, "Trump Gets Taj, Merv Gets Resorts," *The Press,* April 15, 1988, p. 1.
29. Thomas J. Peters, *Thriving on Chaos—Handbook for a Management Revolution* (New York: Alfred A. Knopf, 1987), p. 9.
30. Daniel Heneghan, "It's Official, Trump, Griffin Sign Resorts Deal," *The Press,* May 28, 1988, p. 1.
31. "The Essentials for Survival," *Industry Week,* January 26, 1987, p. 36.
32. Norm Alster, "What Flexible Workers Can Do," *Fortune,* February 13, 1989, p. 63.
33. Robert H. Waterman, Jr., *The Renewal Factor—How the Best Get and Keep the Competitive Edge* (New York: Bantam Books, 1987), p. 229.
34. Ibid., p. 229.
35. Dick Schory, *The Magical Music of Walt Disney* (Glenville, Ill.: Ovation Incorporated, 1978), p. 10.
36. Stephen Koepp, "Why Is This Mouse Smiling?" *Time,* April 25, 1988, pp. 67–73.
37. Ron Grover, *The Disney Touch* (Homewood, Ill.: Business One Irwin, 1991).
38. Maurice Sendak, "Walt Disney's Triumph: The Art of Pinocchio," *The Washington Post,* July 10, 1988, p. 10 (Book World).
39. Peters, *Thriving on Chaos,* p. 66.
40. Paul Blustein, "Japan Inc. Stretches Its Global Foothold—Strategic Shifts Bring New Heights of Success," *The Washington Post,* March 24, 1991, p. H1.
41. "U.S. Industries Unfinished Struggle to Compete," *The New York Times,* February 21, 1988, Sec. 3, p. 2.
42. Peters, *Thriving on Chaos,* p. 66.
43. Ibid., p. 70.
44. Claudia H. Deutsch, "Business Graduates: Shying Away from Wall Street— In MBA-land Corporate America Has Won Back the Loyalties," *The New York Times,* February 25, 1990, p. F8.
45. Sheila Mullan, "Fewer MBAs Going for the Gold—Students Opting for Assembly Lines, Not Wall Street," *The Washington Post,* April 21, 1988, p. F1.
46. Stepp, "In Search of Ethics," p. H1.
47. Andrea Knox, "500 Area Disciples Hear the Gospel According to Deming," *The Philadelphia Inquirer,* March 20, 1988, pp. D1–2.
48. Ronald Henkoff, "Make Your Office More Productive," *Fortune,* February 25, 1991, p. 72.

49. Robert B. Reich, *Tales of a New America—The American Liberal's Guide to the Future* (New York: Vintage Books, a division of Random House, 1987), p. 90.

50. G. R. Horton and Saeid Y. Eidgaby, "Retirement Should Be Obsolete," *HRMagazine,* December 1990, p. 61.

51. Tamar Lewin, "Too Much Retirement Time? A Move Is Afoot to Change It," *The New York Times,* April 22, 1990, p. 1.

52. Lee Smith, "The War between the Generations," *Fortune,* July 20, 1987, p. 78.

53. David Kirkpatrick, "Will You Be Able to Retire?" *Fortune,* July 31, 1989, p. 56.

54. Albert B. Crenshaw, "Whose Pension Money Is It?" *The Washington Post,* July 26, 1988, p. C1.

55. Amanda Bennett, "The Baby Busters: New Generation Asks More than Its Elders of Corporate World," *The Wall Street Journal,* October 26, 1988, p. 1.

56. Lewin, "Too Much Retirement Time?", p. 1.

57. Bennett, "The Baby Busters," p. 1.

58. Tom Forrester, *High Tech Society* (Cambridge, Mass.: The MIT Press, 1987), pp. 134–35.

59. Ibid., p. 146.

60. Gene Bylinsky, "Technology in the Year 2000," *Fortune,* July 18, 1988, p. 92.

61. Liz Spayd, "Increasingly in Area, Home Is Where the Workplace Is," *The Washington Post,* April 22, 1991, p. A15.

62. Sam Hankin, "Zoning Change Could Hit Home Offices," *The Washington Post,* August 6, 1988, p. F3.

63. Roger K. Lewis, "Montgomery Proposal Targets Individuals Who Work at Home," *The Washington Post,* October 15, 1988, p. F14.

64. Terri Shaw, "Transforming Today's Home Offices," *Washington Home,* July 6, 1989, p. 7.

65. Peter H. Lewis, "Electronic Cottages Take Root," *The New York Times,* October 16, 1988, p. F10.

66. John Hillkirk, "PCs Finding a Niche in Home Offices," *USA Today,* June 17, 1988, p. 1B.

67. Forrester, *High Tech Society,* p. 146.

68. Society for Human Resource Management, "Telecommuting Considered a Plus by Employees, Employers," *Visions,* March/April 1990, p. 5.

69. Deirdre Fanning, "Fleeing the Office, and Its Distractions," *The New York Times,* August 12, 1990, p. F25.

70. John Naisbitt, *Megatrends—Ten New Directions Transforming Our Lives* (New York: Warner Books Inc., 1982), p. 45.

71. John A. Byrne, "Is Your Company Too Big?" *Business Week,* March 27, 1989, p. 84.

72. Society for Human Resource Management, "Telecommuting", p. 5.

73. Alvin Toffler, *Powershift* (New York: Bantam Books, 1990), p. 182.

74. Laurie P. Cohen, "Use of Legal Temps Is on the Rise—But Practice Faces Bar Challenge," *The Wall Street Journal,* May 12, 1988, p. 25.

75. Robert Silverberg, an interview.

76. Brit Hume, "PCs May Hold Key to Election-Year Questions on Jobs, Day Care," *The Washington Post,* September 5, 1988, p. 16 (Washington Business).
77. Alvin Toffler, *Future Shock* (New York: Random House, 1970), p. 127.
78. John Gardner, *Self-Renewal* (Evanston, Ill.: Harper & Row, 1963), p. 83.
79. Jon Berry, "Nation's Low Jobless Rate Belies Regional Occupational Wasteland," *The Washington Post,* September 4, 1988, p. H4.
80. Naisbitt, *Megatrends,* (1982) p. 163.
81. Jennefer Kingston, "The Northeast (Is) Faring Well—For Now," *The New York Times,* May 1, 1988, p. F25.
82. David Osborne and Doug Ross, "Catching the Third Wave—Beyond the Beltway, a Post-Industrial Revolution," *The Washington Post,* July 22, 1990, p. C3.
83. Clyde H. Farnsworth in an interview with Mark A. De Bernardo of the U.S. Chamber of Commerce, "A Disincentive to Job Growth," *The New York Times,* May 8, 1988, p. E5.
84. Jennefer A. Kingston, "Massachusetts Living with a Voluntary Law," *The New York Times,* May 8, 1988, p. E5.
85. Martha M. Hamilton, "States Assuming New Power As Federal Policy Role Ebbs," *The Washington Post,* August 30, 1988, p. A1.
86. Paul M. Barret, "Attorney Generals Flex Their Muscles," *The Wall Street Journal,* July 13, 1988, p. 25.
87. Vickey Cohen, Dean Foust, and Ellyn Spragins, "States versus Raiders: Will Washington Step In?" *Business Week,* August 31, 1987, p. 46.
88. Robert L. Dilenschneider, "The Dark Side of Globalization," *The New York Times,* August 28, 1988, p. F2.
89. Milo Geyelin and Vindu P. Goel, "Pennsylvania Legislators Gird to Battle over Bill that Could Become the Stiffest Anti-Takeover Law," *The Wall Street Journal,* December 20, 1989, p. A16.
90. David Halberstam, *The Next Century* (New York: William Morrow & Co., 1991), p. 124.
91. Susan Duffy, "The Real Villain in *Roger & Me*? Big Business," *Business Week,* January 8, 1990, p. 42.
92. Jay, *Corporation Man,* p. 300.
93. Ibid., p. 300.
94. Cindy Skrzycki quoting Richard Moon, "Just Who's in Charge Here, Anyway?" *The Washington Post,* January 29, 1989, p. H1.
95. Hedley Donovan, "Managing Your Intellectuals," *Fortune,* October 23, 1989, p. 177.
96. Toffler, *Powershift,* p. 214.
97. Alan Farnham, "The Trust Gap," *Fortune,* December 4, 1989, p. 58.
98. Daniel W. Kendall, "Rights across the Waters," *The Personnel Administrator,* March 1988, p. 61.
99. Toffler, *Powershift,* p. 211.
100. Pamela Mendels, "Fighting to Bring Bill of Rights into the Workplace," *The Philadelphia Inquirer,* June 23, 1990, p. 8-C.
101. Ibid.

102. Stephanie Overman, "A Delicate Balance Protects Everyone's Rights," *HRMagazine,* November 1990, p. 39.
103. Society for Human Resource Management, "The Constitution in the Workplace," *Visions,* March/April 1990, p. 7.
104. Toffler, *Powershift,* pp. 216–17.

Chapter 4

1. Charles Handy, *The Age Of Unreason* (Boston, Mass.: Harvard Business School Press, 1989), p. 177–78.
2. Dan Lacey, *The Paycheck Disruption—Finding Success in the Workplace of the '90s* (New York: Hippocrene Books, 1988), p. 23.
3. Nina Killham, "Setting a New Course," *The Washington Post,* February 7, 1989, p. D5.
4. William Ouchi, *Theory Z: How American Business Can Meet the Japanese Challenge* (Reading, Mass.: Addison-Wesley Publishing, 1981), pp. 17–21.
5. Society for Human Resource Management, "EEOC May Take on Wrongful Discharge Claims," *Visions,* March/April 1990, p. 7.
6. Jeremy B. Fox and Hugh D. Hindman, "States to Address Model Termination Law," *HRNews,* January 1992, p. A1.
7. Donald J. Trump with Tony Schwartz, *Trump—The Art Of The Deal* (New York: Random House, 1987).
8. L. Z. Lorber et al., *Fear of Firing—A Legal and Personnel Analysis of Employment-at-Will* (Alexandria, Va.: The ASPA Foundation, 1984), p. vii.
9. Peter F. Drucker, *The Frontiers of Management* (New York: Harper & Row 1986), p. 190.
10. Ibid., p. 192.
11. Editorial, "Firing Policy: There Is a Middle Ground," *Business Week,* October 17, 1988, p. 122.
12. Stephen P. Pepe and Scott H. Dunham, *Avoiding and Defending Wrongful Discharge Claims* (Wilmette, Ill.: Callaghan & Company, 1987), p. 15:04.
13. Joseph E. Herman, "Arbitrate, Don't Litigate, at Work," *The New York Times,* April 14, 1991, p. F11.
14. Aaron Bernstein, "More Dismissed Workers Are Telling It to the Judge," *Business Week,* October 17, 1988, p. 68.
15. Peter F. Drucker, *Management—Tasks—Responsibilities—Practices* (New York: Harper & Row, 1974), p. 673.
16. Thomas J. Peters, *Thriving on Chaos—Handbook for a Management Revolution* (New York: Alfred A. Knopf, 1987), p. 14.
17. Claudia H. Deutsch, "What's New in Management Consulting," *The New York Times,* July 10, 1988, p. F17.
18. Amanda Bennett, "Wave of Mergers Hits Consulting Firms," *The Wall Street Journal,* February 20, 1991, p. B1.
19. John A. Byrne, "Is Your Company Too Big?" *Business Week,* March 27, 1989, p. 84.

20. Paul Hirsch, *Pack Your Own Parachute* (Reading, Mass.: Addison-Wesley Publishing, 1987), pp. 168–69.
21. Deutsch, "What's New in Management Consulting," p. 17.
22. Hirsch, *Pack Your Own Parachute,* pp. 166–67.
23. Peter F. Drucker, *The Age Of Discontinuity* (New York: Harper & Row, 1968), p. 264.
24. Lee Berton, "Accounting Firms Face a Deepening Division over Consultant's Pay," *The Wall Street Journal,* July 26, 1988, p. 1.
25. Nina Killham, "Setting a New Course," *The Washington Post,* February 7, 1989, p. D5.
26. Deirdre Fanning, "Fleeing the Office, and Its Distractions," *The New York Times,* August 12, 1990, p. F25.
27. Liz Spayd, "Increasingly in Area, Home Is Where the Workplace Is," *The Washington Post,* April 22, 1991, p. A15.
28. Marvin Bower, *The Will to Manage* (New York: McGraw-Hill, 1966), p. 225.
29. Frank Swoboda quoting Frank Doyle, "A Coming Shift in the Power Balance," *The Washington Post,* October 8, 1989, p. H3.
30. Thomas J. Peters and Robert H. Waterman, Jr., *In Search of Excellence* (New York: Harper & Row, 1982), p. 211.
31. Alvin Toffler, *The Third Wave* (New York: William Morrow & Co., 1980), p. 262.
32. Walter Kiechel III, "The Microbusiness Alternative," *Fortune,* October 24, 1988, p. 220.
33. Editorial, "When the Bonds of Loyalty Are Broken," *Business Week,* October 7, 1991, p. 158.

Chapter 5

1. Michael Schrage, "Rather than Spreadsheets, Companies Need Scenario Software," *The Washington Post,* April 12, 1991, p. C3.
2. Walter Kiechel III, "The Organization that Learns," *Fortune,* March 12, 1990, p. 136.
3. Charles Handy, *The Age Of Unreason* (Boston, Mass.: Harvard Business School Press, 1989), p. 65.
4. *Ideas and Trends in Personnel,* Commerce Clearing House, Inc., July 26, 1988, p. 116.
5. Karen Pennar, "The Productivity Paradox," *Business Week,* June 6, 1988, p. 100.
6. Peter F. Drucker, "Workers' Hands Bound by Tradition," *The Wall Street Journal,* August 2, 1988, p. 20.
7. Robert M. Tomasko, *Downsizing—Shaping the Corporation of the Future* (New York: AMACOM, 1987), pp. 17–20.
8. Ibid.
9. Robert J. Samuelson, "What Good Are B-Schools?" *Newsweek,* May 14, 1990, p. 49.

10. Thomas J. Peters, "The Destruction of Hierarchy," *Industry Week,* August 15, 1988, p. 33.

11. Jeremy Main, "The Winning Organization," *Fortune,* September 26, 1988, p. 50.

12. Carl Bernstein and Bob Woodward, *All the President's Men* (New York: Simon & Schuster, 1974).

13. John A. Byrne, "The Flap over Executive Pay," *Business Week,* May 6, 1991, p. 90.

14. Alan Farnham, "The Trust Gap," *Fortune,* December 4, 1989, p. 74.

15. Kenneth H. Blanchard and Spencer Johnson, *The One Minute Manager* (New York: William Morrow & Co., 1982).

16. Stanley J. Modic, "What Makes Deming Run," *Industry Week,* June 20, 1988, p. 91.

17. Robert Levering, *A Great Place to Work* (New York: Random House, 1988), pp. 134–35.

18. Thomas J. Peters' remarks on "Good Morning America," August 22, 1988.

19. Kenneth R. Noble, "Paying Workers to Be Their Own Efficiency Experts," *The New York Times,* August 28, 1988, p. E7.

20. Daniel Forbes, "One Step Backward, Two Steps Forward," *Business Month,* August 1987, p. 34.

21. Joseph Weber, Lisa Driscoll, and Richard Brandt, "Farewell, Fast Track," *Business Week,* December 10, 1990, p. 192.

22. Rudolph A. Pyatt, Jr., "The Silent Tragedy of Hostile Takeover Attempts Hit Home," *The Washington Post,* August 25, 1988, p. B3.

23. Alan Farnham, "The Trust Gap," *Fortune,* December 4, 1989, p. 62.

24. Brian S. Moskal, "Tomorrow's Best Managers," *Industry Week,* July 18, 1988, p. 34.

25. William Ouchi, *Theory Z: How American Business Can Meet the Japanese Challenge* (Reading, Mass.: Addison-Wesley Publishing, 1981), p. 71.

26. Carol Skryzcki, "New Ideas for the New Year: More Teamwork at the Top," *The Washington Post,* January 1, 1989, p. H4.

27. Peter F. Drucker, *The Age of Discontinuity* (New York: Harper & Row, 1968), p. 254.

28. Dr. Stephen H. Cohen, *When the Going Gets Rough—Best Strategies for a Job Gone Sour* (New York: Bantam Books, 1987), p. 180.

Chapter 6

1. George Bernard Shaw, "Maxims for a Revolution," p. 238, reported in *The Oxford Dictionary of Quotations* (London: Oxford University Press, 1966) p. 490.

2. Charles F. Hendricks, "Routine Restructuring Is the Employee Relations Challenge," *HRMagazine,* May 1990, pp. 95–96.

3. *Les Misérables,* The Complete Symphonic Recording (London: Exallshow Ltd, 1990).

4. Charles Handy, *The Age Of Unreason* (Boston, Mass.: Harvard Business School Press, 1989), pp. 179–80.
5. Ibid., p. 25.
6. Peter Schwartz, *The Art of the Long View* (New York: Doubleday, 1991).
7. Lee Iaccoca: "We believe being competitive is the only way to make 'Made in America' mean something again," in an advertisement in *Fortune,* Spring/ Summer 1991, p. 1.
8. Marc Kaufman, "A generation's vast wealth is a baby boomer windfall," *The Philadelphia Inquirer,* May 26, 1991, p. 1A.
9. Ibid.
10. John Naisbitt, *Megatrends—Ten New Directions Transforming Our Lives* (New York: Warner Books Inc., 1982), pp. 3–4.
11. George F. Will, "Arid Lives, Lurid Falsehoods," *The Washington Post,* April 14, 1991, p. B7.
12. Frank Gerrity, "Give Columbus His Due," *The Philadelphia Inquirer,* October 13, 1991, p. 7E.
13. Michael Schrage, "Rather than Spreadsheets, Companies Need Scenario Software," *The Washington Post,* April 12, 1991, p. C3.
14. Thomas A. Stewart, "Brainpower," *Fortune,* June 3, 1991, p. 44.
15. Ibid., p. 50.
16. Michael Schrage, "Consultant's Maxim for Management: Ignore Markets; Build on Competence," *The Washington Post,* May 17, 1991, p. F3.
17. Ibid.
18. Thomas Mc Carroll, "Whose Bright Idea?" *Time,* June 10, 1991, p. 44.
19. Jeffrey J. Hallett, "The Changing Social Contract," *Visions,* March/April 1990, p. 6.
20. Ronald Henkoff, "Cost Cutting: How to Do It Right," *Fortune,* April 9, 1990, p. 40.
21. Larry Reibstein with Lourdes Rosado, "Seeing Red at Big Blue," *Newsweek,* June 10, 1991, p. 40.
22. Graef S. Crystal, "How Much CEOs Really Make," *Fortune,* June 17, 1991, p. 73.
23. "IBM—As Markets and Technology Change, Can Big Blue Remake Its Culture?" *Business Week,* June 17, 1991, p. 26.
24. Janice Castro, "CEOs: No Pain, Just Gain," *Time,* April 15, 1991, p. 40.
25. Joani Nelson-Horcher, "What's Your Boss Worth?—35 Times Your Salary? 1,000 Times? The Workforce Gets Angry," *The Washington Post,* August 5, 1990, p. D3.
26. Castro, "CEOs: No Pain, Just Gain."
27. Nelson-Horcher, "What's Your Boss Worth?"
28. Ibid.
29. Robert J. McCartney, "When Mega-Pay and Mini-Profits Collide," *The Washington Post,* March 24, 1991, p. H1.
30. Ibid.
31. Kathleen Day, "SEC May Give Shareholders More Say in Executive Pay," *The Washington Post,* May 16, 1991, p. B10.

32. Christeen D. Keen, "CEO's Pay and Philosophy Cause Trust Gap," *HRNews,* May 1990, p. 9.
33. Ibid.
34. "IBM—As Markets and Technology Change."
35. Keith H. Hammonds, "Why Big Companies Are So Tough to Change," *Business Week,* June 17, 1991, p. 28.
36. Handy, *The Age of Unreason,* p. 126.
37. Tom Lewis: an interview.
38. Hallett, "The Changing Social Contract," p. 4.
39. Ibid.
40. Robert J. Samuelson, "What Good Are B-Schools?" *Newsweek,* May 14, 1990, p. 49.
41. Garry Trudeau, "Doonesbury," *The Washington Post,* June 4, 1991, p. B3.
42. Associated Press, "Odd Jobs," *The Washington Post,* May 26, 1991, p. H2.
43. David Gergen, "Bringing Home the 'Storm'," *The Washington Post,* April 28, 1991, p. C2.
44. Paul Taylor, "Two Faces of Fatherhood," *The Washington Post,* June 16, 1991, p. A8.
45. Liz Spayd, "More Women Trading Paychecks for Payoffs of Full-Time Parenting," *The Washington Post,* July 8, 1991, p. A1.
46. Hallett, "The Changing Social Contract," p. 7.
47. Handy, *The Age of Unreason,* pp. 177–78.
48. Nancy J. Perry, "The Workers of the Future," *Fortune,* Spring/Summer 1991, p. 68.
49. Carol Skryzcki, "New Ideas for the New Year: More Teamwork at the Top," *The Washington Post,* January 1, 1989, p. H4.
50. Thomas J. Cody: an interview.
51. Raymond L. Hilgert, "Employers Protected by At-Will Statements," *HRMagazine,* March 1991, p. 60.
52. James Heller and Douglas Huron: an interview.
53. John Ross, "Effective Ways to Hire Contingent Personnel," *HRMagazine,* February 1991, p. 52.
54. Jackson C. Tuttle: an interview.
55. James W. Buttimer, "After Downsizing, How to Rebuild," *Boardroom,* December 15, 1988.
56. Bruce Nussbaum, "I'm Worried About My Job!" *Business Week,* October 7, 1991, p. 95.
57. Walter K. Olson, "Suing Ourselves to Death," *The Washington Post,* April 28, 1991, p. C2.
58. Jonathan A. Segal, "Follow the Yellow-Brick Road," *HRMagazine,* February 1990, p. 83.
59. Robert J. Samuelson, "The Numskull Factor," *The Washington Post,* June 26, 1991, p. A19.
60. Ibid.
61. Ibid.
62. Carol J. Loomis, "Can John Akers Save IBM?" *Fortune,* June 15, 1991, p. 42.

63. Brian Dumaine, "The Bureaucracy Busters," *Fortune*, June 17, 1991, p. 36.
64. Alvin Toffler, *Powershift* (New York: Bantam Books, 1990), p. 227.
65. Kara Swisher, "A Mall for America?" *The Washington Post*, June 30, 1991, p. H1.
66. Toffler, *Powershift*, p. 228.
67. Steve Painter, "Middle-Management Spread Hits Corporate America," *The Washington Post*, May 26, 1991, p. H2.
68. Dumaine, "The Bureaucracy Busters."

Epilogue

1. *Les Misérables, The Complete Symphonic Recording* (London: Exallshow, Ltd, 1990).
2. George Perry, *The Complete Phantom of the Opera* (New York: Henry Holt and Company, 1988) p. 164.
3. *Les Misérables,* The Complete Symphonic Recording.
4. David Kirkpatrick, "The New Executive Unemployed," *Fortune*, April 8, 1991, p. 48.

INDEX

INFORMATION ABOUT SHRM FOR
"THE RIGHTSIZING REMEDY"

The Society for Human Resource Management (SHRM) defines the state-of-the-art for the human resource profession through publications, emerging issue analysis and research, governmental and media representation, seminars and products. Formerly the American Society for Personnel Administration, SHRM represents the interests of local and national members through its network of more than 400 chapters.

An array of benefits are available to SHRM members. SHRM has the professional network, the information, and the educational resources to help you attain your professional goals. More than 45,000 members turn to SHRM as their primary resource for information.

Award winning publications—**HRMagazine, HRNews**, and **The Quarterly**—keep members up-to-date on current industry trends. And answers to technical questions are available through our Information Center. Our unique service—MemberNet—provides access to professionals who have faced the same problems and are willing to share their solutions. To keep members current with the ever-changing field of HR management, SHRM offers frequent, cost-effective seminars. SHRM also offers certification, PHR, and SPHR, through the Human Resource Certification Institute. And, legislative action is monitored that could affect HR management issues. The annual membership dues are only $160. For more information, call SHRM at (703) 548-3440.

Provides practical advice for organizations struggling to respond to on-going change. Pope shows how to integrate business and employee needs in order to recruit and retain the best employees. She shows how you can manage work force problems before they become critical, work collaboratively to develop human resource programs and policies that match business plans, jobs, and people, and much more!
ISBN: 1-55623-537-2 $24.95

TEAM-BASED ORGANIZATIONS
Developing a Successful Team Environment
James H. Shonk

Shonk shows you how to structure and manage an organization that is built around teams versus forcing a team approach into an existing structure. He identifies the advantages and challenges associated with team-based organizations so that you'll be prepared to deal with and resolve any issues that arise. You'll find valuable planning tools to assist you in implementation and help you avoid wasted time.
ISBN: 1-55623-703-0 $34.95

SURVIVE INFORMATION OVERLOAD
The 7 Best Ways to Manage Your Workload by Seeing the Big Picture
Kathryn Alesandrini

Gives you a step-by-step action plan to survive the information onslaught and still have time to effectively manage people, increase productivity, and best serve customers. You'll find innovative techniques, such as Priority Mapping, Context Analysis, Visual Organization, and the use of a Master Control System to manage details by seeing the big picture.
ISBN: 1-55623-721-9 $22.95

Prices quoted are in U.S. currency and are subject to change without notice.
Available at fine bookstores and libraries everywhere.